THE POWER
OF YOUR
SUBCONSCIOUS
MIND

THE POWER OF YOUR SUBCONSCIOUS MIND

The Complete Original Edition

Plus Bonus Material

JOSEPH MURPHY, Ph.D., D.D.

ST. MARTIN'S
ESSENTIALS
NEW YORK

First published in the United States by St. Martin's Essentials,
an imprint of St. Martin's Publishing Group

Introduction copyright © 2019 by Joel Fotinos. All rights reserved.
Printed in the United States of America. For information,
address St. Martin's, Publishing Group
120 Broadway, New York, NY 10271.

www.stmartins.com

The Library of Congress Cataloging-in-Publication Data
is available upon request.

ISBN 9781250236630 (trade paperback)
ISBN 9781250236647 (ebook)

Our books may be purchased in bulk for promotional, educational, or
business use. Please contact your local bookseller or the Macmillan Corporate
and Premium Sales Department at 1-800-221-7945, extension 5442, or by email
at MacmillanSpecialMarkets@macmillan.com.

First Edition: November 2019

11   12   13   14   15   16   17   18   19   20

CONTENTS

INTRODUCTION

The book you are holding in your hands right now has changed the lives of millions of people. That isn't a claim made lightly, that is something that is proven by the many millions of copies it has sold over the years, and the fact that it is still in print nearly sixty years after its initial publication. *The Power of Your Subconscious Mind* is considered to be a classic work on how the mind works, and how to use your mind effectively to succeed in ways far beyond your expectations.

What makes this book so profoundly important, and life-changing? There are probably a lot of reasons, but the first and foremost is the fact that Joseph Murphy was able to take complex ideas about the brain, the mind, the subconscious, and our desires, and turn them into an easy-to-read book that is practical, understandable, chockful of important information, and filled with exercises that you can begin immediately. When

I say "easy-to-read" I mean that he takes ideas found in academic journals and studies, as well as his own experiences and those he has taught over the years, and somehow makes it all engrossing to read, nothing dry about this book!

Originally published in 1963 to immediate acclaims and bestseller sales, *The Power of Your Subconscious Mind* is still one of the leading books on the power of the mind to heal, to bring success, and to help in every area of your life. You'll find as you read the book that the ideas contained within can be applied to you, no matter your age, geographical location, your gender, your background, or any other circumstances. You can find inspiration on nearly every page of this book, and get more out of it each time you read it.

Joseph Murphy himself was a "floor sample" for these principles. Born in County Cork, Ireland, in 1898 into a largely Catholic family and culture, he left for the United States, became a pharmacist and opened his own drugstore. He later joined the U.S. Army, as a pharmacist, and after his service he decided to study religion and philosophy. His interest also included New Thought principles, especially those from Judge Thomas Troward, a pillar of New Thought philosophy.

By then, Murphy moved to Los Angeles, California, had become an independent minister, and started a church. His Sunday services became so popular he eventually moved them to the famous Wilshire Ebell Theatre, and even then it was standing room only. He also began a weekly radio show, which eventually would reach more than a million listeners each week. Murphy also wrote more than thirty books, which were translated around the world.

If you are picking up this book and reading it for the first time, there are several ways you can approach it. You could, of course, just read it from start to finish, or dip into any chapter that you think sounds intriguing. However, perhaps you might be open to reading it a different way, to get the maximum benefit. I would suggest starting from the first chapter, then rereading it, study it, underline it, write notes in the margin or in your journal, and try to see how the ideas he talks about can be applied to your life. Then, after you've done that, move to the next chapter and do the same, and continue this way through the whole book. In this way, you will not just read the words, but you will be applying them, and therefore embodying them.

Enjoy *The Power of Your Subconscious Mind*, and I hope you will use it in positive ways to create positive effects in your life.

—*Joel Fotinos*

THE POWER
OF YOUR
SUBCONSCIOUS
MIND

HOW THIS BOOK
CAN WORK
MIRACLES
IN YOUR LIFE

I have seen miracles happen to men and women in all walks of life all over the world. Miracles will happen to you, too—when you begin using the magic power of your subconscious mind. This book is designed to teach you that your habitual thinking and imagery mold, fashion, and create your destiny; for as a man thinketh in his subconscious mind, so is he.

DO YOU KNOW THE ANSWERS?

Why is one man sad and another man happy? Why is one man joyous and prosperous and another man poor and miserable? Why is one man fearful and anxious and another full of faith and confidence? Why does one man have a beautiful, luxurious home while another man lives out a meager existence in a slum? Why is one man a great success and another an abject failure? Why is one speaker outstanding and immensely popular and another mediocre and unpopular? Why is one man a genius in his work or profession while the other man toils and moils all his life without doing or accomplishing anything worthwhile? Why is one man healed of a so-called incurable disease and another isn't? Why is it so many good, kind religious people suffer the tortures of the damned in their mind and body? Why is it many immoral and irreligious people succeed and prosper and enjoy radiant health? Why is one woman happily married and her sister very unhappy and frustrated? Is there an answer to these questions in the workings of your conscious and subconscious minds? There most certainly is.

REASON FOR WRITING THIS BOOK

It is for the express purpose of answering and clarifying the above questions and many others of a similar nature that motivated me to write this book. I have endeavored to explain the great fundamental truths of your mind in the simplest language possible. I believe that it is perfectly possible to explain the basic, foundational, and fundamental laws of life and of your mind in ordinary everyday language. You will find that the language of this book is that used in your daily papers, current periodicals, in your business offices, in your home, and in the daily workshop. I urge you to study this book and apply the techniques outlined therein; and as you do, I feel absolutely convinced that you will lay hold of a miracle-working power that will lift you up from confusion, misery, melancholy, and failure, and guide you to your true place, solve your difficulties, sever you from emotional and physical bondage, and place you on the royal road to freedom, happiness, and peace of mind. This miracle-working power of your subconscious mind can heal you of your sickness, make you vital and strong again. In learning how to use your inner powers, you will open the prison door of fear and enter into a life described by Paul as the glorious liberty of the sons of God.

RELEASING THE MIRACLE-WORKING POWER

A personal healing will ever be the most convincing evidence of our subconscious powers. Over forty-two years ago I resolved a malignancy—in medical terminology it was called a sarcoma—by using the healing power of my subconscious mind which created me and still maintains and governs all my vital functions. The technique I applied is elaborated on in this book, and I feel sure that it will help others to trust the same Infinite Healing Presence lodged in the subconscious depths of all men. Through the kindly offices of my doctor friend, I suddenly realized that it was natural to assume that the Creative Intelligence which made all my organs, fashioned my body, and started my heart, could heal its own handiwork. The ancient proverb says, "The doctor dresses the wound and God heals it."

WONDERS HAPPEN WHEN YOU PRAY EFFECTIVELY

Scientific prayer is the harmonious interaction of the conscious and subconscious levels of mind scientifically directed for a specific purpose. This book will teach you the scientific way to tap the realm of infinite power within you enabling you to get what you really want in life. You desire a happier, fuller, and richer life. Begin to use this miracle-working power and smooth your way in daily affairs, solve business problems, and bring harmony in family relationships. Be sure that you read this book several times. The many chapters will show you how this wonderful power works, and how you can draw out the hidden inspiration and wisdom that is within you. Learn the simple techniques of impressing the subconscious mind. Follow the new scientific way in tapping the infinite storehouse. Read this book carefully, earnestly, and lovingly. Prove to yourself the amazing way it can help you. It could be and I believe it will be the turning point of your life.

EVERYBODY PRAYS

Do you know how to pray effectively? How long is it since you prayed as part of your everyday activities? In an emergency, in time of danger or trouble, in illness, and when death lurks, prayers pour forth—your own and friends. Just read your daily newspaper. It is reported that prayers are being offered up all over the nation for a child stricken with a so-called incurable ailment, for peace among nations, for a group of miners trapped in a flooded mine. Later it is reported that when rescued, the miners said that they prayed while waiting for rescue; an airplane pilot says that he prayed as he made a successful emergency landing. Certainly, prayer is an ever-present help in time of trouble; but you do not have to wait for trouble to make prayer an integral and constructive part of your life. The dramatic answers to prayer make headlines and are the subject of testimonies to the effectiveness of prayer. What of the many humble prayers of children, the simple thanksgiving of grace at the table daily, the faithful devotions wherein the individual seeks only communion with God? My work with people has made it necessary for me to study the various approaches to prayer. I have experienced the power of prayer in my own life, and I have talked and worked with many people who also have enjoyed the help of prayer. The problem usually is how to tell others how to pray. People who are in trouble have difficulty in thinking and acting reasonably. They need an easy formula to follow, an obviously workable pattern that is simple and specific. Often they must be led to approach the emergency.

UNIQUE FEATURE OF THIS BOOK

The unique feature of this book is its down-to-earth practicality. Here you are presented with simple, usable techniques and formulas which you can easily apply in your workaday world. I have taught these simple processes to men and women all over the world, and recently over a thousand men and women of all religious affiliations attended a special class in Los Angeles where I presented the highlights of what is offered in the pages of this book. Many came from distances of two hundred miles for each class lesson. The special features of this book will appeal to you because they show you why oftentimes you get the opposite of what you prayed for and reveal to you the reasons why. People have asked me in all parts of the world and thousands of times, "Why is it I have prayed and prayed and got no answer?" In this book you will find the reasons for this common complaint. The many ways of impressing the subconscious mind and getting the right answers make this an extraordinarily valuable book and an ever-present help in time of trouble.

WHAT DO YOU BELIEVE?

It is not the thing believed in that brings an answer to man's prayer; the answer to prayer results when the individual's subconscious mind responds to the mental picture or thought in his mind. This law of belief is operating in all religions of the world and is the reason why they are psychologically true. The Buddhist, the Christian, the Moslem, and the Hebrew all may get answers to their prayers, not because of the particular creed, religion, affiliation, ritual, ceremony, formula, liturgy, incantation, sacrifices, or offerings, but solely because of belief or mental acceptance and receptivity about that for which they pray. The law of life is the law of belief, and belief could be summed up briefly as a thought in your mind. As a man thinks, feels, and believes, so is the condition of his mind, body, and circumstances. A technique, a methodology based on an understanding of what you are doing and why you are doing it will help you to bring about a subconscious embodiment of all the good things of life. Essentially, answered prayer is the realization of your heart's desire.

DESIRE IS PRAYER

Everyone desires health, happiness, security, peace of mind, true expression, but many fail to achieve clearly defined results. A university professor admitted to me recently, "I know that if I changed my mental pattern and redirected my emotional life, my ulcers would not recur, but I do not have any technique, process, or modus operandi. My mind wanders back and forth on my many problems, and I feel frustrated, defeated, and unhappy." This professor had a desire for perfect health; he needed a knowledge of the way his mind worked which would enable him to fulfill his desire. By practicing the healing methods outlined in this book, he became whole and perfect.

THERE IS ONE MIND COMMON TO ALL
INDIVIDUAL MEN (EMERSON)

The miracle-working powers of your subconscious mind existed before you and I were born, before any church or world existed. The great eternal truths and principles of life antedate all religions. It is with these thoughts in mind that I urge you in the following chapters to lay hold of this wonderful, magical, transforming power which will bind up mental and physical wounds, proclaim liberty to the fear-ridden mind, and liberate you completely from the limitations of poverty, failure, misery, lack, and frustration. All you have to do is unite mentally and emotionally with the good you wish to embody, and the creative powers of your subconscious will respond accordingly. Begin now, today, let wonders happen in your life! Keep on, keeping on until the day breaks and the shadows flee away.

1

THE TREASURE
HOUSE WITHIN YOU

Infinite riches are all around you if you will open your mental eyes and behold the treasure house of infinity within you. There as a gold mine within you from which you can extract everything you need to live life gloriously, joyously, and abundantly.

Many are sound asleep because they do not know about this gold mine of infinite intelligence and boundless love within themselves. Whatever you want, you can draw forth. A magnetized piece of steel will lift about twelve times its own weight, and if you demagnetize this same piece of steel, it will not even lift a feather. Similarly, there are two types of men. There is the magnetized man who is full of confidence and faith. He knows that he is born to win and to succeed. Then, there is the type of man who is demagnetized. He is full of fears and doubts. Opportunities come, and he says, "I might fail; I might lose my money; people will laugh at me." This type of man will not get very far in life because, if he is afraid to go forward, he will simply stay where he is. Become a magnetized man and discover the master secret of the ages.

THE MASTER SECRET OF THE AGES

What, in your opinion, is the master secret of the ages? The secret of atomic energy? Thermonuclear energy? The neutron bomb? Interplanetary travel? No—not any of these. Then, what is this master secret? Where can one find it, and how can it be contacted and brought into action? The answer is extraordinarily simple. This secret is the marvelous, miracle-working power found in your own subconscious mind, the last place that most people would seek it.

THE MARVELOUS POWER OF YOUR SUBCONSCIOUS

You can bring into your life more power, more wealth, more health, more happiness, and more joy by learning to contact and release the hidden power of your subconscious mind.

You need not acquire this power; you already possess it. But, you want to learn how to use it; you want to understand it so that you can apply it in all departments of your life.

As you follow the simple techniques and processes set forth in this book, you can gain the necessary knowledge and understanding. You can be inspired by a new light, and you can generate a new force enabling you to realize your hopes and make all your dreams come true. Decide now to make your life grander, greater, richer, and nobler than ever before.

Within your subconscious depths lie infinite wisdom, infinite power, and infinite supply of all that is necessary, which is waiting for development and expression. Begin now to recognize these potentialities of your deeper mind, and they will take form in the world without.

The infinite intelligence within your subconscious mind can reveal to you everything you need to know at every moment of time and point of space provided you are open -minded and receptive. You can receive new thoughts and ideas enabling you to bring forth new inventions, make new discoveries, or write books and plays. Moreover, the infinite intelligence in your subconscious can impart to you wonderful kinds of knowledge of an original nature. It can reveal to you and open the way for perfect expression and true place in your life.

Through the wisdom of your subconscious mind you can attract the ideal companion, as well as the right business associate or partner. It can find the right buyer for your home, and provide you with all the money you need, and the financial freedom to be, to do, and to go as your heart desires.

It is your right to discover this inner world of thought, feeling, and power, of light, love, and beauty. Though invisible, its forces are mighty. Within your subconscious mind you will find the solution for every problem, and the cause for every effect. Because you can draw out the hidden powers, you come into actual possession of the power and wisdom necessary to move forward in abundance, security, joy, and dominion.

I have seen the power of the subconscious lift people up out of crippled states, making them whole, vital, and strong once more, and free to go out into the world to experience happiness, health, and joyous expression. There is a miraculous healing power in your subconscious that can heal the troubled mind and the broken heart. It can open the prison door of the mind

and liberate you. It can free you from all kinds of material and
physical bondage.

NECESSITY OF A WORKING BASIS

Substantial progress in any field of endeavor is impossible in
the absence of a working basis which is universal in its application. You can become skilled in the operation of your subconscious mind. You can practice its powers with a certainty of
results in exact proportion to your knowledge of its principles
and to your application of them for definite specific purposes
and goals you wish to achieve.

Being a former chemist, I would like to point out that if you
combine hydrogen and oxygen in the proportions of two atoms
of the former to one of the latter, water will be the result. You
are very familiar with the fact that one atom of oxygen and one
atom of carbon will produce carbon monoxide, a poisonous gas.
But, if you add another atom of oxygen, you will get carbon di-
oxide, a harmless gas, and so on throughout the vast realm of
chemical compounds.

You must not think that the principles of chemistry, physics, and mathematics differ from the principles of your subconscious mind. Let us consider a generally accepted principle:
"Water seeks its own level." This is a universal principle which
is applicable to water everywhere.

Consider another principle: "Matter expands when heated."
This is true anywhere, at any time, and under all circumstances.
You can heat a piece of steel, and it will expand regardless
whether the steel is found in China, England, or India. It is
a universal truth that matter expands when heated. It is also a
universal truth that whatever you impress on your subconscious

mind is expressed on the screen of space as condition, experience, and event.

Your prayer is answered because your subconscious mind is principle, and by principle I mean the way a thing works. For example, the principle of electricity is that it works from a higher to a lower potential. You do not change the principle of electricity when you use it, but by cooperating with nature, you can bring forth marvelous inventions and discoveries which bless humanity in countless ways.

Your subconscious mind is principle and works according to the law of belief. You must know what belief is, why it works, and how it works. Your Bible says in a simple, clear, and beautiful way: *Whosoever shall say unto this mountain, Be thou removed, and be thou cast into the sea; and shall not doubt in his heart, but shall believe that those things which he saith shall come to pass; he shall have whatsoever he saith.* MARK 11:23.

The law of your mind is the law of belief. This means to believe in the way your mind works, to believe in belief itself. The belief of your mind is the thought of your mind—that is simple—just that and nothing else.

All your experiences, events, conditions, and acts are the reactions of your subconscious mind to your thoughts. Remember, it is not the thing believed in, but the belief in your own mind which brings about the result. Cease believing in the false beliefs, opinions, superstitions, and fears of mankind. Begin to believe in the eternal verities and truths of life which never change. Then, you will move onward, upward, and Godward.

Whoever reads this book and applies the principles of the subconscious mind herein set forth, will be able to pray scientifically and effectively for himself and for others. Your prayer is answered according to the universal law of action and reaction. Thought is incipient action. The reaction is the response from your subconscious mind which corresponds with the nature of your thought. Busy your mind with the concepts of harmony, health, peace, and good will, and wonders will happen in your life.

THE DUALITY OF MIND

You have only one mind, but your mind possesses two distinctive characteristics. The line of demarcation between the two is well known to all thinking men and women today. The two functions of your mind are essentially unlike. Each is endowed with separate and distinct attributes and powers. The nomenclature generally used to distinguish the two functions of your mind is as follows: The objective and subjective mind, the conscious and subconscious mind, the waking and sleeping mind, the surface self and the deep self, the voluntary mind and the involuntary mind, the male and the female, and many other terms. You will find the terms "conscious" and "subconscious" used to represent the dual nature of your mind throughout this book.

THE CONSCIOUS AND SUBCONSCIOUS MINDS

An excellent way to get acquainted with the two functions of your mind is to look upon your own mind as a garden. You are a gardener, and you are planting seeds (thoughts) in your subconscious mind all day long, based on your habitual thinking. As you sow in your subconscious mind, so shall you reap in your body and environment.

Begin now to sow thoughts of peace, happiness, right action, good will, and prosperity. Think quietly and with interest on these qualities and accept them fully in your conscious reasoning mind. Continue to plant these wonderful seeds (thoughts) in the garden of your mind, and you will reap a glorious harvest. Your subconscious mind may be likened to the soil which will grow all kinds of seeds, good or bad. *Do men gather grapes of thorns, or figs of thistles?* Every thought is, therefore, a cause, and every condition is an effect. For this reason, it is essential that you take charge of your thoughts so as to bring forth only desirable conditions.

When your mind thinks correctly, when you understand the truth, when the thoughts deposited in your subconscious mind are constructive, harmonious, and peaceful, the magic working power of your subconscious will respond and bring about harmonious conditions, agreeable surroundings, and the best of everything. When you begin to control your thought processes, you can apply the powers of your subconscious to any problem or difficulty. In other words, you will actually be consciously cooperating with the infinite power and omnipotent law which governs all things.

Look around you wherever you live and you will notice that the vast majority of mankind lives in the world without; the more enlightened men are intensely interested in the world within. Remember, it is the world within, namely, your thoughts, feelings, and imagery that makes your world without. It is, therefore, the only creative power, and everything which you find in your world of expression has been created by you in the inner world of your mind consciously or unconsciously.

A knowledge of the interaction of your conscious and subconscious minds will enable you to transform your whole life. In order to change external conditions, you must change the cause. Most men try to change conditions and circumstances by working with conditions and circumstances. To remove discord, confusion, lack, and limitation, you must remove the cause, and the cause is the way you are using your conscious mind. In other words, the way you are thinking and picturing in your mind.

You are living in a fathomless sea of infinite riches. Your subconscious is very sensitive to your thoughts. Your thoughts form the mold or matrix through which the infinite intelligence, wisdom, vital forces, and energies of your subconscious flow. The practical application of the laws of your mind as illustrated in each chapter of this book will cause you to experience abundance for poverty, wisdom for superstition and ignorance, peace for pain, joy for sadness, light for darkness, harmony for discord, faith and confidence for fear, success for failure, and freedom from the law of averages. Certainly, there can be no more wonderful blessing than these from a mental, emotional, and material standpoint.

Most of the great scientists, artists, poets, singers, writers, and inventors have a deep understanding of the workings of the conscious and subconscious minds.

One time Caruso, the great operatic tenor, was struck with stage fright. He said his throat was paralyzed due to spasms caused by intense fear which constricted the muscles of his throat. Perspiration poured copiously down his face. He was ashamed because in a few minutes he had to go out on the stage, yet he was shaking with fear and trepidation. He said, "They will laugh at me. I can't sing." Then he shouted in the presence of those behind the stage, "The Little Me wants to strangle the Big Me within."

He said to the Little Me, "Get out of here, the Big Me wants to sing through me."

By the Big Me, he meant the limitless power and wisdom of his subconscious mind, and he began to shout, "Get out, get out, the Big Me is going to sing!"

His subconscious mind responded, releasing the vital forces within him. When the call came, he walked out on the stage and sang gloriously and majestically, enthralling the audience.

It is obvious to you now that Caruso must have understood the two levels of mind—the conscious or rational, and the subconscious or irrational level. Your subconscious mind is reactive and responds to the nature of your thoughts. When your conscious mind (the Little Me) is full of fear, worry, and anxiety, the negative emotions engendered in your subconscious mind (the Big Me) are released and flood the conscious mind with a sense of panic, foreboding, and despair. When this happens, you can, like Caruso, speak affirmatively and with a deep sense of authority to the irrational emotions generated in your deeper mind as follows: "Be still, be quiet, I am in control, you must obey me, you are subject to my command, you cannot intrude where you do not belong."

It is fascinating and intensely interesting to observe how you can speak authoritatively and with conviction to the irrational movement of your deeper self bringing silence, harmony, and peace to your mind. The subconscious is subject to the conscious mind, and that is why it is called subconscious or subjective.

OUTSTANDING DIFFERENCES AND MODES OF OPERATION

You will perceive the main differences by the following illustrations: The conscious mind is like the navigator or captain at the bridge of a ship. He directs the ship and signals orders to men in the engine room, who in turn control all the boilers, instruments, gauges, etc. The men in the engine room do not know where they are going; they follow orders. They would go on the rocks if the man on the bridge issued faulty or wrong instructions based on his findings with the compass, sextant, or other instruments. The men in the engine room obey him because he is in charge and issues orders which are automatically obeyed. Members of the crew do not talk back to the captain; they simply carry out orders.

The captain is the master of his ship, and his decrees are carried out. Likewise, your conscious mind is the captain and the master of your ship, which represents your body, environment, and all your affairs. Your subconscious mind takes the orders you give it based upon what your conscious mind believes and accepts as true.

When you repeatedly say to people, "I can't afford it," then your subconscious mind takes you at your word and sees to it that you will not be in a position to purchase what you want. As long as you persist in saying, "I can't afford that car, that trip to Europe, that home, that fur coat or ermine wrap," you can rest assured that your subconscious mind will follow your orders, and you will go through life experiencing the lack of all these things.

Last Christmas Eve a beautiful young university student looked at an attractive and rather expensive traveling bag in a store window. She was going home to Buffalo, New York, for the holidays. She was about to say, "I can't afford that bag," when she recalled something she had heard at one of my lectures which was, "Never finish a negative statement; reverse it immediately, and wonders will happen in your life."

She said, "That bag is mine. It is for sale. I accept it mentally, and my subconscious sees to it that I receive it."

At eight o'clock Christmas Eve her fiancé presented her

with a bag exactly the same as the one she had looked at and mentally identified herself with at ten o'clock the same morning. She had filled her mind with the thought of expectancy and released the whole thing to her deeper mind which has the "know-how" of accomplishment.

This young girl, a student at the University of Southern California, said to me, "I didn't have the money to buy that bag, but now I know where to find money and all the things I need, and that is in the treasure house of eternity within me."

Another simple illustration is this: When you say, "I do not like mushrooms," and the occasion subsequently comes that you are served mushrooms in sauces or salads, you will get indigestion because your subconscious mind says to you, "The boss (your conscious mind) does not like mushrooms." This is an amusing example of the outstanding differences and modes of operation of your conscious and subconscious minds.

A woman may say, "I wake up at three o'clock, if I drink coffee at night." Whenever she drinks coffee, her subconscious mind nudges her, as if to say, "The boss wants you to stay awake tonight."

Your subconscious mind works twenty-four hours a day and makes provisions for your benefit, pouring all the fruit of your habitual thinking into your lap.

HOW HER SUBCONSCIOUS RESPONDED

A woman wrote me a few months ago as follows: "I am seventy-five years old, a widow with a grown family. I was living alone and on a pension. I heard your lectures on the powers of the subconscious mind wherein you said that ideas could be conveyed to the subconscious mind by repetition, faith, and expectancy.

"I began to repeat frequently with feeling, 'I am wanted. I am happily married to a kind, loving, and spiritual-minded man. I am secure!'

"I kept on doing this many times a day for about two weeks, and one day at the corner drugstore I was introduced to a retired pharmacist. I found him to be kind, understanding, and very religious. He was a perfect answer to my prayer. Within a week he proposed to me, and now we are on our honeymoon in Europe. I know that the intelligence within my subconscious mind brought both of us together in divine order."

This woman discovered that the treasure house was within her. Her prayer was felt as true in her heart, and her affirmation sank down by osmosis into her subconscious mind, which is the creative medium. The moment she succeeded in bringing about a subjective embodiment, her subconscious mind brought about the answer through the law of attraction. Her deeper mind, full of wisdom and intelligence, brought both of them together in divine order.

Be sure that you think on *whatsoever things are true, whatsoever things are honest, whatsoever things are just, whatsoever things are pure, whatsoever things are lovely, whatsoever things are of good report; if there be any virtue, and if there be any praise, think on these things.* PHILIPPIANS 4:8.

BRIEF SUMMARY OF IDEAS WORTH REMEMBERING

1. The treasure house is within you. Look within for the answer to your heart's desire.

2. The great secret possessed by the great men of all ages was their ability to contact and release the powers of their subconscious mind. You can do the same.

3. Your subconscious has the answer to all problems. If you

suggest to your subconscious prior to sleep, "I want to get up at 6 A.M.," it will awaken you at that exact time.

4. Your subconscious mind is the builder of your body and can heal you. Lull yourself to sleep every night with the idea of perfect health, and your subconscious, being your faithful servant, will obey you.

5. Every thought is a cause, and every condition is an effect.

6. If you want to write a book, write a wonderful play, give a better talk to your audience, convey the idea lovingly and feelingly to your subconscious mind, and it will respond accordingly.

7. You are like a captain navigating a ship. He must give the right orders, and likewise, you must give the right orders (thoughts and images) to your subconscious mind which controls and governs all your experiences.

8. Never use the terms "I can't afford it" or "I can't do this." Your subconscious mind takes you at your word and sees to it that you do not have the money or the ability to do what you want to do. Affirm, "I can do all things through the power of my subconscious mind."

9. The law of life is the law of belief. A belief is a thought in your mind. Do not believe in things to harm or hurt you. Believe in the power of your subconscious to heal, inspire, strengthen, and prosper you. According to your belief is it done unto you.

10. Change your thoughts, and you change your destiny.

2

HOW YOUR OWN
MIND WORKS

You have a mind, and you should learn how to use it. There are two levels of your mind—the conscious or rational level, and the subconscious or irrational level. You think with your conscious mind, and whatever you habitually think sinks down into your subconscious mind, which creates according to the nature of your thoughts. Your subconscious mind is the seat of your emotions and is the creative mind. If you think good, good will follow; if you think evil, evil will follow. This is the way your mind works.

The main point to remember is once the subconscious mind accepts an idea, it begins to execute it. It is an interesting and subtle truth that the law of the subconscious mind works for good and bad ideas alike. This law, when applied in a negative way, is the cause of failure, frustration, and unhappiness.

However, when your habitual thinking is harmonious and constructive, you experience perfect health, success, and prosperity.

Peace of mind and a healthy body are inevitable when you begin to think and feel in the right way. Whatever you claim mentally and feel as true, your subconscious mind will accept and bring forth into your experience. The only thing necessary for you to do is to get your subconscious mind to accept your idea, and the law of your own subconscious mind will bring forth the health, peace, or the position you desire. You give the command or decree, and your subconscious will faithfully reproduce the idea impressed upon it. The law of your mind is this: You will get a reaction or response from your subconscious mind according to the nature of the thought or idea you hold in your conscious mind.

Psychologists and psychiatrists point out that when thoughts are conveyed to your subconscious mind, impressions are made in the brain cells. As soon as your subconscious accepts any idea, it proceeds to put it into effect immediately. It works by association of ideas and uses every bit of knowledge that you have gathered in your lifetime to bring about its purpose. It draws on the infinite power, energy, and wisdom within you. It lines up all the laws of nature to get its way. Sometimes it seems to bring about an immediate solution to your difficulties, but at other times it may take days, weeks, or longer. . . . *Its ways are past finding out.*

CONSCIOUS AND SUBCONSCIOUS
TERMS DIFFERENTIATED

You must remember that these are not two minds. They are merely two spheres of activity within one mind. Your conscious mind is the reasoning mind. It is that phase of mind which chooses. For example, you choose your books, your home, and your partner in life. You make all your decisions with your conscious mind. On the other hand, without any conscious choice on your part, your heart is kept functioning automatically, and the process of digestion, circulation, and breathing are carried on by your subconscious mind through processes independent of your conscious control.

Your subconscious mind accepts what is impressed upon it or what you consciously believe. It does not reason things out like your conscious mind, and it does not argue with you controversially. Your subconscious mind is like the soil which accepts any kind of seed, good or bad. Your thoughts are active and might be likened unto seeds. Negative, destructive thoughts continue to work negatively in your subconscious mind, and in due time will come forth into outer experience which corresponds with them.

Remember, your subconscious mind does not engage in proving whether your thoughts are good or bad, true or false, but it responds according to the nature of your thoughts or suggestions. For example, if you consciously assume something as true, even though it may be false, your subconscious mind will accept it as true and proceed to bring about results which must necessarily follow, because you consciously assumed it to be true.

EXPERIMENTS BY PSYCHOLOGISTS

Innumerable experiments by psychologists and others on persons in the hypnotic state have shown that the subconscious mind is incapable of making selections and comparisons which are necessary for a reasoning process. They have shown repeat-edly that your subconscious mind will accept any suggestions, however false. Having once accepted any suggestion, it re-sponds according to the nature of the suggestion given.

To illustrate the amenability of your subconscious mind to suggestion, if a practiced hypnotist suggests to one of his sub-jects that he is Napoleon Bonaparte, or even a cat or a dog, he will act out the part with inimitable accuracy. His personality becomes changed for the time being. He believes himself to be whatever the operator tells him he is.

A skilled hypnotist may suggest to one of his students in the hypnotic state that his back itches, to another that his nose is bleeding, to another that he is a marble statue, to another that he is freezing and the temperature is below zero. Each one will follow out the line of his particular suggestion, totally oblivious to all his surroundings which do not pertain to his idea.

These simple illustrations portray clearly the difference be-tween your conscious reasoning mind and your subconscious mind which is impersonal, nonselective, and accepts as true whatever your conscious mind believes to be true. Hence, the importance of selecting thoughts, ideas, and premises which bless, heal, inspire, and fill your soul with joy.

THE TERMS OBJECTIVE AND SUBJECTIVE
MIND CLARIFIED

Your conscious mind is sometimes referred to as your objective mind because it deals with outward objects. The objective mind takes cognizance of the objective world. Its media of observa-tion are your five physical senses. Your objective mind is your guide and director in your contact with your environment. You gain knowledge through your five senses. Your objective mind learns through observation, experience, and education. As previously pointed out, the greatest function of the objective mind is that of reasoning.

Suppose you are one of the thousands of tourists who come to Los Angeles annually. You would come to the conclusion that it is a beautiful city based upon your observation of the parks, pretty gardens, majestic buildings, and lovely homes. This is the working of your objective mind.

Your subconscious mind is oftentimes referred to as your subjective mind. Your subjective mind takes cognizance of its environment by means independent of the five senses. Your subjective mind perceives by intuition. It is the seat of your emotion and the storehouse of memory. Your subjective mind performs its highest functions when your objective senses are in abeyance. In a word, it is that intelligence which makes itself manifest when the objective mind is suspended or in a sleepy, drowsy state.

Your subjective mind sees without the use of the natural organs of vision. It has the capacity of clairvoyance and clairaudience. Your subjective mind can leave your body, travel to distant lands, and bring back information oftentimes of the most exact and truthful character. Through your subjective mind you can read the thoughts of others, read the contents of sealed envelopes and closed safes. Your subjective mind has the ability to apprehend the thoughts of others without the use of the ordinary objective means of communication. It is of the greatest importance that we understand the interaction of the objective and subjective mind in order to learn the true art of prayer.

THE SUBCONSCIOUS CANNOT REASON LIKE
YOUR CONSCIOUS MIND

Your subconscious mind cannot argue controversially. Hence, if you give it wrong suggestions, it will accept them as true and will proceed to bring them to pass as conditions, experiences, and events. All things that have happened to you are based on thoughts impressed on your subconscious mind through belief. If you have conveyed erroneous concepts to your subconscious mind, the sure method of overcoming them is by the repetition of constructive, harmonious thoughts frequently repeated which your subconscious mind accepts, thus forming new and healthy habits of thought and life, for your subconscious mind is the seat of habit.

The habitual thinking of your conscious mind establishes deep grooves in your subconscious mind. This is very favorable for you if your habitual thoughts are harmonious, peaceful, and constructive.

If you have indulged in fear, worry, and other obstructive forms of thinking, the remedy is to recognize the omnipotence of your subconscious mind and decree freedom, happiness, and perfect health. Your subconscious mind, being creative and one with your divine source, will proceed to create the freedom and happiness which you have earnestly decreed.

THE TREMENDOUS POWER OF SUGGESTION

You must realize by now that your conscious mind is the "watchman at the gate," and its chief function is to protect your subconscious mind from false impressions. You are now aware of one of the basic laws of mind: Your subconscious mind is amenable to suggestion. As you know, your subconscious mind does not make comparisons, or contrasts, neither does it reason and think things out for itself. This latter function belongs to your conscious mind. It simply reacts to the impressions given to it by your conscious mind. It does not show a preference for one course of action over another.

The following is a classic example of the tremendous power of suggestion. Suppose you approach a timid-looking passenger on board ship and say to him something like this: "You look very ill. How pale you are! I feel certain you are going to be seasick. Let me help you to your cabin." The passenger turns pale. Your suggestion of seasickness associates itself with his own fears and forebodings. He accepts your aid down to the berth, and there your negative suggestion, which was accepted by him, is realized.

DIFFERENT REACTIONS TO
THE SAME SUGGESTION

It is true that different people will react in different ways to the same suggestion because of their subconscious conditioning or belief. For example, if you go to a sailor on the ship and say to him sympathetically, "My dear fellow, you're looking very ill. Aren't you feeling sick? You look to me as if you were going to be seasick."

According to his temperament he either laughs at your "joke," or expresses a mild irritation. Your suggestion fell on deaf ears in this instance because your suggestion of seasickness was associated in his mind with his own immunity from it. Therefore, it called up not fear or worry, but self-confidence.

The dictionary says that a suggestion is the act or instance of putting something into one's mind, the mental process by which the thought or idea suggested is entertained, accepted, or put into effect. You must remember that a suggestion cannot impose something on the subconscious mind against the will of the conscious mind. In other words, your conscious mind has the power to reject the suggestion given. In the case of the sailor, he had no fear of seasickness. He had convinced himself of his immunity, and the negative suggestion had absolutely no power to evoke fear.

The suggestion of seasickness to the other passenger called forth his indwelling fear of seasickness. Each of us has his own inner fears, beliefs, opinions, and these inner assumptions rule and govern our lives. A suggestion has no power in and of itself except it is accepted mentally by you. This causes your subconscious powers to flow in a limited and restricted way according to the nature of the suggestion.

HOW HE LOST HIS ARM

Every two or three years I give a series of lectures at the London Truth Forum in Caxton Hall. This is a Forum I founded a number of years ago. Dr. Evelyn Fleet, the director, told me about an article which appeared in the English newspapers dealing with the power of suggestion. This is the suggestion a man gave to his subconscious mind over a period of about two years: "I would give my right arm to see my daughter cured." It appeared that his daughter had a crippling form of arthritis together with a so-called incurable form of skin disease. Medical treatment had failed to alleviate the condition, and the father had an intense longing for his daughter's healing, and expressed his desire in the words just quoted.

Dr. Evelyn Fleet said that the newspaper article pointed out that one day the family was out riding when their car collided with another. The father's right arm was torn off at the shoulder, and immediately the daughter's arthritis and skin condition vanished.

You must make certain to give your subconscious only suggestions which heal, bless, elevate, and inspire you in all your ways. Remember that your subconscious mind cannot take a joke. It takes you at your word.

HOW AUTOSUGGESTION BANISHES FEAR

Illustrations of autosuggestion: Autosuggestion means suggesting something definite and specific to oneself. Herbert Parkyn, in his excellent manual of autosuggestion,* records the following incident. It has its amusing side, so that one remembers it. "A New York visitor in Chicago looks at his watch, which is set an hour ahead of Chicago time, and tells a Chicago friend that it is twelve o'clock. The Chicago friend, not considering the difference in time between Chicago and New York, tells the New Yorker that he is hungry and that he must go to lunch."

Autosuggestion may be used to banish various fears and other negative conditions. A young singer was invited to give an audition. She had been looking forward to the interview, but on three previous occasions she had failed miserably due to fear of failure. This young lady had a very good voice, but she had been saying to herself, "When the time comes for me to sing, maybe they won't like me. I will try, but I'm full of fear and anxiety."

Her subconscious mind accepted these negative autosuggestions as a request and proceeded to manifest them and bring them into her experience. The cause was an involuntary autosuggestion, i.e., silent fear thoughts emotionalized and subjectified.

She overcame it by the following technique: Three times a

---

* Herbert Parkyn, *Autosuggestion* (London: Fowler, 1916).

day she isolated herself in a room. She sat down comfortably in an armchair, relaxed her body, and closed her eyes. She stilled her mind and body as best she could. Physical inertia favors mental passivity and renders the mind more receptive to suggestion. She counteracted the fear suggestion by saying to herself, "I sing beautifully. I am poised, serene, confident, and calm." She repeated this statement slowly, quietly, and with feeling from five to ten times at each sitting. She had three such "sittings" every day and one immediately prior to sleep. At the end of a week she was completely poised and confident. When the invitation to audition came, she gave a remarkable, wonderful audition.

HOW SHE RESTORED HER MEMORY

A woman, aged seventy-five, was in the habit of saying to herself, "I am losing my memory." She reversed the procedure and practiced induced autosuggestion several times a day as follows: "My memory from today on is improving in every department. I shall always remember whatever I need to know at every moment of time and point of space. The impressions received will be clearer and more definite. I shall retain them automatically and with ease. Whatever I wish to recall will immediately present itself in the correct form in my mind. I am improving rapidly every day, and very soon my memory will be better than it has ever been before." At the end of three weeks, her memory was back to normal, and she was delighted.

HOW HE OVERCAME A NASTY TEMPER

Many men who complained of irritability and bad temper proved to be very susceptible to autosuggestion and obtained marvelous results by using the following statements three or four times a day—morning, noon, and at night prior to sleep for about a month. "Henceforth, I shall grow more good-humored. Joy, happiness, and cheerfulness are now becoming my normal states of mind. Every day I am becoming more and more lovable and understanding. I am now becoming the center of cheer and good will to all those about me, infecting them with good humor. This happy, joyous, and cheerful mood is now becoming my normal, natural state of mind. I am grateful."

THE CONSTRUCTIVE AND DESTRUCTIVE POWER OF SUGGESTION

Some illustrations and comments on heterosuggestion: Heterosuggestion means suggestions from another person. In all ages the power of suggestion has played a part in the life and thought of man in every period of time and in each country of the earth. In many parts of the world it is the controlling power in religion.

Suggestion may be used to discipline and control ourselves, but it can also be used to take control and command over others who do not know the laws of mind. In its constructive form it is wonderful and magnificent. In its negative aspects it is one of the most destructive of all the response patterns of the mind, resulting in patterns of misery, failure, suffering, sickness, and disaster.

HAVE YOU ACCEPTED ANY OF THESE?

From infancy on the majority of us have been given many negative suggestions. Not knowing how to thwart them, we unconsciously accepted them. Here are some of the negative suggestions: "You can't." "You'll never amount to anything." "You mustn't." "You'll fail." "You haven't got a chance." "You're all wrong." "It's no use." "It's not what you know, but who you know." "The world is going to the dogs." "What's the use, nobody cares." "It's no use trying so hard." "You're too old now." "Things are getting worse and worse." "Life is an endless grind." "Love is for the birds." "You just can't win." "Pretty soon you'll be bankrupt." "Watch out, you'll get the virus." "You can't trust a soul," etc.

Unless, as an adult, you use constructive autosuggestion, which is a reconditioning therapy, the impressions made on you in the past can cause behavior patterns that cause failure in your personal and social life. Autosuggestion is a means releasing you from the mass of negative verbal conditioning that might otherwise distort your life pattern, making the development of good habits difficult.

YOU CAN COUNTERACT NEGATIVE SUGGESTIONS

Pick up the paper any day, and you can read dozens of items that could sow the seeds of futility, fear, worry, anxiety, and impending doom. If accepted by you, these thoughts of fear could cause you to lose the will for life. Knowing that you can reject all these negative suggestions by giving your subconscious mind constructive autosuggestions, you counteract all these destructive ideas.

Check regularly on the negative suggestions that people make to you. You do not have to be influenced by destructive heterosuggestion. All of us have suffered from it in our childhood and in our teens. If you look back, you can easily recall how parents, friends, relatives, teachers, and associates contributed in a campaign of negative suggestions. Study the things said to you, and you will discover much of it was in the form of propaganda. The purpose of much of what was said was to control you or instill fear into you.

This heterosuggestion process goes on in every home, office, factory, and club. You will find that many of these suggestions are for the purpose of making you think, feel, and act as others want you to and in ways that are to their advantage.

HOW SUGGESTION KILLED A MAN

Here is an illustration of heterosuggestion: A relative of mine went to a crystal gazer in India who told him that he had a bad heart and predicted that he would die at the next new moon. He began to tell all members of his family about this prediction, and he arranged his will.

This powerful suggestion entered into his subconscious mind because he accepted it completely. My relative also told me that this crystal gazer was believed to have some strange occult powers, and he could do harm or good to a person. He died as predicted not knowing that he was the cause of his own death. I suppose many of us have heard similar stupid, ridiculous, superstitious stories.

Let us look at what happened in the light of our knowledge of the way the subconscious mind works. Whatever the conscious, reasoning mind of man believes, the subconscious mind will accept and act upon. My relative was happy, healthy, vigorous, and robust when he went to see the fortune-teller. She gave him a very negative suggestion which he accepted. He became terrified, and constantly dwelt upon the fact that he was going to die at the next new moon. He proceeded to tell everyone about it, and he prepared for the end. The activity took place in his own mind, and his own thought was the cause. He brought about his own so-called death, or rather destruction of the physical body, by his fear and expectation of the end.

The woman who predicted his death had no more power than the stones and sticks in the field. Her suggestion had no power to create or bring about the end she suggested. If he had known the laws of his mind, he would have completely rejected the negative suggestion and refused to give her words any attention, knowing in his heart that he was governed and controlled by his own thought and feeling. Like tin arrows aimed at a battleship, her prophecy could have been completely neutralized and dissipated without hurting him.

The suggestions of others in themselves have absolutely no power whatever over you except the power that you give them through your own thoughts. You have to give your mental consent; you have to entertain the thought. Then, it becomes your thought, and you do the thinking. Remember, you have the capacity to choose. Choose life! Choose love! Choose health!

THE POWER OF AN ASSUMED MAJOR PREMISE

Your mind works like a syllogism. This means that whatever major premise your conscious mind assumes to be true determines the conclusion your subconscious mind comes to in regard to any particular question or problem in your mind. If your premise is true, the conclusion must be true as in the following example:

Every virtue is laudable;
Kindness is a virtue;
Therefore, kindness is laudable.

Another example is as follows:

All formed things change and pass away;
The Pyramids of Egypt are formed things;
Therefore, some day the Pyramids will pass away.

The first statement is referred to as the major premise, and the right conclusion must necessarily follow the right premise.

A college professor, who attended some of my science of mind lectures in May 1962, at Town Hall, New York, said to me, "Everything in my life is topsy-turvy, and I have lost health, wealth, and friends. Everything I touch turns out wrong."

I explained to him that he should establish a major premise in his thinking, that the infinite intelligence of his subconscious mind was guiding, directing, and prospering him spiritually, mentally, and materially. Then, his subconscious mind would automatically direct him wisely in his investments, decisions, and also heal his body and restore his mind to peace and tranquility.

This professor formulated an overall picture of the way he wanted his life to be, and this was his major premise:

"Infinite intelligence leads and guides me in all my ways. Perfect health is mine, and the Law of Harmony operates in my mind and body. Beauty, love, peace, and abundance are mine. The principle of right action and divine order govern my entire life. I know my major premise is based on the eternal truths of life, and I know, feel, and believe that my subconscious mind responds according to the nature of my conscious mind thinking."

He wrote me as follows: "I repeated the above statements slowly, quietly, and lovingly several times a day knowing that they were sinking deep down into my subconscious mind, and that results must follow. I am deeply grateful for the interview you gave me, and I would like to add that all departments of my life are changing for the better. It works!"

THE SUBCONSCIOUS DOES NOT ARGUE
CONTROVERSIALLY

Your subconscious mind is all-wise and knows the answers to all questions. It does not argue with you or talk back to you. It does not say, "You must not impress me with that." For example, when you say, "I can't do this," "I am too old now," "I can't meet this obligation," "I was born on the wrong side of the tracks," "I don't know the right politician," you are impregnating your subconscious with these negative thoughts, and it responds accordingly. You are actually blocking your own good, thereby bringing lack, limitation, and frustration into your life.

When you set up obstacles, impediments, and delays in your conscious mind, you are denying the wisdom and intelligence resident in your subconscious mind. You are actually saying in effect that your subconscious mind cannot solve your problem. This leads to mental and emotional congestion, followed by sickness and neurotic tendencies.

To realize your desire and overcome your frustration, affirm boldly several times a day: "The infinite intelligence which gave me this desire leads, guides, and reveals to me the perfect plan for the unfolding of my desire. I know the deeper wisdom of my subconscious is now responding, and what I feel and claim within is expressed in the without. There is a balance, equilibrium, and equanimity."

If you say, "There is no way out; I am lost; there is no way out of this dilemma; I am stymied and blocked," you will get no answer or response from your subconscious mind. If you want the subconscious to work for you, give it the right request, and attain its cooperation. It is always working for you. It is controlling your heartbeat this minute and also your breathing. It heals a cut on your finger, and its tendency is lifeward, forever seeking to take care of you and preserve you. Your subconscious has a mind of its own, but it accepts your patterns of thought and imagery.

When you are seeking an answer to a problem, your subconscious will respond, but it expects you to come to a decision and to a true judgment in your conscious mind. You must acknowledge the answer is in your subconscious mind. However, if you say, "I don't think there is any way out; I am all mixed up and confused; why don't I get an answer?" you are neutralizing your prayer. Like the soldier marking time, you do not get anywhere.

Still the wheels of your mind, relax, let go, and quietly affirm: "My subconscious knows the answer. It is responding to me now. I give thanks because I know the infinite intelligence of my subconscious knows all things and is revealing the perfect answer to me now. My real conviction is now setting free the majesty and glory of my subconscious mind. I rejoice that it is so."

REVIEW OF HIGHLIGHTS

1. Think good, and good follows. Think evil, and evil follows. You are what you think all day long.
2. Your subconscious mind does not argue with you. It accepts what your conscious mind decrees. If you say, "I can't afford it," it may be true, but do not say it. Select a better thought, decree, *"I'll buy it. I accept it in my mind."*
3. You have the power to choose. Choose health and happiness. You can choose to be friendly, or you can choose to be unfriendly. Choose to be cooperative, joyous, friendly, lovable, and the whole world will respond. This is the best way to develop a wonderful personality.
4. Your conscious mind is the "watchman at the gate." Its chief function is to protect your subconscious mind from false

impressions. Choose to believe that something good can happen and is happening now. Your greatest power is your capacity to choose. *Choose happiness and abundance.*

5. The suggestions and statements of others have no power to hurt you. The only power is the movement of your own thought. You can choose to reject the thoughts or statements of others and affirm the good. You have the power to choose how you will react.

6. Watch what you say. You have to account for every idle word. Never say, "I will fail; I will lose my job; I can't pay the rent." *Your subconscious cannot take a joke.* It brings all these things to pass.

7. Your mind is not evil. No force of nature is evil. It depends how you use the powers of nature. Use your mind to bless, heal, and inspire all people everywhere.

8. Never say, "I can't." Overcome that fear by substituting the following: "I can do all things through the power of my own subconscious mind."

9. Begin to think from the standpoint of the eternal truths and principles of life and not from the standpoint of fear, ignorance, and superstition. *Do not let others do your thinking for you.* Choose your own thoughts and make your own decisions.

10. You are the captain of your soul (subconscious mind) and the master of your fate. Remember, you have the capacity to choose. Choose life! Choose love! Choose health! Choose happiness!

11. Whatever your conscious mind assumes and believes to be true, your subconscious mind will accept and bring to pass. Believe in good fortune, divine guidance, right action, and all the *blessings* of life.

3

THE MIRACLE-WORKING POWER OF YOUR SUBCONSCIOUS

The power of your subconscious is enormous. It inspires you, it guides you, and it reveals to you names, facts, and scenes from the storehouse of memory. Your subconscious started your heartbeat, controls the circulation of your blood, regulates your digestion, assimilation, and elimination. When you eat a piece of bread, your subconscious mind transmutes it into tissue, muscle, bone, and blood. This process is beyond the ken of the wisest man who walks the earth. Your subconscious mind controls all the vital processes and functions of your body and knows the answer to all problems.

Your subconscious mind never sleeps, never rests. It is always on the job. You can discover the miracle-working power of your subconscious by plainly stating to your subconscious prior to sleep that you wish a certain specific thing accomplished. You will be delighted to discover that forces within you will be released, leading to the desired result. Here, then, is a source of power and wisdom which places you in touch with omnipotence or the power that moves the world, guides the planets in their course, and causes the sun to shine.

Your subconscious mind is the source of your ideals, aspirations, and altruistic urges. It was through the subconscious mind that Shakespeare perceived great truths hidden from the average man of his day. Undoubtedly, it was the response of his subconscious mind that caused the Greek sculptor, Phidias, to portray beauty, order, symmetry, and proportion in marble and bronze. It enabled the Italian artist, Raphael, to paint Madonnas, and Ludwig van Beethoven to compose symphonies.

In 1955 I lectured at the Yoga Forest University, Rishikesh, India, and there I chatted with a visiting surgeon from Bombay. He told me about Dr. James Esdaille, a Scotch surgeon, who worked in Bengal before ether or other modern methods of anesthesia were discovered. Between 1843 and 1846, Dr. Esdaille performed about four hundred major operations of all kinds, such as amputations, removal of tumors and cancerous growths, as well as operations on the eye, ear, and throat. All operations were conducted under mental anesthesia only. This Indian doctor at Rishikesh informed me that the postoperative mortality rate of patients operated on by Dr. Esdaille was extremely low, probably two or three percent. Patients felt no pain, and there were no deaths during the operations.

Dr. Esdaille suggested to the subconscious minds of all his patients, who were in a hypnotic state, that no infection or septic condition would develop. You must remember that this was before Louis Pasteur, Joseph Lister, and others who pointed out the bacterial origin of disease and causes of infection due to unsterilized instruments and virulent organisms.

This Indian surgeon said that the reason for the low mortality rate and the general absence of infection, which was reduced to a minimum, was undoubtedly due to the suggestions of Dr. Esdaille to the subconscious minds of his patients. They responded according to the nature of his suggestion.

It is simply wonderful, when you conceive how a surgeon, over one hundred twenty years ago, discovered the miraculous wonder-working powers of the subconscious mind. Doesn't it cause you to be seized with a sort of mystic awe when you stop and think of the transcendental powers of your subconscious mind? Consider its extrasensory perceptions, such as its capacity for clairvoyance and clairaudience, its independence of time and space, its capacity to render you free from all pain and suffering, and its capacity to get the answer to all problems, be they what they may. All these and many more reveal to you that there is a power and an intelligence within you that far transcends your intellect, causing you to marvel at the wonders of it all. All these experiences cause you to rejoice and believe in the miracle-working powers of your own subconscious mind.

YOUR SUBCONSCIOUS IS YOUR BOOK OF LIFE

Whatever thoughts, beliefs, opinions, theories, or dogmas you write, engrave, or impress on your subconscious mind, you shall experience them as the objective manifestation of circumstances, conditions, and events. What you write on the inside, you will experience on the outside. You have two sides to your life, objective and subjective, visible and invisible, thought and its manifestation.

Your thought is received by your brain, which is the organ of your conscious reasoning mind. When your conscious or objective mind accepts the thought completely, it is sent to the solar plexus, called the brain of your abdomen, where it becomes flesh and is made manifest in your experience.

As previously outlined, your subconscious cannot argue. It acts only from what you write on it. It accepts your verdict or the conclusions of your conscious mind as final. This is why you are always writing on the book of life, because your thoughts become your experiences. The American essayist Ralph Waldo Emerson said, "Man is what he thinks all day long."

WHAT IS IMPRESSED IN THE SUBCONSCIOUS
IS EXPRESSED

William James, the father of American psychology, said that the power to move the world is in your subconscious mind. Your subconscious mind is one with infinite intelligence and boundless wisdom. It is fed by hidden springs, and is called the law of life. Whatever you impress upon your subconscious mind, the latter will move heaven and earth to bring it to pass. You must, therefore, impress it with right ideas and constructive thoughts.

The reason there is so much chaos and misery in the world is because people do not understand the interaction of their conscious and subconscious minds. When these two principles work in accord, in concord, in peace, and synchronously together, you will have health, happiness, peace, and joy. There is no sickness or discord when the conscious and subconscious work together harmoniously and peacefully.

The tomb of Hermes was opened with great expectancy and a sense of wonder because people believed that the greatest secret of the ages was contained therein. The secret was *as within, so without; as above, so below.*

In other words, whatever is impressed in your subconscious mind is expressed on the screen of space. This same truth was proclaimed by Moses, Isaiah, Jesus, Buddha, Zoroaster, Laotze, and the illumined seers of the ages. Whatever you feel as true subjectively is expressed as conditions, experiences, and events. Motion and emotion must balance. *As in heaven* [your own mind], *so on earth* [in your body and environment]. This is the great law of life.

You will find throughout all nature the law of action and re-action, of rest and motion. These two must balance, then there will be harmony and equilibrium. You are here to let the life principle flow through you rhythmically and harmoniously. The intake and the outgo must be equal. The impression and the expression must be equal. All your frustration is due to unfulfilled desire.

If you think negatively, destructively, and viciously, these thoughts generate destructive emotions which must be expressed and find an outlet. These emotions, being of a negative nature, are frequently expressed as ulcers, heart trouble, tension, and anxieties.

What is your idea or feeling about yourself now? Every part of your being expresses that idea. Your vitality, body, financial status, friends, and social status represent a perfect reflection of the idea you have of yourself. This is the real meaning of what is impressed in your subconscious mind, and which is expressed in all phases of your life.

We injure ourselves by the negative ideas which we entertain. How often have you wounded yourself by getting angry, fearful, jealous, or vengeful? These are the poisons that enter your subconscious mind. You were not born with these negative attitudes. Feed your subconscious mind life-giving thoughts, and you will wipe out all the negative patterns lodged therein. As you continue to do this, all the past will be wiped out and remembered no more.

THE SUBCONSCIOUS HEALS A MALIGNANCY
OF THE SKIN

A personal healing will ever be the most convincing evidence of the healing power of the subconscious mind. Over forty years ago I resolved a malignancy of the skin through prayer. Medical therapy had failed to check the growth, and it was getting progressively worse.

A clergyman, with a deep psychological knowledge, explained to me the inner meaning of the 139th Psalm wherein it says, *In thy book all my members were written, which in continuance were fashioned, when as yet there was none of them.* He explained that the term *book* meant my subconscious mind which fashioned and molded all my organs from an invisible cell. He also pointed out that inasmuch as my subconscious mind made my body, it could also recreate it and heal it according to the perfect pattern within it.

This clergyman showed me his watch and said, "This had a maker, and the watchmaker had to have the idea first in mind before the watch became an objective reality, and if the watch was out of order, the watchmaker could fix it." My friend reminded me that the subconscious intelligence which created my body was like a watchmaker, and it also knew exactly how to heal, restore, and direct all the vital functions and processes of my body, but that I had to give it the perfect idea of health. This would act as cause, and the effect would be a healing.

I prayed in a very simple way as follows: "My body and all its organs were created by the infinite intelligence in my subconscious mind. It knows how to heal me. Its wisdom fashioned all my organs, tissues, muscles, and bones. This infinite healing presence within me is now transforming every atom of my being making me whole and perfect now. I give thanks for the healing I know is taking place now. Wonderful are the works of the creative intelligence within me."

I prayed aloud for about five minutes two or three times a day repeating the above simple prayer. In about three months my skin was whole and perfect.

As you can see, all I did was give life-giving patterns of wholeness, beauty, and perfection to my subconscious mind, thereby obliterating the negative images and patterns of thought lodged in my subconscious mind which were the cause of all my trouble. Nothing appears on your body except when the mental equivalent is first in your mind, and as you change your mind by drenching it with incessant affirmatives, you change your body. This is the basis of all healing. . . . *Marvelous are thy works; and that my soul* [subconscious mind] *knoweth right well.* PSALMS 139:14.

HOW THE SUBCONSCIOUS CONTROLS ALL FUNCTIONS OF THE BODY

While you are awake or sound asleep upon your bed, the ceaseless, tireless action of your subconscious mind controls all the vital functions of your body without the help of your conscious mind. For example, while you are asleep your heart continues to beat rhythmically, your lungs do not rest, and the process of inhalation and exhalation, whereby your blood absorbs fresh air, goes on just the same as when you are awake. Your subconscious controls your digestive processes and glandular secretions, as well as all the other mysterious operations of your body. The hair on your face continues to grow whether you are asleep or awake. Scientists tell us that the skin secretes much more perspiration during sleep than during the waking hours. Your eyes, ears, and other senses are active during sleep. For instance, many of our great scientists have received answers to perplexing problems while they were asleep. They saw the answers in a dream.

Oftentimes your conscious mind interferes with the normal rhythm of the heart, lungs, and functioning of the stomach and intestines by worry, anxiety, fear, and depression. These patterns of thought interfere with the harmonious functioning of your subconscious mind. When mentally disturbed, the best procedure is to let go, relax, and still the wheels of your thought processes. Speak to your subconscious mind, telling it to take over in peace, harmony, and divine order. You will find that all the functions of your body will become normal again. Be sure to speak to your subconscious mind with authority and conviction, and it will conform to your command.

Your subconscious seeks to preserve your life and restore you to health at all costs. It causes you to love your children which also illustrates an instinctive desire to preserve all life. Let us suppose you accidentally ate some bad food. Your subconscious mind would cause you to regurgitate it. If you inadvertently took some poison, your subconscious powers would proceed to neutralize it. If you completely entrusted yourself to its wonder-working power, you would be entirely restored to health.

HOW TO GET THE SUBCONSCIOUS
TO WORK FOR YOU

The first thing to realize is that your subconscious mind is always working. It is active night and day, whether you act upon it or not. Your subconscious is the builder of your body, but you cannot consciously perceive or hear that inner silent process. Your business is with your conscious mind and not your subconscious mind. Just keep your conscious mind busy with the expectation of the best, and make sure the thoughts you habitually think are based on whatsoever things are lovely, true, just, and of good report. Begin now to take care of your conscious mind, knowing in your heart and soul that your subconscious mind is always expressing, reproducing, and manifesting according to your habitual thinking.

Remember, just as water takes the shape of the pipe it flows through, the life principle in you flows through you according to the nature of your thoughts. Claim that the healing presence in your subconscious is flowing through you as harmony, health, peace, joy, and abundance. Think of it as a living intelligence, a lovely companion on the way. Firmly believe it is continually flowing through you vivifying, inspiring, and prospering you. It will respond exactly this way. It is done unto you as you believe.

HEALING PRINCIPLE OF THE SUBCONSCIOUS
RESTORES ATROPHIED OPTIC NERVES

There is the well-known, duly authenticated case of Madame Bire of France, recorded in the archives of the medical department of Lourdes, France. She was blind, the optic nerves were atrophied and useless. She visited Lourdes and had what she termed a miraculous healing. Ruth Cranston, a Protestant young lady who investigated and wrote about healings at Lourdes in *McCall's* magazine, November, 1955, writes about Madame Bire as follows: "At Lourdes she regained her sight incredibly, with the optic nerves still lifeless and useless, as several doctors could testify after repeated examinations. A month later, upon reexamination, it was found that the seeing mechanism had been restored to normal. But at first, so far as medical examination could tell, she was seeing with 'dead eyes.'"

I have visited Lourdes several times where I, too, witnessed some healings, and of course, as we shall explain in the next chapter, there is no doubt that healings take place at many shrines throughout the world, Christian and non-Christian.

Madame Bire, to whom we just referred, was not healed by the waters of the shrine, but by her own subconscious mind which responded to her belief. The healing principle within her subconscious mind responded to the nature of her thought. Belief is a thought in the subconscious mind. It means to accept something as true. The thought accepted executes itself automatically. Undoubtedly, Madame Bire went to the shrine with expectancy and great faith, knowing in her heart she would receive a healing. Her subconscious mind responded accordingly, releasing the ever present healing forces. The subconscious mind which created the eye can certainly bring a dead nerve back to life. What the creative principle created, it can recreate. *According to your belief is it done unto you.*

HOW TO CONVEY THE IDEA OF PERFECT HEALTH
TO YOUR SUBCONSCIOUS MIND

A Protestant minister I knew in Johannesburg, South Africa, told me the method he used to convey the idea of perfect health to his subconscious mind. He had cancer of the lung. His technique, as given to me in his own handwriting, is exactly as follows: "Several times a day I would make certain that I was completely relaxed mentally and physically. I relaxed my body by speaking to it as follows, 'My feet are relaxed, my ankles are relaxed, my legs are relaxed, my abdominal muscles are relaxed, my heart and lungs are relaxed, my head is relaxed, my whole being is completely relaxed.' After about five minutes I would be in a sleepy drowsy state, and then I affirmed the following truth: 'The perfection of God is now being expressed through me. The idea of perfect health is now filling my subconscious mind. The image God has of me is a perfect image, and my subconscious mind recreates my body in perfect accordance with the perfect image held in the mind of God.'" This minister had a remarkable healing. This is a simple easy way of conveying the idea of perfect health to your subconscious mind.

Another wonderful way to convey the idea of health to your subconscious is through disciplined or scientific imagination. I told a man who was suffering from functional paralysis to make a vivid picture of himself walking around in his office, touching the desk, answering the telephone, and doing all the things he ordinarily would do if he were healed. I explained to him that this idea and mental picture of perfect health would be accepted by his subconscious mind.

He lived the role and actually felt himself back in the office. He knew that he was giving his subconscious mind something definite to work upon. His subconscious mind was the film upon which the picture was impressed. One day, after several weeks of frequent conditioning of the mind with this mental picture, the telephone rang by prearrangement and kept ringing while his wife and nurse were out. The telephone was about twelve feet away, but nevertheless he managed to answer it. He was healed at that hour. The healing power of his subconscious mind responded to his mental imagery, and a healing followed.

This man had a mental block, which prevented impulses from the brain reaching his legs; therefore, he said he could not walk. When he shifted his attention to the healing power within him, the power flowed through his focused attention, enabling him to walk.

Whatsoever ye shall ask in prayer, believing, ye shall receive. MATTHEW 21:22.

IDEAS WORTH REMEMBERING

1. Your subconscious mind controls all the vital processes of your body and knows the answer to all problems.

2. Prior to sleep, turn over a specific request to your subconscious mind and prove its miracle-working power to yourself.

3. Whatever you impress on your subconscious mind is expressed on the screen of space as conditions, experiences, and events. Therefore, you should carefully watch all ideas and thoughts entertained in your conscious mind.

4. The law of action and reaction is universal. Your thought is action, and the reaction is the automatic response of your subconscious mind to your thought. Watch your thoughts!

5. All frustration is due to unfulfilled desires. If you dwell on obstacles, delays, and difficulties, your subconscious mind responds accordingly, and you are blocking your own good.

6. The Life Principle will flow through you rhythmically and harmoniously if you consciously affirm: "I believe that the subconscious power which gave me this desire is now fulfilling it through me." This dissolves all conflicts.

7. You can interfere with the normal rhythm of your heart, lungs, and other organs by worry, anxiety, and fear. Feed your subconscious with thoughts of harmony, health, and peace, and all the functions of your body will become normal again.

8. Keep your conscious mind busy with the expectation of the best, and your subconscious will faithfully reproduce your habitual thinking.

9. Imagine the happy ending or solution to your problem, feel the thrill of accomplishment, and what you imagine and feel will be accepted by your subconscious mind and bring it to pass.

4

MENTAL HEALINGS
IN ANCIENT TIMES

Down through the ages men of all nations have somehow in-
stinctively believed that somewhere there resided a healing
power which could restore to normal the functions and sensations of man's body. They believed that this strange power
could be invoked under certain conditions, and that the alle-
viation of human suffering would follow. The history of all
nations presents testimony in support of this belief.

In the early history of the world the power of secretly influ-
encing men for good or evil, including the healing of the sick,
was said to be possessed by the priests and holy men of all nations. Healing of the sick was supposed to be a power derived
directly by them from God, and the procedures and processes
of healing varied throughout the world. The healing processes
took the form of supplications to God attended by various

ceremonies, such as the laying on of hands, incantations, and the application of amulets, talismans, rings, relics, and images.

For example, in the religions of antiquity priests in the ancient temples gave drugs to the patient and practiced hypnotic suggestions prior to the patient's sleep, telling him that the gods would visit him in his sleep and heal him. Many healings followed. Obviously, all this was the work of potent suggestions to the subconscious mind.

After the performance of certain mysterious rites, the devotees of Hecate would see the goddess during sleep, provided that before going to sleep they had prayed to her according to weird and fantastic instructions. They were told to mix lizards with resin, frankincense, and myrrh, and pound all this together in the open air under the crescent moon. Healings were reported in many cases following this grotesque procedure.

It is obvious that these strange procedures, as mentioned in the illustrations given, favored suggestion and acceptance by the subconscious mind of these people by making a powerful appeal to their imagination. Actually, in all these healings, the subconscious mind of the subject was the healer.

In all ages unofficial healers have obtained remarkable results in cases where authorized medical skill has failed. This gives cause for thought. How do these healers in all parts of the world effect their cures? The answer to all these healings is due to the blind belief of the sick person which released the healing power resident in his subconscious mind. Many of the remedies and methods employed were rather strange and fantastic which fired the imagination of the patients, causing an aroused emotional state. This state of mind facilitated the suggestion of health, and was accepted both by the conscious and subconscious mind of the sick. This will be elaborated on further in the next chapter.

BIBLICAL ACCOUNTS ON THE USE
OF THE SUBCONSCIOUS POWERS

What things soever ye desire, when ye pray, believe that ye receive them, and ye shall have them. MARK 11:24.

Note the difference in tenses. The inspired writer tells us to believe and accept as true the fact that our desire has already been accomplished and fulfilled, that it is already completed, and that its realization will follow as a thing in the future.

The success of this technique depends on the confident conviction that the thought, the idea, the picture is already a fact in mind. In order for anything to have substance in the realm of mind, it must be thought of as actually existing there.

Here in a few cryptic words is a concise and specific direction for making use of the creative power of thought by impressing upon the subconscious the particular thing which you desire. Your thought, idea, plan, or purpose is as real on its own plane as your hand or your heart. In following the Biblical technique, you completely eliminate from your mind all consideration of conditions, circumstances, or anything which might imply adverse contingencies. You are planting a seed (concept) in the mind which, if you leave it undisturbed, will infallibly germinate into external fruition.

The prime condition which Jesus insisted upon was faith. Over and over again you read in the Bible, *According to your faith is it done unto you.* If you plant certain types of seeds in the ground, you have faith they will grow after their kind. This is the way of seeds, and trusting the laws of growth and agriculture, you know that the seeds will come forth after their kind. Faith as mentioned in the Bible is a way of thinking, an attitude of mind, an inner certitude, knowing that the idea you fully accept in your conscious mind will be embodied in your subconscious mind and made manifest. Faith is, in a sense, accepting as true what your reason and senses deny, i.e., a shutting out of the little, rational, analytical, conscious mind and embracing an attitude of complete reliance on the inner power of your subconscious mind.

A classical instance of Bible technique is recorded in MATTHEW 9:28–30. *And when he was come into the house, the blind men came to him: and Jesus saith unto them, Believe ye that I am able to do this? They said unto him, Yea, Lord. Then touched he their eyes, saying, according to your faith be it unto you. And their eyes were opened; and Jesus straitly charged them, saying, See that no man know it.*

In the words *according to your faith be it unto you,* you can see that Jesus was actually appealing to the cooperation of the subconscious mind of the blind men. Their faith was their great expectancy, their inner feeling, their inner conviction that something miraculous would happen, and that their prayer would be answered, and it was. This is the time-honored technique of healing, utilized alike by all healing groups throughout the world regardless of religious affiliation.

In the words *see that no man know it,* Jesus enjoins the newly healed patients not to discuss their healing because they might be subjected to the skeptical and derogatory criticisms of the unbelieving. This might tend to undo the benefits they had received at the hand of Jesus by depositing thoughts of fear, doubt, and anxiety in the subconscious mind.

. . . for with authority and power he commandeth the unclean spirits, and they come out. LUKE 4:36.

When the sick came to Jesus to be healed, they were healed by their faith together with his faith and understanding of the healing power of the subconscious mind. Whatever he decreed, he felt inwardly to be true. He and the people needing help were in the one universal subjective mind, and his silent inner knowing and conviction of the healing power changed the negative destructive patterns in the patients' subconscious. The resultant healings were the automatic response to the internal mental change. His command was his appeal to the subconscious mind of the patients plus his awareness, feeling, and absolute trust in the response of the subconscious mind to the words which he spoke with authority.

MIRACLES AT VARIOUS SHRINES
THROUGHOUT THE WORLD

It is an established fact that cures have taken place at various shrines throughout the world, such as in Japan, India, Europe, and America. I have visited several of the famous shrines in Japan. At the world famous shrine called Diabutsu is a gigantic divinity of bronze where Buddha is seated with folded hands, and the head is inclined in an attitude of profound contemplative ecstasy. It is 42 feet in height and is called the great Buddha. Here I saw young and old making offerings at its feet. Money, fruit, rice, and oranges were offered. Candles were lit, incense was burned, and prayers of petition recited.

The guide explained the chant of a young girl as she murmured a prayer, bowed low, and placed two oranges as an offering. She also lit a candle. He said she had lost her voice, and it was restored at the shrine. She was thanking Buddha for restoring her voice. She had the simple faith that Buddha would give her back her singing voice if she followed a certain ritual, fasted, and made certain offerings. All this helped to kindle faith and expectancy, resulting in a conditioning of her mind to the point of belief. Her subconscious mind responded to her belief.

To illustrate further the power of imagination and blind belief I will relate the case of a relative of mine who had tuberculosis. His lungs were badly diseased. His son decided to heal his father. He came home to Perth, Western Australia, where his father lived, and said to him that he had met a monk who had returned from one of the healing shrines in Europe. This monk sold him a piece of the true cross. He said that he gave the monk the equivalent of $500 for it.

This young man had actually picked up a splinter of wood from the sidewalk, went to the jeweler's, and had it set in a ring so that it looked real. He told his father that many were healed just by touching the ring or the cross. He inflamed and fired his father's imagination to the point that the old gentleman snatched the ring from him, placed it over his chest, prayed silently, and went to sleep. In the morning he was healed. All the clinic's tests proved negative.

You know, of course, it was not the splinter of wood from the sidewalk that healed him. It was his imagination aroused to an intense degree, plus the confident expectancy of a perfect healing. Imagination was joined to faith or subjective feeling, and the union of the two brought about a healing. The father never learned of the trick that had been played upon him. If he had, he probably would have had a relapse. He remained completely cured and passed away fifteen years later at the age of 89.

ONE UNIVERSAL HEALING PRINCIPLE

It is a well-known fact that all of the various schools of healing effect cures of the most wonderful character. The most obvious conclusion, which strikes your mind is that there must be some underlying principle which is common to them all, namely, the subconscious mind, and the one process of healing is faith.

It will now be in order to recall to your mind once more the following fundamental truths:

First that you possess mental functions which have been distinguished by designating one the conscious mind and the other the subconscious mind.

Secondly, your subconscious mind is constantly amenable to the power of suggestion. Furthermore, your subconscious mind has complete control of the functions, conditions, and sensations of your body.

I venture to believe that all the readers of this book are familiar with the fact that symptoms of almost any disease can be induced in hypnotic subjects by suggestion. For example, a subject in the hypnotic state can develop a high temperature, flushed face, or chills according to the nature of the suggestion given. By experiment, you can suggest to the person that he is paralyzed and cannot walk: it will be so. By illustration, you can hold a cup of cold water under the nose of the hypnotic subject and tell him, "This is full of pepper; smell it!" He will proceed to sneeze. What do you think caused him to sneeze, the water or the suggestion?

If a man says he is allergic to Timothy grass, you can place a synthetic flower or an empty glass in front of his nose, when he is in a hypnotic state, and tell him it is Timothy grass. He will portray the usual allergic symptoms. This indicates that the cause of the disease is in the mind. The healing of the disease can also take place mentally.

You realize that remarkable healings take place through osteopathy, chiropractic medicine, and naturopathy, as well as through all the various religious bodies throughout the world, but it is obvious that all of these healings are brought about through the subconscious mind—the only healer there is.

Notice how it heals a cut on your face caused by shaving. It knows exactly how to do it. The doctor dresses the wound and says, "Nature heals it!" Nature refers to natural law, the law of the subconscious mind, or self-preservation which is the function of the subconscious mind. The instinct of self-preservation is the first law of nature. Your strongest instinct is the most potent of all autosuggestions.

WIDELY DIFFERENT THEORIES

It would be tedious and unprofitable to discuss to any great extent the numerous theories advanced by different religious sects and prayer therapy groups. There are a great number who claim that because their theory produces results it is, therefore, the correct one. This, as explained in this chapter, cannot be true.

You are aware that there are all types of healing. Franz Anton Mesmer, a German physician (1734–1815) who practiced in Paris, discovered that by applying magnets to the diseased body, he could cure that disease miraculously. He also performed cures with various other pieces of glass and metals. He discontinued this form of healing and claimed that his cures were due to "animal magnetism," theorizing that this substance was projected from the healer to the patient.

His method of treating disease from then on was by hypnotism, which was called mesmerism in his day. Other physicians said that all his healings were due to suggestion and nothing else.

All of these groups, such as psychiatrists, psychologists,

osteopaths, chiropractors, physicians, and all the churches are using the one universal power resident in the subconscious mind. Each may proclaim the healings are due to their theory. The process of all healing is a definite, positive, mental attitude, an inner attitude, or a way of thinking, called faith. Healing is due to a confident expectancy, which acts as a powerful suggestion to the subconscious mind releasing its healing potency.

One man does not heal by a different power than another. It is true he may have his own theory or method. There is only one process of healing and that is faith. There is only one healing power, namely, your subconscious mind. Select the theory and method you prefer. You can rest assured, if you have faith, you shall get results.

VIEWS OF PARACELSUS

Philippus Paracelsus, a famous Swiss alchemist and physician, who lived from 1493 to 1541, was a great healer in his day. He stated what is now an obvious scientific fact when he uttered these words, "Whether the object of your faith be real or false, you will nevertheless obtain the same effects. Thus, if I believed in Saint Peter's statue as I should have believed in Saint Peter himself, I shall obtain the same effects that I should have obtained from Saint Peter. But that is superstition. Faith, however, produces miracles; and whether it is true or false faith, it will always produce the same wonders."

The views of Paracelsus were also entertained in the sixteenth century by Pietro Pomponazzi, an Italian philosopher and contemporary of Paracelsus, who said, "We can easily conceive the marvelous effects which confidence and imagination can produce, particularly when both qualities are reciprocated between the subjects and the person who influences them. The cures attributed to the influence of certain relics are the effect of their imagination and confidence. Quacks and philosophers know that if the bones of any skeleton were put in place of the saint's bones, the sick would nonetheless experience beneficial effects, if they believed that they were veritable relics."

Then, if you believe in the bones of saints to heal, or if you believe in the healing power of certain waters, you will get results because of the powerful suggestion given to your subconscious mind. It is the latter that does the healing.

BERNHEIM'S EXPERIMENTS

Hippolyte Bernheim, professor of medicine at Nancy, France, 1910–1919, was the expounder of the fact that the suggestion of the physician to the patient was exerted through the subconscious mind.

Bernheim, in his *Suggestive Therapeutics*, page 197, tells a story of a man with paralysis of the tongue which had yielded to no form of treatment. His doctor told the patient that he had a new instrument with which he promised to heal him. He introduced a pocket thermometer into the patient's mouth. The patient imagined it to be the instrument, which was to save him. In a few moments he cried out joyfully that he could once more move his tongue freely.

"Among our cases," continues Bernheim, "facts of the same sort will be found. A young girl came into my office, having suffered from complete loss of speech for nearly four weeks. After making sure of the diagnosis, I told my students that loss of speech sometimes yielded instantly to electricity, which might act simply by its suggestive influence. I sent for the induction apparatus. I applied my hand over the larynx and moved a little, and said, 'Now you can speak aloud.' In an instant I made her say 'a,' then 'b,' then 'Maria.' She continued to speak distinctly; the loss of voice had disappeared."

Here Bernheim is showing the power of faith and expectancy on the part of the patient which acts as a powerful suggestion to the subconscious mind.

PRODUCING A BLISTER BY SUGGESTION

Bernheim states that he produced a blister on the back of a patient's neck by applying a postage stamp and suggesting to the patient that it was a fly-plaster. This has been confirmed by the experiments and experiences of many doctors in many parts of the world, which leave no doubt that structural changes are a possible result of oral suggestion to patients.

THE CAUSE OF BLOODY STIGMATA

In Hudson's *Law of Psychic Phenomena*, page 153, he states, "Hemorrhages and bloody stigmata may be induced in certain subjects by means of suggestion.

"Dr. M. Bourru put a subject into the somnambulistic condition, and gave him the following suggestion: 'At four o'clock this afternoon, after the hypnosis, you will come into my office, sit down in the armchair, cross your arms upon your breast, and your nose will begin to bleed.' At the hour appointed the young man did as directed. Several drops of blood came from the left nostril.

"On another occasion the same investigator traced the patient's name on both his forearms with the dull point of an instrument. Then when the patient was in the somnambulistic condition, he said, 'At four o'clock this afternoon you will go to sleep, and your arms will bleed along the lines which I have traced, and your name will appear written on your arms in letters of blood.' He was watched at four o'clock and seen to fall asleep. On the left arm the letters stood out in bright relief, and in several places there were drops of blood. The letters were still visible three months afterward, although they had gradually grown faint."

These facts demonstrate at once the correctness of the two fundamental propositions previously stated, namely, the constant amenability of the subconscious mind to the power of suggestion and the perfect control, which the subconscious mind exercises over the functions, sensations, and conditions of the body.

All the foregoing phenomena dramatize vividly abnormal conditions induced by suggestion, and are conclusive proof that *as a man thinketh in his heart* [subconscious mind] *so is he.*

HEALING POINTS IN REVIEW

1. Remind yourself frequently that the healing power is in your own subconscious mind.
2. Know that faith is like a seed planted in the ground; it grows after its kind. Plant the idea (seed) in your mind, water and fertilize it with expectancy, and it will manifest.
3. The idea you have for a book, new invention, or play is real in your mind. This is why you can believe you have it now. Believe in the reality of your idea, plan, or invention, and as you do, it will become manifest.
4. In praying for another, know that your silent inner knowing of wholeness, beauty, and perfection can change the negative patterns of the other's subconscious mind and bring about wonderful results.
5. The miraculous healings you hear about at various shrines

are due to imagination and blind faith which act on the subconscious mind, releasing the healing power.

6. All disease originates in the mind. Nothing appears on the body unless there is a mental pattern corresponding to it.

7. The symptoms of almost any disease can be induced in you by hypnotic suggestion. This shows you the power of your thought.

8. There is only one process of healing and that is faith. There is only one healing power, namely, your subconscious mind.

9. Whether the object of your faith is real or false, you will get results. Your subconscious mind responds to the thought in your mind. Look upon faith as a thought in your mind, and that will suffice.

5

MENTAL HEALINGS IN MODERN TIMES

Everyone is definitely concerned with the healing of bodily conditions and human affairs. What is it that heals? Where is this healing power? These are questions asked by everyone. The answer is that this healing power is in the subconscious mind of each person, and a changed mental attitude on the part of the sick person releases this healing power.

No mental or religious science practitioner, psychologist, psychiatrist, or medical doctor ever healed a patient. There is an old saying, "The doctor dresses the wound, but God heals it." The psychologist or psychiatrist proceeds to remove the mental blocks in the patient so that the healing principle may be released, restoring the patient to health. Likewise, the surgeon removes the physical block enabling the healing currents to function normally. No physician, surgeon, or mental science practitioner claims that "he healed the patient." The one healing power is called by many names—Nature, Life, God, Creative Intelligence, and Subconscious Power.

As previously outlined, there are many different methods used to remove the mental, emotional, and physical blocks which inhibit the flow of the healing life principle animating all of us. The healing principle resident in your subconscious mind can and will, if properly directed by you or some other person, heal your mind and body of all disease. This healing principle is operative in all men regardless of creed, color, or race. You do not have to belong to some particular church in order to use and participate in this healing process. Your subconscious will heal the burn or cut on your hand even though you profess to be an atheist or agnostic.

The modern mental therapeutic procedure is based on the truth that the infinite intelligence and power of your subconscious mind responds according to your faith. The mental science practitioner or minister follows the injunction of the Bible, i.e., he goes into his closet and shuts the door, which means he stills his mind, relaxes, lets go, and thinks of the infinite healing presence within him. He closes the door of his mind to all outside distractions as well as appearances, and then he quietly and knowingly turns over his request or desire to his subconscious mind, realizing that the intelligence of his mind will answer him according to his specific needs.

The most wonderful thing to know is this: Imagine the end desired and feel its reality; then the infinite life principle will respond to your conscious choice and your conscious request. This is the meaning of *believe you have received, and you shall receive.* This is what the modern mental scientist does when he practices prayer therapy.

ONE PROCESS OF HEALING

There is only one universal healing principle operating through everything—the cat, the dog, the tree, the grass, the wind, the earth—for everything is alive. This life principle operates through the animal, vegetable, and mineral kingdoms as instinct and the law of growth. Man is consciously aware of this life principle, and he can consciously direct it to bless himself in countless ways.

There are many different approaches, techniques, and methods in using the universal power, but there is only one process of healing, which is faith, for *according to your faith is it done unto you.*

THE LAW OF BELIEF

All religions of the world represent forms of belief, and these beliefs are explained in many ways. The law of life is belief. What do you believe about yourself, life, and the universe? *It is done unto you as you believe.*

Belief is a thought in your mind, which causes the power of your subconscious to be distributed into all phases of your life according to your thinking habits. You must realize the Bible is not talking about your belief in some ritual, ceremony, form, institution, man, or formula. It is talking about belief itself. The belief of your mind is simply the thought of your mind. *If thou canst believe, all things are possible to him that believeth.* MARK 9:23.

It is foolish to believe in something to hurt or harm you. Remember, it is not the thing believed in that hurts or harms you, but the belief or thought in your mind, which creates the result. All your experiences, all your actions, and all the events and circumstances of your life are but the reflections and reactions to your own thought.

PRAYER THERAPY IS THE COMBINED FUNCTION OF THE CONSCIOUS AND SUBCONSCIOUS MIND SCIENTIFICALLY DIRECTED

Prayer therapy is the synchronized, harmonious, and intelligent function of the conscious and subconscious levels of mind specifically directed for a definite purpose. In scientific prayer or prayer therapy, you must know what you are doing and why you are doing it. You trust the law of healing. Prayer therapy is sometimes referred to as mental treatment, and another term is scientific prayer.

In prayer therapy you consciously choose a certain idea, mental picture, or plan which you desire to experience. You realize your capacity to convey this idea or mental image to your subconscious by feeling the reality of the state assumed. As you remain faithful in your mental attitude, your prayer will be answered. Prayer therapy is a definite mental action for a definite specific purpose.

Let us suppose that you decide to heal a certain difficulty by prayer therapy. You are aware that your problem or sickness, whatever it may be, must be caused by negative thoughts charged with fear and lodged in your subconscious mind, and that if you can succeed in cleansing your mind of these thoughts, you will get a healing.

You, therefore, turn to the healing power within your own subconscious mind and remind yourself of its infinite power and intelligence and its capacity to heal all conditions. As you dwell on these truths, your fear will begin to dissolve, and the recollection of these truths also corrects the erroneous beliefs.

You give thanks for the healing that you know will come, and then you keep your mind off the difficulty until you feel guided, after an interval, to pray again. While you are praying, you absolutely refuse to give any power to the negative conditions or to admit for a second that the healing will not come. This attitude of mind brings about the harmonious union of the conscious and subconscious mind, which releases the healing power.

FAITH HEALING, WHAT IT MEANS, AND HOW BLIND FAITH WORKS

What is popularly termed faith healing is not the faith mentioned in the Bible, which means knowledge of the interaction of the conscious and subconscious mind. A faith healer is one who heals without any real scientific understanding of the powers and forces involved. He may claim that he has a special gift of healing, and the sick person's blind belief in him or his powers may bring results.

The voodoo doctor in South Africa and other parts of the world may heal by incantations, or a person may be healed by touching the so-called bones of saints, or anything else which cause the patients to honestly believe in the method or process.

Any method which causes you to move from fear and worry to faith and expectancy will heal. There are many persons, each of whom claims that because his personal theory produces results, it is, therefore, the correct one. This, as already explained in this chapter, cannot be true.

To illustrate how blind faith works: You will recall our discussion of the German physician Franz Anton Mesmer. In 1776 he claimed many cures when he stroked diseased bodies with artificial magnets. Later on he threw away his magnets and evolved the theory of animal magnetism. This he held to be a fluid, which pervades the universe, but is most active in the human organism.

He claimed that this magnetic fluid, which was going forth from him to his patients healed them. People flocked to him, and many wonderful cures were effected.

Mesmer moved to Paris, and while there the Government appointed a commission composed of physicians and members of the Academy of Science, of which Benjamin Franklin was a member, to investigate his cures. The report admitted the leading facts claimed by Mesmer, but held that there was no evidence to prove the correctness of his magnetic fluid theory, and said the effects were due to the imagination of the patients.

Soon after this, Mesmer was driven into exile, and died in 1815. Shortly afterward, Dr. Braid of Manchester undertook to show that magnetic fluid had nothing to do with the production of the healings of Dr. Mesmer. Dr. Braid discovered that patients could be thrown into hypnotic sleep by suggestion, during which many of the well-known phenomena ascribed to magnetism by Mesmer could be produced.

You can readily see that all these cures were undoubtedly brought about by the active imagination of the patients together with a powerful suggestion of health to their subconscious minds. All this could be termed blind faith as there was no understanding in those days as to how the cures were brought about.

SUBJECTIVE FAITH AND WHAT IT MEANS

You will recall the proposition, which need not be repeated at length, that the subjective or subconscious mind of an individual is as amenable to the control of his own conscious objective mind as it is by the suggestions of another. It follows that whatever may be your objective belief, if you will assume to have faith actively or passively, your subconscious mind will be controlled by the suggestion, and your desire will be fulfilled.

The faith required in mental healings is a purely subjective faith, and it is attainable upon the cessation of active opposition on the part of the objective or conscious mind.

In the healing of the body it is, of course, desirable to secure the concurrent faith of both the conscious and subconscious mind. However, it is not always essential if you will enter into a state of passivity and receptivity by relaxing the mind and the body and getting into a sleepy state. In this drowsy state your passivity becomes receptive to subjective impression.

Recently, I was asked by a man, "How is it that I got a healing through a minister? I did not believe what he said when he told me that there is no such thing as disease and that matter does not exist."

This man at first thought his intelligence was being insulted, and he protested against such a palpable absurdity. The explanation is simple. He was quieted by soothing words and told to get into a perfectly passive condition, to say nothing, and think of nothing for the time being. His minister also became passive, and affirmed quietly, peacefully, and constantly for about one half hour that this man would have perfect health, peace, harmony, and wholeness. He felt immense relief and was restored to health.

It is easy to see that his subjective faith had been made manifest by his passivity under treatment, and the suggestions of perfect healthfulness by the minister were conveyed to his subconscious mind. The two subjective minds were men *en rapport*.

The minister was not handicapped by antagonistic autosuggestions of the patient arising from objective doubt of the power of the healer or the correctness of the theory. In this sleepy, drowsy state the conscious mind resistance is reduced to a minimum, and results followed. The subconscious mind of the patient being necessarily controlled by such suggestion exercised its functions in accordance therewith, and a healing followed.

THE MEANING OF ABSENT TREATMENT

Suppose you learned that your mother was sick in New York City and you lived in Los Angeles. Your mother would not be physically present where you are, but you could pray for her. *It is the Father within which doeth the work.*

The creative law of mind (subconscious mind) serves you and will do the work. Its response to you is automatic. Your treatment is for the purpose of inducing an inner realization of health and harmony in your mentality. This inner realization, acting through the subconscious mind, operates through your mother's subconscious mind as there is but one creative mind. Your thoughts of health, vitality, and perfection operate through the one universal subjective mind, and set a law in motion on the subjective side of life, which manifests through her body as a healing.

In the mind principle there is no time or space. It is the same mind that operates through your mother no matter where she may be. In reality there is no absent treatment as opposed to present treatment for the universal mind is omnipresent. You do not try to send out thoughts or hold a thought. Your treatment is a conscious movement of thought, and as you become conscious of the qualities of health, well-being, and relaxation, these qualities will be resurrected in the experience of your mother, and results will follow.

The following is a perfect example of what is called absent treatment. Recently, a listener of our radio program in Los Angeles prayed as follows for her mother in New York who had a coronary thrombosis: "The healing presence is right where my mother is. Her bodily condition is but a reflection of her thought-life like shadows cast on the screen. I know that in order to change the images on the screen I must change the projection reel. My mind is the projection reel, and I now project in my own mind the image of wholeness, harmony, and perfect health for my mother. The infinite healing presence, which created my mother's body and all her organs is now saturating every atom of her being, and a river of peace flows through every cell of her body. The doctors are divinely guided and directed, and whoever touches my mother is guided to do the right thing. I know that disease has no ultimate reality; if it had, no one could be healed. I now align myself with the infinite principle of love and life, and I know and decree that harmony, health, and peace are now being expressed in my mother's body."

She prayed in the above manner several times daily, and her mother had a most remarkable recovery after a few days, much to the amazement of her specialist. He complimented her on her great faith in the power of God.

The conclusion arrived at in the daughter's mind set the creative law of mind in motion on the subjective side of life, which manifested itself through her mother's body as perfect health and harmony. What the daughter felt as true about her mother was simultaneously resurrected in the experience of her mother.

RELEASING THE KINETIC ACTION
OF THE SUBCONSCIOUS MIND

A psychologist friend of mine told me that one of his lungs was infected. X rays and analysis showed the presence of tuberculosis. At night before going to sleep he would quietly affirm,

"Every cell, nerve, tissue, and muscle of my lungs is now being made whole, pure, and perfect. My whole body is being restored to health and harmony."

These are not his exact words, but they represent the essence of what he affirmed. A complete healing followed in about a month's time. Subsequent X rays showed a perfect healing.

I wanted to know his method, so I asked him why he repeated the words prior to sleep. Here is his reply: "The kinetic action of the subconscious mind continues throughout your sleep-time period. Hence, give the subconscious mind something good to work on as you drop off into slumber." This was a very wise answer. In thinking of harmony and perfect health, he never mentioned his trouble by name.

I strongly suggest that you cease talking about your ailments or giving them a name. The only sap from which they draw life is your attention and fear of them. Like the above-mentioned psychologist, become a mental surgeon. Then your troubles will be cut off like dead branches are pruned from a tree.

If you are constantly naming your aches and symptoms, you inhibit the kinetic action, which means the release of the healing power and energy of your subconscious mind. Furthermore, by the law of your own mind, these imaginings tend to take shape, *As the thing I greatly feared*. Fill your mind with the great truths of life and walk forward in the light of love.

SUMMARY OF YOUR AIDS TO HEALTH

1. Find out what it is that heals you. Realize that correct directions given to your subconscious mind will heal your mind and body.
2. Develop a definite plan for turning over your requests or desires to your subconscious mind.

3. Imagine the end desired and feel its reality. Follow it through, and you will get definite results.

4. Decide what belief is. Know that belief is a thought in your mind, and what you think you create.

5. It is foolish to believe in sickness as something to hurt or to harm you. Believe in perfect health, prosperity, peace, wealth, and divine guidance.

6. Great and noble thoughts upon which you habitually dwell become great acts.

7. Apply the power of prayer therapy in your life. Choose a certain plan, idea, or mental picture. Mentally and emotionally unite with that idea, and as you remain faithful to your mental attitude, your prayer will be answered.

8. Always remember, if you really want the power to heal, you can have it through faith, which means knowledge of the working of your conscious and subconscious mind. Faith comes with understanding.

9. Blind faith means that a person may get results in healing without any scientific understanding of the powers and forces involved.

10. Learn to pray for your loved ones who may be ill. Quiet your mind, and your thoughts of health, vitality, and perfection operating through the one universal subjective mind will be felt and resurrected in the mind of your loved one.

6

PRACTICAL TECHNIQUES IN MENTAL HEALINGS

An engineer has a technique and a process for building a bridge or an engine. Like the engineer, your mind also has a technique for governing, controlling, and directing your life. You must realize that methods and techniques are primary.

In building the Golden Gate bridge, the chief engineer understood mathematical principles, stresses, and strains. Secondly, he had a picture of the ideal bridge across the bay. The third step was his application of tried and proven methods by which the principles were implemented until the bridge took form and we drive on it. There also are techniques and methods by which your prayers are answered. If your prayer is answered, there is a way in which it is answered, and this is a scientific way. Nothing happens by chance. This is a world of law and order. In this chapter you will find practical techniques for the unfolding and nurture of your spiritual life. Your prayers must not remain up in the air like a balloon. They must go somewhere and accomplish something in your life.

When we come to analyze prayer we discover there are many different approaches and methods. We will not consider in this book the formal, ritual prayers used in religious services. These have an important place in group worship. We are immediately concerned with the methods of personal prayer as it is applied in your daily life and as it is used to help others.

Prayer is the formulation of an idea concerning something we wish to accomplish. Prayer is the soul's sincere desire. Your desire is your prayer. It comes out of your deepest needs and it reveals the things you want in life. *Blessed are they that hunger and thirst after righteousness: for they shall be filled.* That is really prayer, life's hunger and thirst for peace, harmony, health, joy, and all the other blessings of life.

THE PASSING-OVER TECHNIQUE
FOR IMPREGNATING THE SUBCONSCIOUS

This consists essentially in inducing the subconscious mind to take over your request as handed it by the conscious mind. This passing-over is best accomplished in the reverie-like state. Know that in your deeper mind are Infinite Intelligence and Infinite Power. Just calmly think over what you want; see it coming into fuller fruition from this moment forward. Be like the little girl who had a very bad cough and a sore throat. She declared firmly and repeatedly, "It is passing away now. It is passing away now." It passed away in about an hour. Use this technique with complete simplicity and naïveté.

YOUR SUBCONSCIOUS WILL ACCEPT
YOUR BLUEPRINT

If you were building a new home for yourself and family, you know that you would be intensely interested in regard to the blueprint for your home; you would see to it that the builders conformed to the blueprint. You would watch the material and select only the best wood, steel, in fact, the best of everything. What about your mental home and your mental blueprint for happiness and abundance? All your experiences and everything that enters into your life depend upon the nature of the mental building blocks which you use in the construction of your mental home.

If your blueprint is full of mental patterns of fear, worry, anxiety, or lack, and if you are despondent, doubtful, and cynical, then the texture of the mental material you are weaving into your mind will come forth as more toil, care, tension, anxiety, and limitation of all kinds.

The most fundamental and the most far-reaching activity in life is that which you build into your mentality every waking hour. Your word is silent and invisible; nevertheless, it is real.

You are building your mental home all the time, and your thought and mental imagery represent your blueprint. Hour by hour, moment by moment, you can build radiant health, success, and happiness by the thoughts you think, the ideas which you harbor, the beliefs that you accept, and the scenes that you rehearse in the hidden studio of your mind. This stately mansion, upon the construction of which you are perpetually engaged, is your personality, your identity in this plane, your whole life story on this earth.

Get a new blueprint; build silently by realizing peace, harmony, joy, and good will in the present moment. By dwelling upon these things and claiming them, your subconscious will accept your blueprint and bring all these things to pass. *By their fruits ye shall know them.*

THE SCIENCE AND ART OF TRUE PRAYER

The term "science" means knowledge which is coordinated, arranged, and systematized. Let us think of the science and art of true prayer as it deals with the fundamental principles of life and the techniques and processes by which they can be demonstrated in your life, as well as in the life of every human being when he applies them faithfully. The art is your technique or process, and the science behind it is the definite response of creative mind to your mental picture or thought.

Ask, and it shall be given you; seek, and ye shall find; knock, and it shall be opened unto you. MATTHEW 7:7.

Here you are told you shall receive that for which you ask. It shall be opened to you when you knock, and you shall find that for which you are searching. This teaching implies the definiteness of mental and spiritual laws. There is always a direct response from the Infinite Intelligence of your subconscious mind to your conscious thinking. If you ask for bread, you will not receive a stone. You must ask *believing,* if you are to receive. Your mind moves from the thought to the thing. Unless there is first an image in the mind, it cannot move, for there would be nothing for it to move toward. Your prayer, which is your mental act, must be accepted as an image in your mind before the power from your subconscious will play upon it and make it productive. You must reach a point of acceptance in your mind, an unqualified and undisputed state of agreement.

This contemplation should be accompanied by a feeling of joy and restfulness in foreseeing the certain accomplishment of your desire. The sound basis for the art and science of true prayer is your knowledge and complete confidence that the movement of your conscious mind will gain a definite response from your subconscious mind, which is one with boundless wisdom and infinite power. By following this procedure, your prayers will be answered.

THE VISUALIZATION TECHNIQUE

The easiest and most obvious way to formulate an idea is to visualize it, to see it in your mind's eye as vividly as if it were alive. You can see with the naked eye only what already exists in the external world; in a similar way, that which you can visualize in your mind's eye already exists in the invisible realms of your mind. Any picture, which you have in your mind, is *the substance of things hoped for and the evidence of things not seen*. What you form in your imagination is as real as any part of your body. The idea and the thought are real and will one day appear in your objective world if you are faithful to your mental image.

This process of thinking forms impressions in your mind; these impressions in turn become manifested as facts and experiences in your life. The builder visualizes the type of building he wants; he sees it as he desires it to be completed. His imagery and thought processes become a plastic mold from which the building will emerge—a beautiful or an ugly one, a skyscraper or a very low one. His mental imagery is projected as it is drawn on paper. Eventually, the contractor and his workers gather the essential materials, and the building progresses until it stands finished, conforming perfectly to the mental patterns of the architect.

I use the visualization technique prior to speaking from the platform. I quiet the wheels of my mind in order that I may present to the subconscious mind my images of thought. Then, I picture the entire auditorium and the seats filled with men and women, and each one of them illumined and inspired by the infinite healing presence within each one. I see them as radiant, happy, and free.

Having first built up the idea in my imagination, I quietly sustain it there as a mental picture while I imagine I hear men and women saying, "I am healed," "I feel wonderful," "I've had an instantaneous healing," "I'm transformed." I keep this up for about ten minutes or more, knowing and feeling that each person's mind and body are saturated with love, wholeness, beauty, and perfection. My awareness grows to the point where in my mind I can actually hear the voices of the multitude proclaiming their health and happiness; then I release the whole picture and go onto the platform. Almost every Sunday some people stop and say that their prayers were answered.

MENTAL MOVIE METHOD

The Chinese say, "A picture is worth a thousand words." William James, the father of American psychology, stressed the fact that the subconscious mind will bring to pass any picture held in the mind and backed by faith. *Act as though I am, and I will be.*

A number of years ago I was in the Middle West lecturing in several states, and I desired to have a permanent location in the general area from which I could serve those who desired help. I traveled far, but the desire did not leave my mind. One evening, while in a hotel in Spokane, Washington, I relaxed completely on a couch, immobilized my attention, and in a quiet, passive manner imagined that I was talking to a large audience, saying in effect, "I am glad to be here; I have prayed for the ideal opportunity." I saw in my mind's eye the imaginary audience, and I felt the reality of it all. I played the role of the actor, dramatized this mental movie, and felt satisfied that this picture was being conveyed to my subconscious mind, which would bring it to pass in its own way. The next morning, on awakening, I felt a great sense of peace and satisfaction, and in a few days' time I received a telegram asking me to take over an organization in the Midwest, which I did, and I enjoyed it immensely for several years.

The method outlined here appeals to many who have described it as "the mental movie method." I have received numerous letters from people who listen to my radio talks and weekly public lectures, telling me of the wonderful results they get using this technique in the sale of their property. I suggest to those who have homes or property for sale that they satisfy themselves in their own mind that their price is right. Then, I claim that the Infinite Intelligence is attracting to them the buyer who really wants to have the property and who will love it and prosper in it. After having done this I suggest that they quiet their mind, relax, let go, and get into a drowsy, sleepy state, which reduces all mental effort to a minimum. Then, they are to picture the check in their hands, rejoice in the check, give thanks for the check, and go off to sleep feeling the naturalness of the whole mental movie created in their own mind. They must act as though it were an objective reality, and the subconscious mind will take it as an impression, and through the deeper currents of the mind the buyer and the seller are brought together. A mental picture held in the mind, backed by faith, will come to pass.

THE BAUDOIN TECHNIQUE

Charles Baudoin was a professor at the Rousseau Institute in France. He was a brilliant psychotherapist and a research director of the New Nancy School of Healing, who in 1910 taught that the best way to impress the subconscious mind was to enter into a drowsy, sleepy state, or a state akin to sleep in which all effort was reduced to a minimum. Then in a quiet, passive, receptive way, by reflection, he would convey the idea to the subconscious. The following is his formula: "A very simple way of securing this (impregnation of the subconscious mind) is to condense the idea which is to be the object of suggestion, to sum it up in a brief phrase which can be readily graven on the memory, and to repeat it over and over again as a lullaby."

Some years ago, a young lady in Los Angeles was engaged in a prolonged bitter family lawsuit over a will. Her husband had bequeathed his entire estate to her, and his sons and daughters by a previous marriage were bitterly fighting to break the will. The Baudoin technique was outlined to her, and this is what she did: She relaxed her body in an armchair, entered into the sleepy state and, as suggested, condensed the idea of her need into a phrase consisting of six words easily graven on the memory. "It is finished in Divine Order." The significance to her of these words meant that Infinite Intelligence operating through the laws of her subconscious mind would bring about a harmonious adjustment through the principle of harmony. She continued this procedure every night for about ten nights. After she got into a sleepy state, she would affirm slowly, quietly, and feelingly the statement: "It is finished in Divine Order," over and over again, feeling a sense of inner peace and an all-pervading tranquility; then she went off into her deep, normal sleep.

On the morning of the eleventh day, following the use of

the above technique, she awakened with a sense of well-being, a conviction that *it was finished*. Her attorney called her the same day, saying that the opposing attorney and his clients were willing to settle. A harmonious agreement was reached, and litigation was discontinued.

THE SLEEPING TECHNIQUE

By entering into a sleepy, drowsy state, effort is reduced to a minimum. The conscious mind is submerged to a great extent when in a sleepy state. The reason for this is that the highest degree of outcropping of the subconscious occurs prior to sleep and just after we awaken. In this state the negative thoughts, which tend to neutralize your desire and so prevent acceptance by your subconscious mind, are no longer present.

Suppose you want to get rid of a destructive habit. Assume a comfortable posture, relax your body, and be still. Get into a sleepy state, and in that sleepy state, say quietly, over and over again as a lullaby, "I am completely free from this habit; harmony and peace of mind reign supreme." Repeat the above slowly, quietly, and lovingly for five or ten minutes night and morning. Each time you repeat the words the emotional value becomes greater. When the urge comes to repeat the negative habit, repeat the above formula out loud by yourself. By this means you induce the subconscious to accept the idea, and a healing follows.

THE "THANK YOU" TECHNIQUE

In the Bible, Paul recommends that we make known our requests with praise and thanksgiving. Some extraordinary results follow this simple method of prayer. The thankful heart is always close to the creative forces of the universe, causing countless blessings to flow toward it by the law of reciprocal relationship, based on a cosmic law of action and reaction.

For instance, a father promises his son a car for graduation; the boy has not yet received the car, but he is very thankful and happy, and is as joyous as though he had actually received the car. He knows his father will fulfill his promise, and he is full of gratitude and joy even though he has not yet received the car, objectively speaking. He has, however, received it with joy and thankfulness in his mind.

I shall illustrate how Mr. Broke applied this technique with excellent results. He said, "Bills are piling up, I am out of work, I have three children and no money. What shall I do?" Regularly every night and morning, for a period of about three weeks, he repeated the words, "Thank you, Father, for my wealth," in a relaxed, peaceful manner until the feeling or mood of thankfulness dominated his mind. He imagined he was addressing the infinite power and intelligence within him knowing, of course, that he could not see the creative intelligence or infinite mind. He was seeing with the inner eye of spiritual perception, realizing that his thought-image of wealth was the *first cause*, relative to the money, position, and food he needed. His thought-feeling was the substance of wealth untrammeled by antecedent conditions of any kind. By repeating, "Thank you, Father," over and over again, his mind and heart were lifted up to the point of acceptance, and when fear, thoughts of lack, poverty, and distress came into his mind, he would say, "Thank you, Father," as often as necessary. He knew that as he kept up the thankful attitude he would recondition his mind to the idea of wealth, which is what happened.

The sequel to his prayer is very interesting. After praying in the above-mentioned manner, he met a former employer of his on the street whom he had not seen for twenty years. The man offered him a very lucrative position and advanced him $500 on a temporary loan. Today, Mr. Broke is vice president of the company for which he works. His recent remark to me was, "I shall never forget the wonders of 'Thank you, Father.' It has worked wonders for me."

THE AFFIRMATIVE METHOD

The effectiveness of an affirmation is determined largely by your understanding of the truth and the meaning back of the words, *"In praying use not vain repetition."* Therefore, the power of your affirmation lies in the intelligent application of definite and specific positives. For example, a boy adds three and three and puts down seven on the blackboard. The teacher affirms with mathematical certainty that three and three are six; therefore, the boy changes his figures accordingly. The teacher's statement did not make three and three equal six because the latter was already a mathematical truth. The mathematical truth caused the boy to rearrange the figures on the blackboard. It is abnormal to be sick; it is normal to be healthy. Health is the truth of your being. When you affirm health, harmony, and peace for yourself or another, and when you realize these are universal principles of your own being, you will rearrange the negative patterns of your subconscious mind based on your faith and understanding of that which you affirm.

The result of the affirmative process of prayer depends on your conforming to the principles of life, regardless of appearances. Consider for a moment that there is a principle of mathematics and none of error; there is a principle of truth but none of dishonesty. There is a principle of intelligence but none of ignorance; there is a principle of harmony and none of discord.

There is a principle of health but none of disease, and there is a principle of abundance but none of poverty.

The affirmative method was chosen by the author for use on his sister who was to be operated on for the removal of gallstones in a hospital in England. The condition described was based on the diagnosis of hospital tests and the usual X-ray procedures. She asked me to pray for her. We were separated geographically about 6,500 miles, but there is no time or space in the mind principle. Infinite mind or intelligence is present in its entirety at every point simultaneously. I withdrew all thought from the contemplation of symptoms and from the corporeal personality altogether. I affirmed as follows: "This prayer is for my sister Catherine. She is relaxed and at peace, poised, balanced, serene, and calm. The healing intelligence of her subconscious mind, which created her body is now transforming every cell, nerve, tissue, muscle, and bone of her being according to the perfect pattern of all organs lodged in her subconscious mind. Silently, quietly, all distorted thought patterns in her subconscious mind are removed and dissolved, and the vitality, wholeness, and beauty of the life principle are made manifest in every atom of her being. She is now open and receptive to the healing currents, which are flowing through her like a river, restoring her to perfect health, harmony, and peace. All distortions and ugly images are now washed away by the infinite ocean of love and peace flowing through her, and it is so."

I affirmed the above several times a day, and at the end of two weeks my sister had an examination, which showed a remarkable healing, and the X ray proved negative.

To affirm is to state that it is so, and as you maintain this attitude of mind as true, regardless of all evidence to the contrary, you will receive an answer to your prayer. Your thought can only affirm, for even if you deny something, you are actually affirming the presence of what you deny. Repeating an affirmation, knowing what you are saying and why you are saying it, leads the mind to that state of consciousness where it accepts that which you state as true. Keep on affirming the truths of life until you get the subconscious reaction, which satisfies.

THE ARGUMENTATIVE METHOD

This method is just what the word implies. It stems from the procedure of Dr. Phineas Parkhurst Quimby of Maine. Dr. Quimby, a pioneer in mental and spiritual healing, lived and practiced in Belfast, Maine, about one hundred years ago. A book called *The Quimby Manuscripts*, published in 1921 by Thomas Y. Crowell Company, New York City, and edited by Horatio Dresser, is available in your library. This book gives newspaper accounts of this man's remarkable results in prayer treatment of the sick. Quimby duplicated many of the healing miracles recorded in the Bible. In brief, the argumentative method employed according to Quimby consists of spiritual reasoning where you convince the patient and yourself that his sickness is due to his false belief, groundless fears, and negative patterns lodged in his subconscious mind. You reason it out clearly in your mind and convince your patient that the disease or ailment is due only to a distorted, twisted pattern of thought, which has taken form in his body. This wrong belief in some external power and external causes has now externalized itself as sickness, and can be changed by changing the thought patterns.

You explain to the sick person that the basis of all healing is a change of belief. You also point out that the subconscious mind created the body and all its organs; therefore, it knows how to heal it, can heal it, and is doing so now as you speak.

You argue in the courtroom of your mind that the disease is a shadow of the mind based on disease-soaked, morbid thought imagery. You continue to build up all the evidence you can muster on behalf of the healing power within, which created all the organs in the first place, and which has a perfect pattern of every cell, nerve, and tissue within it. Then, you render a verdict in the courthouse of your mind in favor of yourself or your patient. You liberate the sick one by faith and spiritual understanding. Your mental and spiritual evidence is overwhelming; there being but one mind, what you feel as true will be resurrected in the experience of the patient. This procedure is essentially the argumentative method used by Dr. Quimby of Maine from 1849 to 1869.

THE ABSOLUTE METHOD IS LIKE
MODERN SOUND WAVE THERAPY

Many people throughout the world practice this form of prayer treatment with wonderful results. The person using the absolute method mentions the name of the patient, such as John Jones, then quietly and silently thinks of God and His qualities and attributes, such as, God is all bliss, boundless love, infinite intelligence, all-powerful, boundless wisdom, absolute harmony, indescribable beauty, and perfection. As he quietly thinks along these lines he is lifted up in consciousness into a new spiritual wave length, at which times he feels the infinite ocean of God's love is now dissolving everything unlike itself in the mind and body of John Jones for whom he is praying. He feels all the power and love of God are now focused on John Jones, and whatever is bothering or vexing him is now completely neutralized in the presence of the infinite ocean of life and love.

The absolute method of prayer might be likened to the sound wave or sonic therapy recently shown me by a distinguished physician in Los Angeles. He has an ultra sound wave machine, which oscillates at a tremendous speed and sends sound waves to any area of the body to which it is directed. These sound waves can be controlled, and he told me of achieving remarkable results in dissolving arthritic calcareous deposits, as well as the healing and removal of other disturbing conditions.

To the degree that we rise in consciousness by contemplating qualities and attributes of God, do we generate spiritual electronic waves of harmony, health, and peace. Many remarkable healings follow this technique of prayer.

A CRIPPLE WALKS

Dr. Phineas Parkhurst Quimby, of whom we spoke previously in this chapter, used the absolute method in the latter years of his healing career. He was really the father of psychosomatic medicine and the first psychoanalyst. He had the capacity to diagnose clairvoyantly the cause of the patient's trouble, pains, and aches.

The following is a condensed account of the healing of a cripple as recorded in Quimby's Manuscripts:

Quimby was called on to visit a woman who was lame, aged, and bedridden. He states that her ailment was due to the fact that she was imprisoned by a creed so small and contracted that she could not stand upright and move about. She was living in the tomb of fear and ignorance; furthermore, she was taking the Bible literally, and it frightened her. "In this tomb," Quimby said, "was the presence and power of God trying to burst the bands, break through the bonds, and rise from the dead." When she would ask others for an explanation of some passage of the Bible, the answer would be a stone; then she would hunger for the bread of life. Dr. Quimby diagnosed her case as a mind cloudy and stagnated, due to excitation and fear, caused by the inability to see clearly the meaning of the passage of the Bible which she had been reading. This showed itself in the body by her heavy and sluggish feeling, which would terminate as paralysis.

At this point Quimby asked her what was meant in the Bible verses: *Yet a little while am I with you, and then I go unto Him that sent me. Ye shall seek me, and shall not find me: and where I am, thither ye cannot come.* JOHN 7:33–34. She replied that it meant Jesus went to heaven. Quimby explained what it really meant by telling her that *being with her a little while* meant his explanation of her symptoms, feelings, and their causes; i.e., he had compassion and sympathy for her momentarily, but he could not remain in that mental state. The next step was *to go to Him that sent us*, which, as Quimby pointed out, was the creative power of God in all of us.

Quimby immediately traveled in his mind and contemplated the divine ideal; i.e., the vitality, intelligence, harmony, and power of God functioning in the sick person. This is why he said to the woman, "Therefore, where I go you cannot come, for you are in your narrow, restricted belief, and I am in health." This prayer and explanation produced an instantaneous sensation, and a change came over her mind. She walked without her crutches! Quimby said it was one of the most singular of all his healings. She was, as it were, dead to error, and to bring her to life or truth was to raise her from the dead. Quimby quoted the resurrection of Christ and applied it to her own Christ or health; this produced a powerful effect on her. He also explained to her that the truth, which she accepted, was the angel or idea, which rolled away the stone of fear, ignorance, and superstition, thereby, releasing the healing power of God, which made her whole.

THE DECREE METHOD

Power goes into our word according to the feeling and faith behind it. When we realize the power that moves the world is moving on our behalf and is backing up our word, our confidence and assurance grow. You do not try and add power to power; therefore, there must be no mental striving, coercion, force, or mental wrestling.

A young girl used the decree method on a young man who was constantly phoning her, pressing her for dates, and meeting her at her place of business; she found it very difficult to get rid of him. She decreed as follows: "I release . . . unto God. He is in his true place at all times. I am free, and he is free. I now decree that my words go forth into infinite mind and it brings it to pass. It is so." She said he vanished and she has never seen him since, adding, "It was as though the ground swallowed him up."

Thou shalt also decree a thing, and it shall be established unto thee: and the light shall shine upon thy ways. Job 22:28.

SERVE YOURSELF WITH SCIENTIFIC TRUTH

1. Be a mental engineer and use tried and proven techniques in building a grander and greater life.
2. Your desire is your prayer. Picture the fulfillment of your desire now and feel its reality, and you will experience the joy of the answered prayer.
3. Desire to accomplish things the easy way—with the sure aid of mental science.

4. You can build radiant health, success, and happiness by the thoughts you think in the hidden studio of your mind.

5. Experiment scientifically until you personally prove that there is always a direct response from the infinite intelligence of your subconscious mind to your conscious thinking.

6. Feel the joy and restfulness in foreseeing the certain accomplishment of your desire. Any mental picture, which you have in your mind is the substance of things hoped for and the evidence of things not seen.

7. A mental picture is worth a thousand words. Your subconscious will bring to pass any picture held in the mind backed by faith.

8. Avoid all effort or mental coercion in prayer. Get into a sleepy, drowsy state and lull yourself to sleep feeling and knowing that your prayer is answered.

9. Remember that the thankful heart is always close to the riches of the universe.

10. To affirm is to state that it is so, and as you maintain this attitude of mind as true, regardless of all evidence to the contrary, you will receive an answer to your prayer.

11. Generate electronic waves of harmony, health, and peace by thinking of the love and the glory of God.

12. What you decree and feel as true will come to pass. Decree harmony, health, peace, and abundance.

7

THE TENDENCY OF
THE SUBCONSCIOUS
IS LIFEWARD

Over 90 percent of your mental life is subconscious, so men and women who fail to make use of this marvelous power live within very narrow limits.

Your subconscious processes are always lifeward and constructive. Your subconscious is the builder of your body and maintains all its vital functions. It is on the job 24 hours a day and never sleeps. It is always trying to help and preserve you from harm.

Your subconscious mind is in touch with infinite life and boundless wisdom, and its impulses and ideas are always lifeward. The great aspirations, inspirations, and visions for a grander and nobler life spring from the subconscious. Your profoundest convictions are those you cannot argue about rationally because they do not come from your conscious mind; they come from your subconscious mind. Your subconscious speaks to you in intuitions, impulses, hunches, intimations, urges, and ideas, and it is always telling you to rise, transcend, grow, advance, adventure, and move forward to greater heights. The urge to love, to save the lives of others comes from the depths of your subconscious. For example, during the great San Francisco earthquake and fire of April 18, 1906, invalids and cripples who had been confined to bed for long periods of time, rose up and performed some of the most amazing feats of bravery and endurance. The intense desire welled up within them to save others at all costs, and their subconscious responded accordingly.

Great artists, musicians, poets, speakers, and writers tune in with their subconscious powers and become animated and inspired. For example, Robert Louis Stevenson, before he went to sleep, used to charge his subconscious with the task of evolving stories for him while he slept. He was accustomed to ask his subconscious to give him a good, marketable thriller when his bank account was low. Stevenson said the intelligence of his deeper mind gave him the story piece by piece, like a serial. This shows how your subconscious will speak lofty and wise sayings through you, which your conscious mind knows nothing about.

Mark Twain confided to the world on many occasions that he never worked in his life. All his humor and all his great writings were due to the fact that he tapped the inexhaustible reservoir of his subconscious mind.

HOW THE BODY PORTRAYS
THE WORKINGS OF THE MIND

The interaction of your conscious and subconscious mind requires a similar interaction between the corresponding system of nerves. The cerebrospinal system is the organ of the conscious mind, and the sympathetic system is the organ of the subconscious mind. The cerebrospinal system is the channel through which you receive conscious perception by means of your five physical senses and exercise control over the movement of your body. This system has its nerves in the brain, and it is the channel of your volitional and conscious mental action.

The sympathetic system, sometimes referred to as the involuntary nervous system, has its center in a ganglionic mass at the back of the stomach known as the solar plexus, and is sometimes spoken of as the abdominal brain. It is the channel of that mental action which unconsciously supports the vital functions of the body.

The two systems may work separately or synchronously. Judge Thomas Troward* says, "The vagus nerve passes out of the cerebral region as a portion of the voluntary system, and through it we control the vocal organs; then it passes onward to the thorax sending out branches to the heart and lungs; finally, passing through the diaphragm, it loses the outer coating which distinguishes the nerves of the voluntary system and becomes identified with those of the sympathetic system, so forming a connecting link between the two and making the man physically a single entity.

"Similarly different areas of the brain indicate their connection with the objective and subjective activities of the mind respectively, and speaking in a general way we may assign the frontal portion of the brain to the former and the posterior

---

* *The Edinburgh Lectures on Menial Science* (New York: Robert McBride & Co., 1909).

portion to the latter, while the intermediate portion partakes of the character of both."

A rather simple way of looking at the mental and physical interaction is to realize that your conscious mind grasps an idea, which induces a corresponding vibration in your voluntary system of nerves. This in turn causes a similar current to be generated in your involuntary system of nerves, thus handling the idea over to your subconscious mind, which is the creative medium. This is how your thoughts become things.

Every thought entertained by your conscious mind and accepted as true is sent by your brain to your solar plexus, the brain of your subconscious mind, to be made into your flesh, and to be brought forth into your world as a reality.

THERE IS AN INTELLIGENCE WHICH TAKES CARE OF THE BODY

When you study the cellular system and the structure of the organs, such as eyes, ears, heart, liver, bladder, etc., you learn they consist of groups of cells which form a group intelligence whereby they function together and are able to take orders and carry them out in deductive function at the suggestion of the master mind (conscious mind).

A careful study of the single-celled organism shows you what goes on in your complex body. Though the monocellular organism has no organs, it still gives evidence of mind action and reaction performing the basic functions of movement, alimentation, assimilation, and elimination.

Many say there is an intelligence, which will take care of your body if you let it alone. That is true, but the difficulty is that the conscious mind always interferes with its five-sense evidence based on outer appearances, leading to the sway of false beliefs, fears, and mere opinion. When fear, false beliefs, and negative patterns are made to register in your subconscious mind through psychological, emotional conditioning, there is no other course open to the subconscious mind except to act on the blueprint specifications offered it.

THE SUBCONSCIOUS MIND WORKS CONTINUALLY FOR THE COMMON GOOD

The subjective self within you works continuously for the general good, reflecting an innate principle of harmony behind all things. Your subconscious mind has its own will, and it is a very real something in itself. It acts night and day whether you act upon it or not. It is the builder of your body, but you cannot see, hear, or feel it building, as all this is a silent process. Your subconscious has a life of its own which is always moving toward harmony, health, and peace. This is the divine norm within it seeking expression through you at all times.

HOW MAN INTERFERES WITH THE INNATE PRINCIPLE OF HARMONY

To think correctly, scientifically, we must know the "Truth." To know the truth is to be in harmony with the infinite intelligence and power of your subconscious mind, which is always moving lifeward.

Every thought or action, which is not harmonious, whether through ignorance or design, will result in discord and limitation of all kinds.

Scientists inform us that you build a new body every eleven months; so you are really only eleven months old from a physical standpoint. If you build defects back into your body by thoughts of fear, anger, jealousy, and ill will, you have no one to blame but yourself.

You are the sum total of your own thoughts. You can keep from entertaining negative thought and imagery. The way to get rid of darkness is with light; the way to overcome cold is with heat; the way to overcome the negative thought is to substitute the good thought. Affirm the good, and the bad will vanish.

WHY IT'S NORMAL TO BE HEALTHY, VITAL, AND STRONG—IT'S ABNORMAL TO BE SICK

The average child born into the world is perfectly healthy with all its organs functioning perfectly. This is the normal state, and we should remain healthy, vital, and strong. The instinct of self-preservation is the strongest instinct of your nature, and it constitutes a most potent, ever-present, and constantly operative truth, inherent in your nature. It is, therefore, obvious that all your thoughts, ideas, and beliefs must operate with greater potentiality when they are in harmony with the innate life-principle in you, which is forever seeking to preserve and protect you along all lines. It follows from this that normal conditions can be restored with greater ease and certainty than abnormal conditions can be induced.

It is abnormal to be sick; it simply means you are going against the stream of life and thinking negatively. The law of life is the law of growth; all nature testifies to the operation of this law by silently, constantly expressing itself in the law of growth. Where there is growth and expression, there must be life; where there is life, there must be harmony; and where there is harmony, there is perfect health.

If your thought is in harmony with the creative principle of your subconscious mind, you are in tune with the innate principle of harmony. If you entertain thoughts which are not in accordance with the principle of harmony, these thoughts cling to you, harass you, worry you, and finally bring about disease, and if persisted in, possibly death.

In the healing of disease, you must increase the inflow and distribution of the vital forces of your subconscious mind throughout your system. This can be done by eliminating thoughts of fear, worry, anxiety, jealousy, hatred, and every other destructive thought which tends to tear down and destroy your nerves and glands—body tissue which controls the elimination of all waste material.

POTT'S DISEASE CURED

In the *Nautilus* magazine of March, 1917, there appears an article about a boy suffering from Pott's disease, or tuberculosis of the spine, who had a remarkable healing. His name was Frederick Elias Andrews of Indianapolis, now minister of Unity School of Christianity, Kansas City, Missouri. His physician pronounced him incurable. He began to pray, and from a crooked, twisted cripple going about on hands and knees, he became a strong, straight, well-formed man. He created his own affirmation, mentally absorbing the qualities he needed.

He affirmed over and over again many times a day, "I am whole, perfect, strong, powerful, loving, harmonious, and happy." He persevered and said that this prayer was the last utterance on his lips at night and the first in the morning. He prayed for others also by sending out thoughts of love and health. This attitude of mind and way of prayer returned to him multiplied many times. His faith and perseverance paid off with big dividends. When thoughts of fear, anger, jealousy, or envy drew his attention, he would immediately start his counteracting force of affirmation going in his mind. His subconscious mind responded according to the nature of his habitual thinking. This is the meaning of the statement in the Bible, *Go thy way, thy faith hath made thee whole.* MARK 10:52.

HOW FAITH IN YOUR SUBCONSCIOUS POWERS MAKES YOU WHOLE

A young man, who came to my lectures on the healing power of the subconscious mind, had severe eye trouble, which his doctor said necessitated an operation. He said to himself, "My subconscious made my eyes, and it can heal me."

Each night, as he went to sleep, he entered into a drowsy, meditative state, the condition akin to sleep. His attention was immobilized and focused on the eye doctor. He imagined the doctor was in front of him, and he plainly heard, or imagined he heard, the doctor saying to him, "A miracle has happened!" He heard this over and over again every night for perhaps five minutes or so before going to sleep. At the end of three weeks he again went to the ophthalmologist who had previously examined his eyes, and the physician said to this man, "This is a miracle!" What happened? This man impressed his subconscious mind using the doctor as an instrument or a means of convincing it or conveying the idea. Through repetition, faith, and expectancy he impregnated his subconscious mind. His subconscious mind made his eye; within it was the perfect pattern, and immediately it proceeded to heal the eye. This is another example of how faith in the healing power of your subconscious can make you whole.

POINTERS TO REVIEW

1. Your subconscious is the builder of your body and is on the job 24 hours a day. You interfere with its life-giving patterns by negative thinking.

2. Charge your subconscious with the task of evolving an answer to any problem, prior to sleep, and it will answer you.

3. Watch your thoughts. Every thought accepted as true is sent by your brain to your solar plexus—your abdominal brain—and is brought into your world as a reality.

4. Know that you can remake yourself by giving a new blueprint to your subconscious mind.

5. The tendency of your subconscious is always lifeward. Your job is with your conscious mind. Feed your subconscious mind with premises, which are true. Your subconscious is always reproducing according to your habitual mental patterns.

6. You build a new body every eleven months. Change your body by changing your thoughts and keeping them changed.

7. It is normal to be healthy. It is abnormal to be ill. There is within the innate principle of harmony.

8. Thoughts of jealousy, fear, worry, and anxiety tear down and destroy your nerves and glands bringing about mental and physical diseases of all kinds.

9. What you affirm consciously and feel as true will be made manifest in your mind, body, and affairs. Affirm the good and enter into the joy of living.

8

HOW TO GET THE
RESULTS YOU WANT

The principle reasons for failure are: lack of confidence and too much effort. Many people block answers to their prayers by failing to fully comprehend the workings of their subconscious mind. When you know how your mind functions, you gain a measure of confidence. You must remember whenever your subconscious mind accepts an idea, it immediately begins to execute it. It uses all its mighty resources to that end and mobilizes all the mental and spiritual laws of your deeper mind. This law is true for good or bad ideas. Consequently, if you use it negatively, it brings trouble, failure, and confusion. When you use it constructively, it brings guidance, freedom, and peace of mind.

The right answer is inevitable when your thoughts are positive, constructive, and loving. From this it is perfectly obvious that the only thing you have to do in order to overcome failure is to get your subconscious to accept your idea or request by feeling its reality now, and the law of your mind will do the rest. Turn over your request with faith and confidence, and your subconscious will take over and answer for you.

You will always fail to get results by trying to use mental coercion—your subconscious mind does not respond to coercion, it responds to your faith or conscious mind acceptance.

Your failure to get results may also arise from such statements as: "Things are getting worse." "I will never get an answer." "I see no way out." "It is hopeless." "I don't know what to do." "I'm all mixed up." When you use such statements, you get no response or cooperation from your subconscious mind. Like a soldier marking time, you neither go forward nor backward; in other words, you don't get anywhere.

If you get into a taxi and give a half dozen different directions to the driver in five minutes, he would become hopelessly confused and probably would refuse to take you anywhere. It is the same when working with your subconscious mind. There must be a clear-cut idea in your mind. You must arrive at the definite decision that there is a way out, a solution to the vexing problem in sickness. Only the infinite intelligence within your subconscious knows the answer. When you come to that clear-cut conclusion in your conscious mind, your mind is then made up, and according to your belief is it done unto you.

EASY DOES IT

A house owner once remonstrated with a furnace repairman for charging two hundred dollars for fixing the boiler. The mechanic said, "I charged five cents for the missing bolt and one hundred ninety-nine dollars and ninety-five cents for knowing what was wrong."

Similarly, your subconscious mind is the master mechanic, the all-wise one, who knows ways and means of healing any organ of your body, as well as your affairs. Decree health, and your subconscious will establish it, but relaxation is the key. "Easy does it." Do not be concerned with details and means, but know the end result. Get the *feel* of the happy solution to your problem whether it is health, finances, or employment. Remember how you felt after you had recovered from a severe state of illness. Bear in mind that your feeling is the touchstone of all subconscious demonstration. Your new idea must be felt subjectively in a finished state, not the future, but as coming about now.

INFER NO OPPONENT, USE IMAGINATION AND NOT WILLPOWER

In using your subconscious mind you infer no opponent, you use no willpower. You imagine the end and the freedom state. You will find your intellect trying to get in the way, but persist in maintaining a simple, childlike, miracle-making faith. Picture yourself without the ailment or problem. Imagine the emotional accompaniment of the freedom state you crave. Cut out all red tape from the process. The simple way is the best.

HOW DISCIPLINED IMAGINATION WORKS WONDERS

A wonderful way to get a response from your subconscious mind is through disciplined or scientific imagination. As previously pointed out, your subconscious mind is the builder of the body and controls all its vital functions.

The Bible says, *Whatsoever ye shall ask in prayer, believing, ye shall receive.* To believe is to accept something as true, or to live in the state of being it. As you sustain this mood, you shall experience the joy of the answered prayer!

THE THREE STEPS TO SUCCESS IN PRAYER
The usual procedure is as follows:

1. Take a look at the problem.
2. Turn to the solution or way out known only to the subconscious mind.
3. Rest in a sense of deep conviction that it is done.

Do not weaken your prayer by saying, "I wish I might be healed." "I hope so." Your feeling about the work to be done is "the boss." Harmony is yours. Know that health is yours. Become intelligent by becoming a vehicle for the infinite healing power of the subconscious mind. Pass on the idea of health to your subconscious mind to the point of conviction; then relax. Get yourself off your hands. Say to the condition and circumstance, "This, too, shall pass." Through relaxation you impress your subconscious mind enabling the kinetic energy behind the idea to take over and bring it into concrete realization.

THE LAW OF REVERSED EFFORT AND WHY YOU
GET THE OPPOSITE OF WHAT YOU PRAY FOR
Coué, the famous psychologist from France who visited America about forty years ago, defined the law of reversed effort as follows: "When your desires and imagination are in conflict your imagination invariably gains the day."

If, for example, you were asked to walk a plank on the floor, you would do so without question. Now suppose the same plank were placed twenty feet up in the air between two walls, would you walk it? Your desire to walk it would be counteracted by your imagination or fear of falling. Your dominant idea, which would be the picture of falling would conquer. Your desire, will, or effort to walk on the plank would be reversed, and the dominant idea of failure would be reinforced.

Mental effort is invariably self-defeated, eventuating always in the opposite of what is desired. The suggestions of powerlessness to overcome the condition dominate the mind; your subconscious is always controlled by the dominant idea. Your subconscious will accept the strongest of two contradictory propositions. The effortless way is the better.

If you say, "I want a healing, but I can't get it," "I try so hard," "I force myself to pray," "I use all the willpower I have," you must realize that your error lies in your effort. Never try to compel the subconscious mind to accept your idea by exercising willpower. Such attempts are doomed to failure, and you get the opposite of what you prayed for.

The following is a rather common experience. Students, when taking examinations and reading through their papers, find that all their knowledge has suddenly deserted them. Their minds become appalling blanks, and they are unable to recall one relevant thought. The more they grit their teeth and summon the powers of the will, the further the answers seem to flee. But, when they have left the examination room and the mental pressure relaxes, the answers they were seeking flow tantalizingly back into their minds. Trying to force themselves to remember was the cause of their failure. This is an example of the law of reversed effort whereby you get the opposite of what you asked or prayed for.

THE CONFLICT OF DESIRE AND IMAGINATION
MUST BE RECONCILED

To use mental force is to presuppose that there is opposition. When your mind is concentrated on the means to overcome a problem, it is no longer concerned with the obstacle. MATTHEW 18:19 says, *If two of you shall agree on earth as touching anything that they shall ask, it shall be done for them of my Father which is in heaven.* Who are these two? It means the harmonious union or agreement between your conscious and subconscious on any idea, desire, or mental image. When there is no longer any quarrel in either part of your mind, your prayer will be answered. The two agreeing may also be represented as you and your desire, your thought and feeling, your idea and emotion, your desire and imagination.

You avoid all conflict between your desires and imagination by entering into a drowsy, sleepy state which brings all effort to a minimum. The conscious mind is submerged to a great extent when in a sleepy state. The best time to impregnate your subconscious is prior to sleep. The reason for this is that the highest degree of outcropping of the subconscious occurs prior to sleep and just after we awaken. In this state the negative thoughts and imagery, which tend to neutralize your desire and so prevent acceptance by your subconscious mind no longer present themselves. When you imagine the reality of the fulfilled desire and feel the thrill of accomplishment, your subconscious brings about the realization of your desire.

A great many people solve all their dilemmas and problems by the play of their controlled, directed, and disciplined imagination, knowing that whatever they imagine and feel as true *will* and *must* come to pass.

The following will clearly illustrate how a young girl overcame the conflict between her desire and her imagination. She desired a harmonious solution to her legal problem, yet her mental imagery was constantly on failure, loss, bankruptcy, and poverty. It was a complicated lawsuit and there was one postponement after another with no solution in sight.

At my suggestion, she got into a sleepy, drowsy state each night prior to sleep, and she began to imagine the happy ending, feeling it to the best of her ability. She knew that the image in her mind had to agree with her heart's desire. Prior to sleep she began to dramatize as vividly as possible her lawyer having an animated discussion with her regarding the outcome. She would ask him questions, and he would answer her appropriately. He would say to her over and over again, "There has been a perfect, harmonious solution. The case has been settled out of court." During the day when fear thoughts came into her mind, she would run her mental movie with gestures, voice, and sound equipment. She could easily imagine the sound of his voice, smile, and mannerism. She ran this mental picture so often, it became a subjective pattern, a regular train track. At the end of a few weeks her attorney called her and confirmed objectively what she had been imagining and feeling as true subjectively.

This is really what the Psalmist meant when he wrote, *Let the words of my mouth* [your thoughts, mental images, good], *and the meditations of my heart* [your feeling, nature, emotion] *be acceptable in thy sight, O Lord* [the law of your subconscious mind], *my strength, and my redeemer* [the power and wisdom of your subconscious mind can redeem you from sickness, bondage, and misery]. PSALMS 19:14.

IDEAS WORTH RECALLING

1. Mental coercion or too much effort shows anxiety and fear, which block your answer. Easy does it.

2. When your mind is relaxed and you accept an idea, your subconscious goes to work to execute the idea.

3. Think and plan independently of traditional methods. Know that there is always an answer and a solution to every problem.

4. Do not be overly concerned with the beating of your heart, with the breathing of your lungs, or the functions of any part of your anatomy. Lean heavily upon your subconscious and proclaim frequently that Divine right action is taking place.

5. The feeling of health produces health, the feeling of wealth produces wealth. How do you feel?

6. Imagination is your most powerful faculty. Imagine what is lovely and of good report. You are what you imagine yourself to be.

7. You avoid conflict between your conscious and subconscious in the sleepy state. Imagine the fulfillment of your desire over and over again prior to sleep. Sleep in peace and wake in joy.

9

HOW TO USE THE POWER OF YOUR SUBCONSCIOUS FOR WEALTH

If you are having financial difficulties, if you are trying to make ends meet, it means you have not convinced your subconscious mind that you will always have plenty and some to spare. You know men and women who work a few hours a week and make fabulous sums of money. They do not strive or slave hard. Do not believe the story that the only way you can become wealthy is by the sweat of your brow and hard labor. It is not so; the effortless way of life is the best. Do the thing you love to do, and do it for the joy and thrill of it.

I know an executive in Los Angeles who receives a salary of $75,000 yearly. Last year he went on a nine-month cruise seeing the world and its beauty spots. He said to me that he had succeeded in convincing his subconscious mind that he is worth that much money. He told me that many men in his organization getting about one hundred dollars a week knew more about the business than he did, and could manage it better, but they had no ambition, no creative ideas, and were not interested in the wonders of their subconscious mind.

WEALTH IS OF THE MIND

Wealth is simply a subconscious conviction on the part of the individual. You will not become a millionaire by saying, "I am a millionaire, I am a millionaire." You will grow into a wealth consciousness by building into your mentality the idea of wealth and abundance.

YOUR INVISIBLE MEANS OF SUPPORT

The trouble with most people is that they have no invisible means of support. When business falls away, the stock market drops, or they lose their investments, they seem helpless. The reason for such insecurity is that they do not know how to tap the subconscious mind. They are unacquainted with the inexhaustible storehouse within.

A man with a poverty-type mind finds himself in poverty-stricken conditions. Another man with a mind filled with ideas of wealth is surrounded with everything he needs. It was never intended that man should lead a life of indigence. You can have wealth, everything you need, and plenty to spare. Your words have power to cleanse your mind of wrong ideas and to instill right ideas in their place.

THE IDEAL METHOD FOR BUILDING
A WEALTH CONSCIOUSNESS

Perhaps you are saying as you read this chapter, "I need wealth and success." This is what you do: Repeat for about five minutes to yourself three or four times a day, "Wealth—Success." These words have tremendous power. They represent the inner power of the subconscious mind. Anchor your mind on this substantial power within you; then conditions and circumstances corresponding to their nature and quality will be manifested in your life. You are not saying, "I am wealthy," you are dwelling on real powers within you. There is no conflict in the mind when you say, "Wealth." Furthermore, the feeling of wealth will well up within you as you dwell on the idea of wealth.

The feeling of wealth produces wealth; keep this in mind at all times. Your subconscious mind is like a bank, a sort of universal financial institution. It magnifies whatever you deposit or impress upon it whether it is the idea of wealth or of poverty. Choose wealth.

WHY YOUR AFFIRMATIONS FOR WEALTH FAIL

I have talked to many people during the past thirty-five years whose usual complaint is, "I have said for weeks and months, 'I am wealthy, I am prosperous,' and nothing has happened." I discovered that when they said, "I am prosperous, I am wealthy," they felt within that they were lying to themselves.

One man told me, "I have affirmed that I am prosperous until I am tired. Things are now worse. I knew when I made the statement that it was obviously not true." His statements were rejected by the conscious mind, and the very opposite of what he outwardly affirmed and claimed was made manifest.

Your affirmation succeeds best when it is specific and when it does not produce a mental conflict or argument; hence the statements made by this man made matters worse because they suggested his lack. Your subconscious accepts what you really feel to be true, not just idle words or statements. The dominant idea or belief is always accepted by the subconscious mind.

HOW TO AVOID MENTAL CONFLICT

The following is the ideal way to overcome this conflict for those who have this difficulty. Make this practical statement frequently, particularly prior to sleep: "By day and by night I am being prospered in all of my interests." This affirmation will not arouse any argument because it does not contradict your subconscious mind's impression of financial lack.

I suggested to one businessman whose sales and finances were very low and who was greatly worried, that he sit down in his office, become quiet, and repeat this statement over and over again: "My sales are improving every day." This statement engaged the cooperation of the conscious and subconscious mind; results followed.

DON'T SIGN BLANK CHECKS

You sign blank checks when you make such statements as, "There is not enough to go around." "There is a shortage." "I will lose the house because of the mortgage," etc. If you are full of fear about the future, you are also writing a blank check and attracting negative conditions to you. Your subconscious mind takes your fear and negative statement as your request and proceeds in its own way to bring obstacles, delays, lack, and limitation into your life.

YOUR SUBCONSCIOUS GIVES YOU
COMPOUND INTEREST

To him that hath the feeling of wealth, more wealth shall be added; to him that hath the feeling of lack, more lack shall be added. Your subconscious multiplies and magnifies whatever you deposit in it. Every morning as you awaken deposit thoughts of prosperity, success, wealth, and peace. Dwell upon these concepts. Busy your mind with them as often as possible. These constructive thoughts will find their way as deposits in your subconscious mind, and bring forth abundance and prosperity.

WHY NOTHING HAPPENED

I can hear you saying, "Oh, I did that and nothing happened." You did not get results because you indulged in fear thoughts perhaps ten minutes later and neutralized the good you had affirmed. When you place a seed in the ground, you do not dig it up. You let it take root and grow.

Suppose, for example, you are going to say, "I shall not be able to make that payment." Before you get further than, "I shall—" stop the sentence and dwell on a constructive statement, such as, "By day and by night I am prospered in all my ways."

TRUE SOURCE OF WEALTH

Your subconscious mind is never short of ideas. There are within it an infinite number of ideas ready to flow into your conscious mind and appear as cash in your pocketbook in countless ways. This process will continue to go on in your mind regardless of whether the stock market goes up or down, or whether the pound sterling or dollar drops in value. Your wealth is never truly dependent on bonds, stocks, or money in the bank; these are really only symbols, necessary and useful, of course, but only symbols.

The point I wish to emphasize is that if you convince your subconscious mind that wealth is yours, and that it is always circulating in your life, you will always and inevitably have it, regardless of the form it takes.

TRYING TO MAKE ENDS MEET AND THE REAL CAUSE

There are people who claim that they are always trying to make ends meet. They seem to have a great struggle to meet their obligations. Have you listened to their conversation? In many instances their conversation runs along this vein: They are constantly condemning those who have succeeded in life and who have raised their heads above the crowd. Perhaps they are saying, "Oh, that fellow has a racket; he is ruthless; he is a crook." This is why they lack; they are condemning the thing they desire and want. The reason they speak critically of their more prosperous associates is because they are envious and covetous of the others' prosperity. The quickest way to cause wealth to take wings and fly away is to criticize and condemn others who have more wealth than you.

A COMMON STUMBLING BLOCK TO WEALTH

There is one emotion which is the cause of the lack of wealth in the lives of many. Most people learn this the hard way. It is envy. For example, if you see a competitor depositing large sums of money in the bank, and you have only a meager amount to deposit, does it make you envious? The way to overcome this emotion is to say to yourself, "Isn't it wonderful! I rejoice in that man's prosperity. I wish for him greater and greater wealth."

To entertain envious thoughts is devastating because it places you in a very negative position; therefore, wealth flows *from* you instead of *to* you. If you are ever annoyed or irritated by the prosperity or great wealth of another, claim immediately that you truly wish for him greater wealth in every possible way. This will neutralize the negative thoughts in your mind and cause an even greater measure of wealth to flow to you by the law of your own subconscious mind.

RUBBING OUT A GREAT MENTAL BLOCK
TO WEALTH

If you are worried and critical about someone whom you claim is making money dishonestly, cease worrying about him. You know such a person is using the law of mind negatively; the law of mind takes care of him. Be careful not to criticize him for the reasons previously indicated. Remember: The block or obstacle to wealth is in your own mind. You can now destroy that mental block. This you may do by getting on mental good terms with everyone.

SLEEP AND GROW RICH

As you go to sleep at night, practice the following technique: Repeat the word "wealth" quietly, easily, and feelingly. Do this over and over again, just like a lullaby. Lull yourself to sleep with the one word, "wealth." You should be amazed at the result. Wealth should flow to you in avalanches of abundance. This is another example of the magic power of your subconscious mind.

SERVE YOURSELF WITH THE POWERS
OF YOUR MIND

1. Decide to be wealthy the easy way, with the infallible aid of your subconscious mind.

2. Trying to accumulate wealth by the sweat of your brow and hard labor is one way to become the richest man in the graveyard. You do not have to strive or slave hard.

3. Wealth is a subconscious conviction. Build into your mentality the idea of wealth.

4. The trouble with most people is that they have no invisible means of support.

5. Repeat the word "wealth" to yourself slowly and quietly for about five minutes prior to sleep and your subconscious will bring wealth to pass in your experience.

6. The feeling of wealth produces wealth. Keep this in mind at all times.

7. Your conscious and subconscious mind must agree. Your subconscious accents what you really feel to be true. The dominant idea is always accepted by your subconscious mind. The dominant idea should be *wealth*, not *poverty*.

8. You can overcome any mental conflict regarding wealth by affirming frequently, "By day and by night I am being prospered in all of my interests."

9. Increase your sales by repeating this statement over and over again, "My sales are improving every day; I am advancing, progressing, and getting wealthier every day."

10. Stop writing blank checks, such as, "There is not enough to go around," or "There is a shortage," etc. Such statements magnify and multiply your loss.

11. Deposit thoughts of prosperity, wealth, and success in your subconscious mind, and the latter will give you compound interest.

12. What you consciously affirm, you must not mentally deny a few moments later. This will neutralize the good you have affirmed.

13. Your true source of wealth consists of the ideas in your mind. You can have an idea worth millions of dollars. Your subconscious will give you the idea you seek.

14. Envy and jealousy are stumbling blocks to the flow of wealth. Rejoice in the prosperity of others.

15. The block to wealth is in your own mind. Destroy that block now by getting on good mental terms with everyone.

10

YOUR RIGHT TO BE RICH

It is your right to be rich. You are here to lead the abundant life and be happy, radiant, and free. You should, therefore, have all the money you need to lead a full, happy, and prosperous life.

You are here to grow, expand, and unfold spiritually, mentally, and materially. You have the inalienable right to fully develop and express yourself along all lines. You should surround yourself with beauty and luxury.

Why be satisfied with just enough to go around when you can enjoy the riches of your subconscious mind? In this chapter you can learn to make friends with money, and you should always have a surplus. Your desire to be rich is a desire for a fuller, happier, more wonderful life. It is a cosmic urge. It is not only good, but very good.

MONEY IS A SYMBOL

Money is a symbol of exchange. It means to you not only freedom from want, but beauty, luxury, abundance, and refinement.

It is merely a symbol of the economic health of the nation. When your blood is circulating freely in your body, you are healthy. When money is circulating freely in your life, you are economically healthy. When people begin to hoard money, to put it away in tin boxes, and become charged with fear, there is economic illness. Money has taken many forms as a medium of exchange down through the centuries, such as salt, beads, and trinkets of various kinds. In early times a man's wealth was determined by the number of sheep and oxen he had. Now we use currency, and other negotiable instruments, as it is much more convenient to write a check than carry some sheep around with you to pay bills.

HOW TO WALK THE ROYAL ROAD TO RICHES

Knowledge of the powers of your subconscious mind is the means to the royal road to riches of all kinds—spiritual, mental, or financial. The student of the laws of mind believes and knows definitely that regardless of economic situations, stock market fluctuation, depression, strikes, war, or other conditions or circumstances, he will always be amply supplied, regardless of what form money takes. The reason for this is that he has conveyed the idea of wealth to his subconscious mind, and it keeps him supplied wherever he may be. He has convinced himself in his mind that money is forever flowing freely in his life and that there is always a wonderful surplus. Should there be a financial collapse of government tomorrow and all the man's present holdings become valueless, as the German marks did after the First World War, he would still attract wealth and be cared for, regardless of the form the new currency took.

WHY YOU DO NOT HAVE MORE MONEY

As you read this chapter, you are probably saying, "I am worthy of a higher salary than I am receiving." I believe most people are inadequately compensated. One of the causes many people do not have more money is that they are silently or openly condemning it. They refer to money as "filthy lucre" or "the love of money is the root of all evil." Another reason they do not prosper is that they have a sneaky subconscious feeling there is some virtue in poverty. This subconscious pattern may be due to early childhood training, superstition, or it could be based on a false interpretation of scriptures.

MONEY AND A BALANCED LIFE

One time a man said to me, "I am broke. I do not like money. It is the root of all evil." These statements represent a confused neurotic mind. Love of money to the exclusion of everything else will cause you to become lopsided and unbalanced. You are here to use your power or authority wisely. Some men crave power, others crave money. If you set your heart on money exclusively and say, "Money is all I want; I am going to give all my attention to amassing money; nothing else matters," you can get money and attain a fortune, but you have forgotten that you are here to lead a balanced life. You must also satisfy the hunger for peace of mind, harmony, love, joy, and perfect health.

By making money your sole aim, you simply made a wrong choice. You thought that was all you wanted, but you found after all your efforts that it was not only the money you needed. You also desired true expression of your hidden talents, true place in life, beauty, and the joy of contributing to the welfare and success of others. By learning the laws of your subconscious mind, you could have a million dollars or many millions, if you wanted them, and still have peace of mind, harmony, perfect health, and perfect expression.

POVERTY IS A MENTAL DISEASE

There is no virtue in poverty; it is a disease like any other mental disease. If you were physically ill, you would think there was something wrong with you. You would seek help and do something about the condition at once. Likewise, if you do not have money constantly circulating in your life, there is something radically wrong with you.

The urge of the life principle in you is toward growth, expansion, and the life more abundant. You are not here to live in a hovel, dress in rags, and go hungry. You should be happy, prosperous, and successful.

WHY YOU MUST NEVER CRITICIZE MONEY

Cleanse your mind of all weird and superstitious beliefs about money. Do not ever regard money as evil or filthy. If you do, you cause it to take wings and fly away from you. Remember that you lose what you condemn. You cannot attract what you criticize.

GETTING THE RIGHT ATTITUDE TOWARD MONEY

Here is a simple technique you may use to multiply money in your experience. Use the following statements several times a day, "I like money, I love it, I use it wisely, constructively, and judiciously. Money is constantly circulating in my life. I release it with joy, and it returns to me multiplied in a wonderful way. It is good and very good. Money flows to me in avalanches of abundance. I use it for good only, and I am grateful for my good and for the riches of my mind."

HOW THE SCIENTIFIC THINKER LOOKS AT MONEY

Suppose, for example, you found gold, silver, lead, copper, or iron in the ground. Would you pronounce these things evil? All evil comes from man's darkened understanding, from his ignorance, from his false interpretation of life, and from his misuse of his subconscious mind. Uranium, lead, or some other metal could have been used as a medium of exchange. We use paper bills, checks, nickel, and silver, surely, these are not evil. Physicists and chemists know today that the only difference between one metal and another is the number and rate of motion of electrons revolving around a central nucleus. They can now change one metal into another through a bombardment of the atoms in the powerful cyclotron. Gold under certain conditions becomes mercury. I believe that our modern scientists in the near future will be able to make gold, silver, and other metals synthetically in the chemical laboratory. The cost may be prohibitive now, but it can be done. I cannot imagine any intelligent person seeing anything evil in electrons, neutrons, protons, and isotopes.

The piece of paper in your pocket is composed of atoms and molecules with their electrons and protons arranged differently. Their number and rate of motion are different. That is the only way the paper differs from the silver in your pocket.

HOW TO ATTRACT THE MONEY YOU NEED

Many years ago I met a young boy in Australia who wanted to become a physician and surgeon, but he had no money. I explained to him how a seed deposited in the soil attracts to itself everything necessary for its unfolding, and that all he had to do was to take a lesson from the seed and deposit the required idea in his subconscious mind. For expenses this young, brilliant boy used to clean out doctors' offices, wash windows, and do odd repair jobs. He told me that every night, as he went to sleep, he used to picture in his mind's eye a medical diploma on a wall with his name on it in big, bold letters. He used to clean and shine the framed diplomas in the medical building where he worked. It was not hard for him to engrave the image of a diploma in his mind and develop it there. Definite results followed as he persisted with his mental picture every night for about four months.

The sequel of this story was very interesting. One of the doctors took a great liking to this young boy and after training him in the art of sterilizing instruments, giving hypodermic injections, and other miscellaneous first-aid work, he employed him as a technical assistant in his office. The doctor later sent him to medical school at his own expense. Today, this young man is a prominent medical doctor in Montreal, Canada. He discovered the law of attraction by using his subconscious mind the right way. He operated an age-old law, which says, "Having seen the end, you have willed the means to the realization of the end." The *end* in this case was to become a medical doctor.

This young man was able to imagine, see, and feel the reality of being a doctor. He lived with that idea, sustained it, nourished it, and loved it until through his imagination it penetrated the layers of his subconscious mind and became a conviction, thereby attracting to him everything necessary for the fulfillment of his dream.

WHY SOME MEN DO NOT GET A RAISE IN PAY

If you are working in a large organization and you are silently thinking of and resenting the fact you are underpaid, that you are not appreciated, and that you deserve more money and greater recognition, you are subconsciously severing your ties with that organization. You are setting a law in motion, and the superintendent or manager will say to you, "We have to let you go." Actually, you dismissed yourself. The manager was simply the instrument through which your own negative mental state was confirmed. It was an example of the law of action and reaction. The action was your thought, and the reaction was the response of your subconscious mind.

OBSTACLES AND IMPEDIMENTS ON
THE PATHWAY TO RICHES

I am sure you have heard men say, "That fellow has a racket." "He is a racketeer." "He is getting money dishonestly." "He is a faker." "I knew him when he had nothing." "He is a crook, a thief, and a swindler."

If you analyze the man who talks like that, you discover he is usually in want or suffering from some financial or physical illness. Perhaps his former college friends went up the ladder of success and excelled him. Now he is bitter and envious of their progress. In many instances this is the cause of his downfall. Thinking negatively of these classmates and condemning their wealth causes the wealth and prosperity he is praying for to vanish and flee away. He is condemning the thing he is praying for.

He is praying two ways. On the one hand he is saying, "Wealth is flowing to me now," and in the next breath, silently or audibly, he is saying, "I resent that fellow's wealth." Always make it a special point to rejoice in the wealth of the other person.

PROTECT YOUR INVESTMENTS

If you are seeking wisdom regarding investments, or if you are worried about your stocks or bonds, quietly claim, "Infinite intelligence governs and watches over all my financial transactions, and whatsoever I do shall prosper." Do this frequently and you will find that your investments will be wise; moreover, you will be protected from loss, as you will be prompted to sell your securities or holdings before any loss accrues to you.

YOU CANNOT GET SOMETHING FOR NOTHING

In large stores the management employs store detectives to prevent people from stealing. They catch a number of people every day trying to get something for nothing. All such people are living in the mental atmosphere of lack and limitation and are stealing from themselves peace, harmony, faith, honesty, integrity, good will, and confidence. Furthermore, they are attracting to themselves all manner of loss, such as loss of character, prestige, social status, and peace of mind. These people lack faith in the source of supply and the understanding of how their minds work. If they would mentally call on the powers of their subconscious mind and claim that they are guided to their true expression, they would find work and constant supply. Then by honesty, integrity, and perseverance, they would become a credit to themselves and to society at large.

YOUR CONSTANT SUPPLY OF MONEY

Recognizing the powers of your subconscious mind and the creative power of your thought or mental image is the way to opulence, freedom, and constant supply. Accept the abundant life in your own mind. Your mental acceptance and expectancy of wealth has its own mathematics and mechanics of expression. As you enter into the mood of opulence, all things necessary for the abundant life will come to pass.

Let this be your daily affirmation; write it in your heart:

"I am one with the infinite riches of my subconscious mind. It is my right to be rich, happy, and successful. Money flows to me freely, copiously, and endlessly. I am forever conscious of my true worth. I give of my talents freely, and I am wonderfully blessed financially. It is wonderful!"

STEP UP THIS WAY TO RICHES

1. Be bold enough to claim that it is your right to be rich and your deeper mind will honor your claim.

2. You don't want just enough to go around. You want all the money you need to do all the things you want to do and when you want to do them. Get acquainted with the riches of your subconscious mind.

3. When money is circulating freely in your life, you are economically healthy. Look at money like the tide and you will always have plenty of it. The ebb and flow of the tide is constant. When the tide is out, you are absolutely sure that it will return.

4. Knowing the laws of your subconscious mind, you will always be supplied regardless of what form money takes.

5. One reason many people simply make ends meet and never have enough money is that they condemn money. What you condemn takes wings and flies away.

6. Do not make a god of money. It is only a symbol. Remember that the real riches are in your mind. You are here to lead a balanced life—this includes acquiring all the money you need.

7. Don't make money your sole aim. Claim wealth, happiness, peace, true expression, and love, and personally radiate love and good will to all. Then your subconscious mind will give you compound interest in all these fields of expression.

8. There is no virtue in poverty. It is a disease of the mind, and you should heal yourself of this mental conflict or malady at once.

9. You are not here to live in a hovel, to dress in rags, or to go hungry. You are here to lead the life more abundant.

10. Never use the terms "filthy lucre" or "I despise money." You lose what you criticize. There is nothing good or bad, but thinking of it in either light makes it so.

11. Repeat frequently, "I like money. I use it wisely, constructively, and judiciously. I release it with joy, and it returns a thousandfold."

12. Money is not evil any more so than copper, lead, tin, or iron which you may find in the ground. All evil is due to ignorance and misuse of the mind's powers.

13. To picture the end result in your mind causes your subconscious to respond and fulfill your mental picture.

14. Stop trying to get something for nothing. There is no such thing as a free lunch. You must give to receive. You must give mental attention to your goals, ideals, and enterprises, and your deeper mind will back you up. The key to wealth is application of the laws of the subconscious mind by impregnating it with the idea of wealth.

YOUR SUBCONSCIOUS MIND AS A PARTNER IN SUCCESS

Success means successful living. A long period of peace, joy, and happiness on this plane may be termed success. The eternal experience of these qualities is the everlasting life spoken of by Jesus. The real things of life, such as peace, harmony, integrity, security, and happiness are intangible. They come from the Deep Self of man. Meditating on these qualities builds these treasures of heaven in our subconscious. It is where *moth nor rust doth corrupt, and where thieves do not break through nor steal.* MATTHEW 6:20.

THE THREE STEPS TO SUCCESS

Let us discuss three steps to success: The first step to success is to find out the thing you love to do, then do it. Success is in loving your work. Although, if a man is a psychiatrist, it is not adequate for him to get a diploma and place it on the wall; he must keep up with the times, attend conventions, and continue studying the mind and its workings. The successful psychiatrist visits clinics and reads the latest scientific articles. In other words, he is informed in the most advanced methods of alleviating human suffering. The successful psychiatrist or doctor must have the interest of his patients at heart.

Someone may say, "How can I put the first step into operation? I do not know what I should do." In such a case, pray for guidance as follows: "The infinite intelligence of my subconscious mind reveals to me my true place in life." Repeat this prayer quietly, positively, and lovingly to your deeper mind. As you persist with faith and confidence, the answer will come to you as a feeling, a hunch, or a tendency in a certain direction. It will come to you clearly and in peace, and as an inner silent awareness.

The second step to success is to specialize in some particular branch of work and know more about it than anyone else. For example, if a young man chooses chemistry as his profession, he should concentrate on one of the many branches in this field. He should give all of his time and attention to his chosen specialty. He should become sufficiently enthusiastic to try to know all there is available about his field; if possible, he should know more than anyone else. The young man should become ardently interested in his work and should desire to serve the world.

He that is greatest among you, let him become your servant. There is a great contrast in this attitude of mind in comparison to that of the man who only wants to make a living or just "get by." "Getting by" is not true success. Man's motive must be greater, nobler, and more altruistic. He must serve others, thereby casting his bread upon the waters.

The third step is the most important one. You must be sure that the thing you want to do does not redound to your success only. Your desire must not be selfish; it must benefit humanity. The path of a complete circuit must be formed. In other words, your idea must go forth with the purpose of blessing or serving the world. It will then come back to you pressed down, shaken together, and running over. If it is to benefit yourself exclusively, the circle or complete circuit is not formed, and you may experience a short circuit in your life which may consist of limitation or sickness.

THE MEASURE OF TRUE SUCCESS

Some people may say, "But, Mr. James made a fortune in selling fraudulent oil stock." A man may seem to succeed for a while, but the money he obtained by fraud usually takes wings and flies away. When we rob from another, we rob from ourselves, because we are in a mood of lack and limitation, which may manifest itself in our body, home life, and affairs. What we think and feel, we create. We create what we believe. Even though a man may have accumulated a fortune fraudulently, he is not successful. There is no success without peace of mind. What good is man's accumulated wealth if he cannot sleep nights, is sick, or has a guilt complex?

I knew a man in London who told me of his exploits. He had been a professional pickpocket and had amassed a large amount of money. He had a summer home in France and lived in a royal fashion in England. His story was that he was in constant dread of being arrested by Scotland Yard. He had many inner disorders, which were undoubtedly caused by his constant fear and deep-seated guilt complex. He knew he had done wrong. This deep sense of guilt attracted all kinds of trouble to him. Subsequently, he voluntarily surrendered to the police and served a prison sentence. After his release from prison, he sought psychological and spiritual counsel and became transformed. He went to work and became an honest, law-abiding citizen. He found what he loved to do and was happy.

A successful person loves his work and expresses himself fully. Success is contingent upon a higher ideal than the more accumulation of riches. The man of success is the man who possesses great psychological and spiritual understanding. Many of the great industrialists today depend upon the correct use of their subconscious minds for their success.

There was an article published some years ago about Flagler, an oil magnate. He admitted that the secret of his success was his ability to see a project in its completion. For instance, in his case, he closed his eyes, imagined a big oil industry, saw trains running on tracks, heard whistles blowing, and saw smoke. Having seen and felt the fulfillment of his prayer, his subconscious mind brought about its realization. If you imagine an objective clearly, you will be provided with the necessities, in ways you know not of, through the wonder-working power of your subconscious mind.

In considering the three steps to success you must never forget the underlying power of the creative forces of your subconscious mind. This is the energy in back of all steps in any plan of success. Your thought is creative. Thought fused with feeling becomes a subjective faith or belief, and *according to your belief be it done unto you.* MATTHEW 9:29.

A knowledge of a mighty force in you, which is capable of bringing to pass all your desires, gives you confidence and a sense of peace. Whatever your field of action may be, you should learn the laws of your subconscious mind. When you know how to apply the powers of your mind, and when you are expressing yourself fully and giving of your talents to others, you are on the sure path to true success. If you are about God's business, or any part of it, God, by His very nature, is for you, so who can be against you? With this understanding there is no power in heaven or on earth to withhold success from you.

HOW HE MADE HIS DREAM COME TRUE

A movie actor told me that he had very little education, but he had a dream as a boy of becoming a successful movie actor. Out in the field mowing hay, driving the cows home, or even when milking them he said, "I would constantly imagine I saw my name in big lights at a large theater. I kept this up for years until finally I ran away from home. I got extra jobs in the motion-picture field, and the day finally came when I saw my name in great, big lights as I did when I was a boy!" Then he added, "I know the power of sustained imagination to bring success."

HIS DREAM PHARMACY BECAME A REALITY

Thirty years ago I knew a young pharmacist who was receiving forty dollars a week plus commission on sales. "After twenty-five years," he said to me, "I will get a pension and retire."

I said to this young man, "Why don't you own your own store? Get out of this place. Raise your sights! Have a dream for your children. Maybe your son wants to be a doctor; perhaps your daughter desires to be a great musician."

His answer was that he had no money! He began to awaken to the fact that whatever he could conceive as true, he could give conception.

The first step toward his goal was his awakening to the powers of his subconscious mind, which I briefly elaborated on for his benefit. His second step was his realization that if he could succeed in conveying an idea to his subconscious mind, the latter would somehow bring it to pass.

He began to imagine that he was in his own store. He mentally arranged the bottles, dispensed prescriptions, and imagined several clerks in the store waiting on customers. He also visualized a big bank balance. Mentally he worked in that imaginary store. Like a good actor he lived the role. *Act as though I am, and I will be.* This pharmacist put himself wholeheartedly into the act, living, moving, and acting on the assumption that he owned the store.

The sequel was interesting. He was discharged from his position. He found new employment with a large chain store, became manager, and later on, district manager. He saved enough money in four years to provide a down payment on a drugstore of his own. He called it his "Dream Pharmacy."

"It was," he said, "exactly the store I saw in my imagination." He became a recognized success in his chosen field, and was happy doing what he loved to do.

USING THE SUBCONSCIOUS MIND IN BUSINESS

Some years ago I gave a lecture to a group of businessmen on the powers of imagination and the subconscious mind. In this lecture I pointed out how Goethe used his imagination wisely when confronted with difficulties and predicaments.

His biographers point out that he was accustomed to fill many hours quietly holding imaginary conversations. It is well known that his custom was to imagine one of his friends before him in a chair answering him in the right way. In other words, if he were concerned over any problems, he imagined his friend giving him the right or appropriate answer, accompanied with the usual gestures and tonal qualities of the voice, and he made the entire imaginary scene as real and as vivid as possible.

One of the men present at this lecture was a young stockbroker. He proceeded to adopt the technique of Goethe. He began to have mental, imaginary conversations with a multimillionaire banker friend of his who used to congratulate him on his wise and sound judgment, and compliment him on his purchase of the right stocks. He used to dramatize this imaginary conversation until he had psychologically fixed it as a form of belief in his mind.

This broker's inner talking and controlled imagination certainly agreed with his aim, which was to make sound investments for his clients. His main purpose in life was to make money for his clients and to see them prosper financially by his wise counsel. He is still using his subconscious mind in his business, and he is a brilliant success in his field of endeavor.

BOY OF SIXTEEN YEARS TURNS
FAILURE INTO SUCCESS

A young boy who was attending high school said to me, "I am getting very poor grades. My memory is failing. I do not know what is the matter." I discovered that the only thing wrong with this boy was his attitude, which was one of indifference and resentment toward some of his teachers and fellow students. I taught him how to use his subconscious mind, and how to succeed in his studies.

He began to affirm certain truths several times a day particularly at night prior to sleep, and also in the morning after awakening. These are the best times to impregnate the subconscious mind.

He affirmed as follows: "I realize that my subconscious mind is a storehouse of memory. It retains everything I read and hear from my teachers. I have a perfect memory, and the infinite intelligence in my subconscious mind constantly reveals to me everything I need to know at all my examinations, whether written or oral. I radiate love and good will to all my teachers and fellow students. I sincerely wish for them success and all good things."

This young man is now enjoying a greater freedom than he has ever known. He is now receiving all "A's." He constantly imagines the teachers and his mother congratulating him on his success in his studies.

HOW TO BECOME SUCCESSFUL
IN BUYING AND SELLING

In buying and selling, remember that your conscious mind is the starter and your subconscious mind is the motor. You must start the motor to enable it to perform its work. Your conscious mind is the dynamo that awakens the power of your subconscious mind.

The first step in conveying your clarified desire, idea, or image to the deeper mind is to relax, immobilize the attention, get still, and be quiet. This quiet, relaxed, and peaceful attitude of mind prevents extraneous matter and false ideas from interfering with your mental absorption of your ideal. Furthermore, in the quiet, passive, and receptive attitude of mind, effort is reduced to a minimum.

The second step is to begin to imagine the reality of that which you desire. For example, you may wish to buy a home, and in your relaxed state of mind affirm as follows: "The infinite intelligence of my subconscious mind is all-wise. It reveals to me now the ideal home, which is central, ideal, is in a lovely environment, meets with all my requirements, and is commensurate with my income. I am now turning this request over to my subconscious mind, and I know it responds according to the nature of my request. I release this request with absolute faith and confidence in the same way that a farmer deposits a seed in the ground, trusting implicitly in the laws of growth."

The answer to your prayer may come through an advertisement in the paper, through a friend, or you may be guided directly to a particular home, which is exactly what you are seeking. There are many ways by which your prayer may be answered. The principal knowledge, in which you may place your confidence, is that the answer always comes, provided you trust the working of your deeper mind.

You may wish to sell a home, land, or any kind of property. In private consultation with real estate brokers I have told them of the way I sold my own home on Orlando Avenue in Los Angeles. Many of them have applied the technique I used with remarkable and speedy results. I placed a sign which read, "For sale by owner" in the garden in front of my home. The day after I said to myself as I was going to sleep, "Supposing you sold your house, what would you do?"

I answered my own question and I said, "I would take that sign down and throw it into the garage." In my imagination I took hold of the sign, pulled it up from the ground, placed it on my shoulder, went to the garage, threw it on the floor, and said jokingly to the sign, "I don't need you any more!" I felt the inner satisfaction of it all, realizing it was finished.

The next day a man gave me a deposit of $1,000 and said to me, "Take your sign down. We will go into escrow now."

Immediately I pulled the sign up and took it to the garage. The outer action conformed to the inner. There is nothing new about this. *As within, so without,* meaning according to the image impressed on your subconscious mind, so it is on the objective screen of your life. The outside mirrors the inside. External action follows internal action.

Here is another very popular method used in selling homes, land, or any kind of property. Affirm slowly, quietly, and feelingly as follows: "Infinite intelligence attracts to me the buyer for this home who wants it and who prospers in it. This buyer is being sent to me by the creative intelligence of my subconscious mind, which makes no mistakes. This buyer may look at many other homes, but mine is the only one he wants and will buy, because he is guided by the infinite intelligence within him. I know the buyer is right, the time is right, and the price is right. Everything about it is right. The deeper currents of my subconscious mind are now in operation bringing both of us together in divine order. I know that it is so."

Remember always, that what you are seeking is also seeking you, and whenever you want to sell a home or property of any kind, there is always someone who wants what you have to offer. By using the powers of your subconscious mind correctly, you free your mind of all sense of competition and anxiety in buying and selling.

HOW SHE SUCCEEDED IN GETTING
WHAT SHE WANTED

There is a young lady who regularly comes to my lectures and classes. She had to change buses three times; it took her one and a half hours each time to come to the lectures. In one lecture I explained how a young man who needed a car in his work received one.

She went home and experimented as outlined in my lecture. Here is her letter in part, narrating her application of my method, and published by her permission:

Dear Dr. Murphy:

This is how I received a Cadillac car—I wanted one to come to the lectures regularly. In my imagination I went through the identical process I would go through, if I were actually driving a car. I went to the showroom, and the salesman took me for a ride in one. I also drove it several blocks. I claimed the Cadillac car as my own over and over again.

I kept the mental picture of getting into the car, driving it, feeling the upholstery, etc., consistently for over two weeks. Last week I drove to your lectures in a Cadillac. My uncle in Inglewood passed away, and left me his Cadillac and his entire estate.

A SUCCESS TECHNIQUE EMPLOYED BY MANY OUTSTANDING EXECUTIVES AND BUSINESSMEN

There are many prominent businessmen who quietly use the abstract term, "success," over and over many times a day until they reach a conviction that *success* is theirs. They know that the *idea of success* contains all the essential elements of success. Likewise, you can begin now to repeat the word, "success," to yourself with faith and conviction. Your subconscious mind will accept it as true of you, and you will be under a subconscious compulsion to succeed.

You are compelled to express your subjective beliefs, impressions, and convictions. What does success imply to you?

You want, undoubtedly, to be successful in your home life and in your relationships with others. You wish to be outstanding in your chosen work or profession. You wish to possess a beautiful home, and all the money you need to live comfortably and happily. You want to be successful in your prayer life and in your contact with the powers of your subconscious mind.

You are a businessman also because you are in the business of living. Become a successful businessman by imagining yourself doing what you long to do, and possessing the things you long to possess. Become imaginative; mentally participate in the reality of the successful state. Make a habit of it. Go to sleep feeling successful every night, and perfectly satisfied, and you will eventually succeed in implanting the idea of success in your subconscious mind. Believe you were born to succeed, and wonders will happen as you pray!

PROFITABLE POINTERS

1. Success means successful living. When you are peaceful, happy, joyous, and doing what you love to do, you are successful.
2. Find out what you love to do, then do it. If you don't know your true expression, ask for guidance, and the *lead* will come.
3. Specialize in your particular field and try to know more about it than anyone else.
4. A successful man is not selfish. His main desire in life is to serve humanity.
5. There is no true success without peace of mind.
6. A successful man possesses great psychological and spiritual understanding.
7. If you imagine an objective clearly, you will be provided

with the necessities through the wonder-working power of your subconscious mind.

8. Your thought fused with feeling becomes a subjective belief, and *according to your belief is it done unto you.*

9. The power of sustained imagination draws forth the miracle-working powers of your subconscious mind.

10. If you are seeking promotion in your work, imagine your employer, supervisor, or loved one congratulating you on your promotion. Make the picture vivid and real. Hear the voice, see the gestures, and feel the reality of it all. Continue to do this frequently, and through frequent occupancy of your mind, you will experience the joy of the answered prayer.

11. Your subconscious mind is a storehouse of memory. For a perfect memory, affirm frequently: "The infinite intelligence of my subconscious mind reveals to me everything I need to know at all times, everywhere."

12. If you wish to sell a home or property of any kind, affirm slowly, quietly, and feelingly as follows: "Infinite intelligence attracts to me the buyer of this house or property, who wants it, and who prospers in it." Sustain this awareness, and the deeper currents of your subconscious mind will bring it to pass.

13. The idea of success contains all the elements of success. Repeat the word, "success," to yourself frequently with faith and conviction, and you will be under a subconscious compulsion to succeed.

12

SCIENTISTS USE THE SUBCONSCIOUS MIND

Many scientists realize the true importance of the subconscious mind. Edison, Marconi, Kettering, Poincaré, Einstein, and many others have used the subconscious mind. It has given them the insight and the "know-how" for all their great achievements in modern science and industry. Research has shown that the ability to bring into action the subconscious power has determined the success of all the great scientific and research workers.

An instance of how a famous chemist, Friedrich von Stradonitz, used his subconscious mind to solve his problem is as follows: He had been working laboriously for a long time trying to rearrange the six carbon and the six hydrogen atoms of the benzine formula, and he was constantly perplexed and unable to solve the matter. Tired and exhausted, he turned the request over completely to his subconscious mind. Shortly afterward, as he was about to board a London bus, his subconscious presented his conscious mind with a sudden flash of a snake biting its own tail and turning around like a pinwheel. This answer, from his subconscious mind, gave him the long-sought answer of the circular rearrangement of the atoms that is known as the benzine ring.

HOW A DISTINGUISHED SCIENTIST BROUGHT
FORTH HIS INVENTIONS

Nikola Tesla was a brilliant electrical scientist who brought forth the most amazing innovations. When an idea for a new invention came into his mind, he would build it up in his imagination, knowing that his subconscious mind would reconstruct and reveal to his conscious mind all the parts needed for its manufacture in concrete form. Through quietly contemplating every possible improvement, he spent no time in correcting defects, and was able to give the technicians the perfect product of his mind.

He said, "Invariably, my device works as I imagined it should. In twenty years there has not been a single exception."

HOW A FAMOUS NATURALIST
SOLVED HIS PROBLEM

Professor Agassiz, a distinguished American naturalist, discovered the indefatigable activities of his subconscious mind while he slept. The following has been reported by his widow in her biography of her famous husband.

"He had been for two weeks striving to decipher the somewhat obscure impression of a fossil fish on the stone slab in which it was preserved. Weary and perplexed, he put his work aside at last, and tried to dismiss it from his mind. Shortly after, he waked one night persuaded that while asleep he had seen his fish with all the missing features perfectly restored. But when he tried to hold and make fast the image it escaped him. Nevertheless, he went early to the Jardin des Plantes, thinking that on looking anew at the impression he should see something, which would put him on the track of his vision. In vain—the blurred record was as black as ever. The next night he saw the fish again, but with no more satisfactory result. When he awoke it disappeared from his memory as before. Hoping that the same experience might be repeated, on the third night he placed a pencil and paper beside his bed before going to sleep.

"Accordingly, toward morning the fish reappeared in his dream, confusedly at first, but at last with such distinctness that he had no longer any doubt as to its zoological characters. Still half dreaming, in perfect darkness, he traced these characters on the sheet of paper at the bedside. In the morning he was surprised to see in his nocturnal sketch features, which he thought it impossible the fossil itself should reveal. He hastened to the Jardin des Plantes, and, with his drawing as a guide, succeeded in chiseling away the surface of the stone under which portions of the fish proved to be hidden. When wholly exposed it corresponded with his dream and his drawing, and he succeeded in classifying it with ease."

AN OUTSTANDING PHYSICIAN SOLVED
THE PROBLEM OF DIABETES

Some years ago I received a clipping from a magazine describing the origin of the discovery of insulin. This is the essence of the article as I recall it.

About forty years ago or more, Dr. Frederick Banting, a brilliant Canadian physician and surgeon, was concentrating his attention on the ravages of diabetes. At that time medical science offered no effective method of arresting the disease. Dr. Banting spent considerable time experimenting and studying the international literature on the subject. One night he was exhausted and fell asleep. While asleep, his subconscious mind instructed him to extract the residue from the degenerated pancreatic duct of dogs. This was the origin of insulin which has helped millions of people.

You will note that Dr. Banting had been consciously dwelling on the problem for some time seeking a solution, a way out, and his subconscious responded accordingly.

It does not follow that you will always get an answer overnight. The answer may not come for some time. Do not be discouraged. Keep on turning the problem over every night to the subconscious mind prior to sleep, as if you had never done it before.

One of the reasons for the delay may be that you look upon it as a major problem. You may believe it will take a long time to solve it.

Your subconscious mind is timeless and spaceless. Go to sleep believing you have the answer now. Do not postulate the answer in the future. Have an abiding faith in the outcome. Become convinced now as you read this book that there is an answer and a perfect solution for you.

HOW A FAMOUS SCIENTIST AND PHYSICIST ESCAPED FROM A RUSSIAN CONCENTRATION CAMP

Dr. Lothar von Blenk-Schmidt, a member of the Rocket Society and an outstanding research electronic engineer, gives the following condensed summary of how he used his subconscious mind to free himself from certain death at the hands of brutal guards in a Russian prison camp coal mine. He states as follows:

"I was a prisoner of war in a coal mine in Russia, and I saw men dying all around me in that prison compound. We were watched over by brutal guards, arrogant officers, and sharp, fast-thinking commissars. After a short medical checkup, a quota of coal was assigned to each person. My quota was three hundred pounds per day. In case any man did not fill his quota, his small food ration was cut down, and in a short time he was resting in the cemetery.

"I started concentrating on my escape. I knew that my subconscious mind would somehow find a way. My home in Germany was destroyed, my family wiped out; all my friends and former associates were either killed in the war or were in concentration camps.

"I said to my subconscious mind, 'I want to go to Los Angeles, and you will find the way.' I had seen pictures of Los Angeles and I remembered some of the boulevards very well as well as some of the buildings.

"Every day and night I would imagine I was walking down Wilshire Boulevard with an American girl whom I met in Berlin prior to the war (she is now my wife). In my imagination we would visit the stores, ride buses, and eat in the restaurants. Every night I made it a special point to drive my imaginary American automobile up and down the boulevards of Los Angeles. I made all this vivid and real. These pictures in my mind were as real and as natural to me as one of the trees outside the prison camp.

"Every morning the chief guard would count the prisoners as they were lined up. He would call out 'one, two, three,' etc., and when seventeen was called out, which was my number in sequence, I stepped aside. In the meantime, the guard was called away for a minute or so, and on his return he started by mistake on the next man as number seventeen. When the crew returned in the evening, the number of men was the same, and I was not missed, and the discovery would take a long time.

"I walked out of the camp undetected and kept walking for twenty-four hours, resting in a deserted town the next day. I was able to live by fishing and killing some wildlife. I found coal trains going to Poland and traveled on them by night, until finally I reached Poland. With the help of friends, I made my way to Lucerne, Switzerland.

"One evening at the Palace Hotel, Lucerne, I had a talk with a man and his wife from the United States of America. This man asked me if I would care to be a guest at his home in Santa Monica, California. I accepted, and when I arrived in Los Angeles, I found that their chauffeur drove me along Wilshire Boulevard and many other boulevards, which I had imagined so vividly in the long months in the Russian coal mines. I recognized the buildings, which I had seen in my mind so often. It actually seemed as if I had been in Los Angeles before. I had reached my goal.

"I will never cease to marvel at the wonders of the subconscious mind. Truly, it has ways we know not of."

HOW ARCHAEOLOGISTS AND PALEONTOLOGISTS RECONSTRUCT ANCIENT SCENES

These scientists know that their subconscious mind has a memory of everything that has ever transpired. As they study the ancient ruins and fossils, through their imaginative perception, their subconscious mind aids them in reconstructing the ancient scenes. The dead past becomes alive and audible once more. Looking at these ancient temples and studying the pottery, statuary, tools, and household utensils of these ancient times, the scientist tells us of an age when there was no language. Communication was done by grunts, groans, and signs.

The keen concentration and disciplined imagination of the scientist awakens the latent powers of his subconscious mind enabling him to clothe the ancient temples with roofs, and surround them with gardens, pools, and fountains. The fossil remains are clothed with eyes, sinews, and muscles, and they again walk and talk. The past becomes the living present, and we find that in mind there is no time or space. Through disciplined, controlled, and directed imagination, you can be a companion of the most scientific and inspired thinkers of all time.

HOW TO RECEIVE GUIDANCE FROM YOUR SUBCONSCIOUS

When you have what you term "a difficult decision" to make, or when you fail to see the solution to your problem, begin at once to think constructively about it. If you are fearful and worried, you are not really thinking. True thinking is free from fear.

Here is a simple technique you can use to receive guidance on any subject: Quiet the mind and still the body. Tell the body to relax; it has to obey you. It has no volition, initiative, or self-conscious intelligence. Your body is an emotional disk, which records your beliefs and impressions. Mobilize your attention; focus your thought on the solution to your problem. Try to solve it with your conscious mind. Think how happy you would be about the perfect solution. Sense the feeling you would have if the perfect answer were yours now. Let your mind play with this mood in a relaxed way; then drop off to sleep. When you awaken, and you do not have the answer, get busy about something else. Probably, when you are preoccupied with something else, the answer will come into your mind like toast pops out of a toaster.

In receiving guidance from the subconscious mind, the simple way is the best. This is an illustration: I once lost a valuable ring, which was an heirloom. I looked everywhere for it and could not locate it. At night I talked to the subconscious in the same manner that I would talk to anyone. I said to it prior to dropping off to sleep, "You know all things; you know where that ring is, and you now reveal to me where it is."

In the morning I awoke suddenly with the words ringing in my ear, "Ask Robert!"

I thought it very strange that I should ask Robert, a young boy about nine years of age; however, I followed the inner voice of intuition.

Robert said, "Oh, yes, I picked it up in the yard while I was playing with the boys. I placed it on the desk in my room. I did not think it worth anything, so I did not say anything about it."

The subconscious mind will always answer you if you trust it.

HIS SUBCONSCIOUS REVEALED
THE LOCATION OF HIS FATHER'S WILL

A young man who attends my lectures had this experience. His father died and apparently left no will. However, this man's sister told him that their father had confided to her that a will had been executed which was fair to all. Every attempt to locate the will failed.

Prior to sleep he talked to his deeper mind as follows: "I now turn this request over the subconscious mind. It knows just where that will is, and reveals it to me." Then he condensed his request down to one word, "Answer," repeating it over and over again as a lullaby. He lulled himself to sleep with the word, "Answer."

The next morning this young man had an overpowering hunch to go to a certain bank in Los Angeles where he found a safe deposit vault registered in the name of his father, the contents of which solved all his problems.

Your thought, as you go to sleep, arouses the powerful latency, which is within you. For example, let us suppose you are wondering whether to sell your home, buy a certain stock, sever partnership, move to New York or stay in Los Angeles, dissolve the present contract or take a new one. Do this: Sit quietly in your armchair or at the desk in your office. Remember that there is a universal law of action and reaction. The action is your thought. The reaction is the response from your subconscious mind. The subconscious mind is reactive and reflexive; this is its nature. It rebounds, rewards, and repays. It is the law of correspondence. It responds by corresponding. As you contemplate right action, you will automatically experience a reaction or response in yourself, which represents the guidance or answer of your subconscious mind.

In seeking guidance, you simply think quietly about right action, which means that you are using the infinite intelligence resident in the subconscious mind to the point where it begins to use you. From there on, your course of action is directed and controlled by the subjective wisdom within you, which is all-wise and omnipotent. Your decision will be right. There will only be right action because you are under a subjective compulsion to do the right thing. I use the word *compulsion* because the law of the subconscious is compulsion.

THE SECRET OF GUIDANCE

The secret of guidance or right action is to mentally devote yourself to the right answer, until you find its response in you. The response is a feeling, an inner awareness, an overpowering hunch whereby you know that you know. You have used the power to the point where it begins to use you. You cannot possibly fail or make one false step while operating under the subjective wisdom within you. You will find that all your ways are pleasantness and all your paths are peace.

HIGHLIGHTS TO RECALL

1. Remember that the subconscious mind has determined the success and wonderful achievements of all great scientific workers.

2. By giving your conscious attention and devotion to the solution of a perplexing problem, your subconscious mind gathers all the necessary information and presents it full-blown to the conscious mind.

3. If you are wondering about the answer to a problem, try to solve it objectively. Get all the information you can from research and also from others. If no answer comes, turn it over to your subconscious mind prior to sleep, and the answer always comes. It never fails.

4. You do not always get the answer overnight. Keep on turning your request over to your subconscious until the day breaks and the shadows flee away.

5. You delay the answer by thinking it will take a long time or that it is a major problem. Your subconscious has no problem, it knows only the answer.

6. Believe that you have the answer now. Feel the joy of the

answer and the way you would feel if you had the perfect answer. Your subconscious will respond to your feeling.

7. Any mental picture, backed by faith and perseverance, will come to pass through the miracle-working power of your subconscious. Trust it, believe in its power, and wonders will happen as you pray.

8. Your subconscious is the storehouse of memory, and within your subconscious are recorded all your experiences since childhood.

9. Scientists meditating on ancient scrolls, temples, fossils, etc., are able to reconstruct scenes of the past and make them alive today. Their subconscious mind comes to their aid.

10. Turn over your request for a solution to your subconscious prior to sleep. Trust it and believe in it, and the answer will come. It knows all and sees all, but you must not doubt or question its powers.

11. The action is your thought, and the reaction is the response of your subconscious mind. If your thoughts are wise, your actions and decisions will be wise.

12. Guidance comes as a feeling, an inner awareness, an overpowering hunch whereby you know that you know. It is an inner sense of touch. Follow it.

13

YOUR SUBCONSCIOUS AND THE WONDERS OF SLEEP

You spend about eight out of every twenty-four hours, or one-third of your entire life, in sleep. This is an inexorable law of life. This also applies to the animal and vegetable kingdoms. Sleep is a divine law, and many answers to our problems come to us when we are sound asleep upon the bed.

Many people have advocated the theory that you get tired during the day, that you go to sleep to rest the body, and that a reparative process takes place while you sleep. Nothing rests in sleep. Your heart, lungs, and all your vital organs function while you are asleep. If you eat prior to sleep, the food is digested and assimilated; also, your skin secretes perspiration, and your nails and hair continue to grow.

Your subconscious mind never rests or sleeps. It is always active, controlling all your vital forces. The healing process takes place more rapidly while you are asleep as there is no interference from your conscious mind. Remarkable answers are given to you while you are asleep.

WHY WE SLEEP

Dr. John Bigelow, a famous research authority on sleep,* demonstrated that at night while asleep you receive impressions showing that the nerves of the eyes, ears, nose, and taste buds are active during sleep, and also that the nerves of your brain are quite active. He says that the main reason we sleep is because "the nobler part of the soul is united by abstraction to our higher nature and becomes a participant in the wisdom and foreknowledge of the gods."

Dr. Bigelow states also, "The results of my studies have not only strengthened my convictions that the supposed exemption from customary toils and activities was not the final purpose of sleep, but have also made clearer to my mind the conviction that no part of a man's life deserves to be considered more indispensable to its symmetrical and perfect spiritual development than the while he is separated from the phenomenal world in sleep."

PRAYER, A FORM OF SLEEP

Your conscious mind gets involved with vexations, strife, and contentions of the day, and it is very necessary to withdraw periodically from sense evidence and the objective world, and

---

* John Bigelow, *The Mystery of Sleep* (New York and London: Harper Brothers, 1903).

commune silently with the inner wisdom of your subconscious mind. By claiming guidance, strength, and greater intelligence in all phases of your life, you will be enabled to overcome all difficulties and solve your daily problems.

This regular withdrawal from sense evidence and the noise and confusion of everyday living is also a form of sleep, i.e., you become asleep to the world of the senses and alive to the wisdom and power of your subconscious mind.

STARTLING EFFECTS OF SLEEP DEPRIVATION

Lack of sleep can cause you to become irritable, moody, and depressed. Dr. George Stevenson of the National Association for Mental Health says, "I believe it can safely be said that all human beings need a minimum of six hours' sleep to be healthy. Most people need more. Those who think they can get along on less are fooling themselves."

Medical research scholars, investigating sleep processes and deprivation of sleep, point out that severe insomnia has preceded psychotic breakdown in some instances. Remember, you are spiritually recharged during sleep, and adequate sleep is essential to produce joy and vitality in life.

YOU NEED MORE SLEEP

Robert O'Brien, in an article, "Maybe You Need More Sleep," in an issue of *The Reader's Digest*, reports the following experiment on sleep:

"For the last three years experiments have been in progress at Walter Reed Army Institute of Research in Washington, D.C. Subjects—more than one hundred military and civilian volunteers—have been kept awake for as long as four days. Thousands of tests have measured the effects on their behavior and personality. Results of these tests have given scientists aston-ishingly new insights into the mysteries of sleep.

"They now know that the tired brain apparently craves sleep so hungrily that it will sacrifice anything to get it. After only a few hours of sleep loss, fleeting stolen naps called 'lapses,' or micro-sleep, occurred at the rate of three or four an hour. As in real sleep, eyelids drooped, heartbeat slowed. Each lapse lasted just a fraction of a second. Sometimes the lapses were periods of blankness; sometimes they were filled with images, wisps of dreams. As hours of sleep loss mounted, the lapses took place more often and lasted longer, perhaps two or three seconds. Even if the subjects had been piloting an air-liner in a thunderstorm, they still couldn't have resisted micro-sleeps for those few priceless seconds. And it can happen to you, as many who have fallen asleep at the wheel of a car can testify.

"Another startling effect of sleep deprivation was its attack on human memory and perception. Many sleep-deprived sub-jects were unable to retain information long enough to relate it to the task they were supposed to perform. They were totally befuddled in situations requiring them to hold several factors in mind and act on them, as a pilot must when he skillfully inte-grates wind direction, air speed, altitude, and glide path to make a safe landing."

SLEEP BRINGS COUNSEL

A young lady in Los Angeles who listens to my morning radio talks told me that she had been offered a lucrative position in New York City at twice her present salary. She was wondering whether to accept or not and prayed prior to sleep as follows: "The creative intelligence of my subconscious mind knows what is best for me. Its tendency is always lifeward, and it reveals to me the right decision, which blesses me and all concerned. I give thanks for the answer which I know will come to me."

She repeated this simple prayer over and over again as a lullaby prior to sleep, and in the morning she had a persistent feeling that she should not accept the offer. She rejected the offer and subsequent events verified her inward sense of knowing, because the company went bankrupt in a few months following their offer of employment to her.

The conscious mind may be correct on the facts objectively known, but the intuitive faculty of her subconscious mind saw the failure of the concern in question, and prompted her accordingly.

SAVED FROM CERTAIN DISASTER

I will illustrate how the wisdom of your subconscious mind can instruct you and protect you relative to your request for right action as you go to sleep.

Many years ago, before the Second World War, I was offered a very lucrative assignment in the Orient, and I prayed for guidance and the right decision as follows: "Infinite intelligence within me knows all things, and the right decision is revealed to me in divine order. I will recognize the answer when it comes."

I repeated this simple prayer over and over again as a lullaby prior to sleep, and in a dream came the vivid realization of things to come three years hence. An old friend appeared in the dream and said, "Read these headlines—do not go!" The headlines of the newspaper, which appeared in the dream, related to war and the attack on Pearl Harbor.

Occasionally, the writer dreams literally. The aforementioned dream was undoubtedly a dramatization of the subconscious mind which projected a person whom I trusted and respected. To some a warning may come in the form of a mother who appears in a dream. She tells the person not to go here or there, and the reason for the warning. Your subconscious mind is all-wise. It knows all things. Oftentimes it will speak to you only in a voice that your conscious mind will immediately accept as true. Sometimes your subconscious will warn you in a voice which sounds like that of your mother or some loved one which may cause you to stop on the street, and you find, if you had gone another foot, a falling object from a window might have struck you on the head.

My subconscious mind is one with the universal subconscious, and it knew the Japanese were planning a war, and it also knew when the war would start.

Dr. Rhine, director of the Department of Psychology at Duke University, has gathered together a vast amount of evidence showing that a great number of people all over the world see events before they happen, and in many instances are, therefore, able to avoid the tragic event which was foreseen vividly in a dream.

The dream which I had showed clearly the headlines in *The New York Times* about three years prior to the tragedy of Pearl Harbor. In consequence of this dream, I immediately canceled the trip as I felt a subconscious compulsion to do so. Three years later the Second World War proved the truth of the inner voice of intuition.

YOUR FUTURE IS IN YOUR SUBCONSCIOUS MIND

Remember that the future, the result of your habitual thinking, is already in your mind except when you change it through prayer. The future of a country, likewise, is in the collective subconscious of the people of that nation. There is nothing strange in the dream I had wherein I saw the headlines of the New York newspapers long before the war began. The war had already taken place in mind, and all the plans of attack were already engraved on that great recording instrument, the subconscious mind or collective unconscious of the universal mind. Tomorrow's events are in your subconscious mind, so are next week's and next month's, and they may be seen by a highly psychic or clairvoyant person.

No disaster or tragedy can happen to you if you decide to pray. Nothing is predetermined or foreordained. Your mental attitude, i.e., the way you think, feel, and believe, determines your destiny. You can, through scientific prayer, which is explained in a previous chapter, mold, fashion, and create your own future. *Whatsoever a man soweth, that shall he also reap.*

A CATNAP NETS HIM $15,000

One of my students mailed me a newspaper clipping three or four years ago about a man called Ray Hammerstrom, a roller at the steel works in Pittsburgh operated by Jones and Laughlin Steel Corporation. He received $15,000 for his dream.

According to the article, the engineers could not fix a faulty switch in a newly installed bar mill which controlled the delivery of straight bars to the cooling beds. The engineers worked on the switch about eleven or twelve times to no avail.

Hammerstrom thought a lot about the problem and tried to figure out a new design, which might work. Nothing worked. One afternoon he lay down for a nap, and prior to sleep he began to think about the answer to the switch problem. He had a dream in which a perfect design for the switch was portrayed. When he awoke, he sketched his new design according to the outline of his dream.

This visionary catnap won Hammerstrom a check for $15,000, the largest award the firm ever gave an employee for a new idea.

HOW A FAMOUS PROFESSOR SOLVED
HIS PROBLEM IN SLEEP

Dr. H. V. Hilprecht, professor of Assyrian at the University of Pennsylvania, wrote as follows: "One Saturday evening . . . I had been wearying myself, in the vain attempt to decipher two small fragments of agate which were supposed to belong to the finger rings of some Babylonians.

"About midnight, weary and exhausted, I went to bed and dreamed the following remarkable dream: A tall, thin priest of Nippur, about forty years of age, led me to the treasure chamber of the temple . . . a small, low-ceilinged room without windows, while scraps of agate and lapis-lazuli lay scattered on the floor. Here he addressed me as follows: 'The two fragments which you have published separately on pages 22 and 26 belong together, are not finger rings. . . . The first two rings served as earrings for the statue of the god; the two fragments (you have) . . . are the portions of them. If you will put them together you will have confirmation of my words.' . . . I awoke at once . . . I examined the fragments . . . and to my astonishment found the dream verified. The problem was then at last solved."

This demonstrates clearly the creative manifestation of

his subconscious mind, which knew the answer to all his problems.

HOW THE SUBCONSCIOUS WORKED FOR A FAMOUS WRITER WHILE HE SLEPT

Robert Louis Stevenson in one of his books, *Across the Plains*, devotes a whole chapter to dreams. He was a vivid dreamer and had the persistent habit of giving specific instructions to his subconscious every night prior to sleep. He would request his subconscious to evolve stories for him while he slept. For example, if Stevenson's funds were at a low ebb, his command to his subconscious would be something like this: "Give me a good thrilling novel which will be marketable and profitable." His subconscious responded magnificently.

Stevenson says, "These little brownies [the intelligences and powers of his subconscious] can tell me a story piece by piece, like a serial, and keep me, its supposed creator, all the while in total ignorance of where they aim." And he added: "That part of my work which is done when I am up and about [while he is consciously aware and awake] is by no means necessarily mine, since all goes to show that the *brownies* have a hand in it even then."

SLEEP IN PEACE AND WAKE IN JOY

To those who suffer from insomnia, you will find the following prayer very effective. Repeat it slowly, quietly, and lovingly prior to sleep: "My toes are relaxed, my ankles are relaxed, my abdominal muscles are relaxed, my heart and lungs are relaxed, my hands and arms are relaxed, my neck is relaxed, my brain is relaxed, my face is relaxed, my eyes are relaxed, my whole mind and body are relaxed. I fully and freely forgive everyone, and I sincerely wish for them harmony, health, peace, and all the blessings of life. I am at peace, I am poised, serene, and calm. I rest in security and in peace. A great stillness steals over me, and a great calm quiets my whole being as I realize the Divine Presence within me. I know that the realization of life and love heals me. I wrap myself in the mantle of love and fall asleep filled with good will for all. Throughout the night peace remains with me, and in the morning I shall be filled with life and love. A circle of love is drawn around me. *I will fear no evil, for Thou art with me.* I sleep in peace, I wake in joy, and *in Him I live, move, and have my being.*"

SUMMARY OF YOUR AIDS TO THE WONDERS OF SLEEP

1. If you are worried that you will not wake up on time, suggest to your subconscious mind prior to sleep the exact time you wish to arise, and it will awaken you. It needs no clock. Do the same thing with all problems. There is nothing too hard for your subconscious.

2. Your subconscious never sleeps. It is always on the job. It controls all your vital functions. Forgive yourself and everyone else before you go to sleep, and healing will take place much more rapidly.

3. Guidance is given you while you are asleep, sometimes in a dream. The healing currents are also released, and in the morning you feel refreshed and rejuvenated.

4. When troubled by the vexations and strife of the day, still the wheels of your mind and think about the wisdom and

intelligence lodged in your subconscious mind, which is ready to respond to you. This will give you peace, strength, and confidence.

5. Sleep is essential for peace of mind and health of body. Lack of sleep can cause irritation, depression, and mental disorders. You need eight hours' sleep.

6. Medical research scholars point out that insomnia precedes psychotic breakdowns.

7. You are spiritually recharged during sleep. Adequate sleep is essential for joy and vitality in life.

8. Your tired brain craves sleep so hungrily that it will sacrifice anything to get it. Many who have fallen asleep at the wheel of an automobile can testify to this.

9. Many sleep-deprived people have poor memories and lack proper coordination. They become befuddled, confused, and disoriented.

10. Sleep brings counsel. Prior to sleep, claim that the infinite intelligence of your subconscious mind is guiding and directing you. Then, watch for the *lead,* which comes, perhaps on awakening.

11. Trust your subconscious completely. Know that its tendency is always lifeward. Occasionally, your subconscious answers you in a very vivid dream and a vision in the night. You can be forewarned in a dream in the same way as the author of this book was warned.

12. Your future is in your mind now, based on your habitual thinking and beliefs. Claim infinite intelligence leads and guides you and that all good is yours, and your future will be wonderful. Believe it and accept it. Expect the best, and invariably the best will come to you.

13. If you are writing a novel, play, or book, or are working on an invention, speak to your subconscious mind at night and claim boldly that its wisdom, intelligence, and power are guiding, directing, and revealing to you the ideal play, novel, book, or revealing the perfect solution whatever it may be. Wonders will happen as you pray this way.

14

YOUR SUBCONSCIOUS MIND AND MARITAL PROBLEMS

Ignorance of the functions and powers of the mind is the cause of all marital trouble. Friction between husband and wife can be solved by each using the law of mind correctly. By praying together they stay together. The contemplation of divine ideals, the study of the laws of life, the mutual agreement on a common purpose and plan, and the enjoyment of personal freedom bring about that harmonious marriage, that wedded bliss, that sense of oneness where the two become one.

The best time to prevent divorce is before marriage. It is not wrong to try to get out of a very bad situation. But, why get into the bad situation in the first place? Would it not be better to give attention to the real cause of marital problems, in other words, to really get at the root of the matter involved?

As with all other problems of men and women, the problems of divorce, separation, annulment, and endless litigation are directly traceable to lack of knowledge of the working and interrelationship of the conscious and subconscious mind.

THE MEANING OF MARRIAGE

Marriage to be real must first be on a spiritual basis. It must be of the heart, and the heart is the chalice of love. Honesty, sincerity, kindness, and integrity are also forms of love. Each partner should be perfectly honest and sincere with the other. It is not a true marriage when a man marries a woman for her money, social position, or to lift his ego, because this indicates a lack of sincerity, honesty, and true love. Such a marriage is a farce, a sham, and a masquerade.

When a woman says, "I am tired working; I want to get married because I want security," her premise is false. She is not using the laws of mind correctly. Her security depends upon her knowledge of the interaction of the conscious and subconscious mind and its application.

For example, a woman will never lack for wealth or health if she applies the techniques outlined in the respective chapters of this book. Her wealth can come to her independent of her husband, father, or anyone else. A woman is not dependent on her husband for health, peace, joy, inspiration, guidance, love, wealth, security, happiness, or anything in the world. Her security and peace of mind come from her knowledge of the inner powers within her and from the constant use of the laws of her own mind in a constructive fashion.

HOW TO ATTRACT THE IDEAL HUSBAND

You are now acquainted with the way your subconscious mind works. You know that whatever you impress upon it will be experienced in your world. Begin now to impress your subconscious mind with the qualities and characteristics you desire in a man.

The following is an excellent technique: Sit down at night in your armchair, close your eyes, let go, relax the body, become very quiet, passive, and receptive. Talk to your subconscious mind and say to it, "I am now attracting a man into my experience who is honest, sincere, loyal, faithful, peaceful, happy, and prosperous. These qualities, which I admire, are sinking down into my subconscious mind now. As I dwell upon these characteristics, they become a part of me and are embodied subconsciously.

"I know there is an irresistible law of attraction and that I attract to me a man according to my subconscious belief. I attract that which I feel to be true in my subconscious mind.

"I know I can contribute to his peace and happiness. He loves my ideals, and I love his ideals. He does not want to make me over; neither do I want to make him over. There is mutual love, freedom, and respect."

Practice this process of impregnating your subconscious mind. Then, you will have the joy of attracting to you a man possessing the qualities and characteristics you mentally dwelt upon. Your subconscious intelligence will open up a pathway, whereby both of you will meet, according to the irresistible and changeless flow of your own subconscious mind. Have a keen desire to give the best that is in you of love, devotion, and cooperation. Be receptive to this gift of love, which you have given to your subconscious mind.

HOW TO ATTRACT THE IDEAL WIFE

Affirm as follows: "I now attract the right woman who is in complete accord with me. This is a spiritual union because it is divine love functioning through the personality of someone with whom I blend perfectly. I know I can give to this woman love, light, peace, and joy. I feel and believe I can make this woman's life full, complete, and wonderful.

"I now decree that she possesses the following qualities and attributes: She is spiritual, loyal, faithful, and true. She is harmonious, peaceful, and happy. We are irresistibly attracted to each other. Only that which belongs to love, truth, and beauty can enter my experience. I accept my ideal companion now."

As you think quietly and with interest on the qualities and attributes, which you admire in the companion you seek, you will build the mental equivalent into your mentality. Then, the deeper currents of your subconscious mind will bring both of you together in divine order.

NO NEED FOR THIRD MISTAKE

Recently a teacher said to me, "I have had three husbands and all three have been passive, submissive, and dependent on me to make all decisions and govern everything. Why do I attract such type men?"

I asked her whether she had known that her second husband was the effeminate type, and she replied, "Of course not. Had I known, I would not have married him." Apparently she had not learned anything from the first mistake. The trouble was with her own personality makeup. She was very masculine, domineering, and unconsciously wanted someone who would be submissive and passive so that she could play the dominant role. All this was unconscious motivation, and her subconscious picture attracted to her what she subjectively wanted. She had to learn to *break the pattern by adopting the right prayer process.*

HOW SHE BROKE THE NEGATIVE PATTERN

The above-mentioned woman learned a simple truth. When you believe you can have the type of man you idealize, it is done unto you as you believe. The following is the specific prayer she used to break the old subconscious pattern and attract to her the ideal mate: "I am building into my mentality the type of man I deeply desire. The man I attract for a husband is strong, powerful, loving, very masculine, successful, honest, loyal, and faithful. He finds love and happiness with me. I love to follow where he leads.

"I know he wants me, and I want him. I am honest, sincere, loving, and kind. I have wonderful gifts to offer him. They are good will, a joyous heart, and a healthy body. He offers me the same. It is mutual. I give and I receive. Divine intelligence knows where this man is, and the deeper wisdom of my subconscious mind is now bringing both of us together in its own way, and we recognize each other immediately. I release this request to my subconscious mind, which knows how to bring my request to pass. I give thanks for the perfect answer."

She prayed in the above manner night and morning, affirming these truths and knowing that through frequent occupation of the mind she would reach the mental equivalent of that which she sought.

THE ANSWER TO HER PRAYER

Several months went by. She had a great number of dates and social engagements, none of which was agreeable to her. When she was about to question, waiver, doubt, and vacillate, she reminded herself that the infinite intelligence was bringing it to pass in its own way and that there was nothing to be concerned about. Her final decree in her divorce proceedings was granted which brought her a great sense of release and mental freedom.

Shortly afterward she went to work as a receptionist in a doctor's office. She told me that the minute she saw the physician she knew he was the man she was praying about. Apparently he knew it, too, because he proposed to her the first week she was in the office, and their subsequent marriage was ideally happy. This physician was not the passive or submissive type, but was a real man, a former football player, an outstanding athlete, and was a deeply spiritual man though he was completely devoid of any sectarian or denominational affiliation.

She got what she prayed for because she claimed it mentally until she reached the point of saturation. In other words, she mentally and emotionally united with her idea, and it became a part of her in the same way that an apple becomes a part of her bloodstream.

SHOULD I GET A DIVORCE?

Divorce is an individual problem. It cannot be generalized. In some cases, of course, there never should have been a marriage. In some cases, divorce is not the solution, no more so than marriage is the solution for a lonely man. Divorce may be right for one person and wrong for another. A divorced woman may be far more sincere and noble than many of her married sisters who perhaps are living a lie.

For example, I once talked with a woman whose husband was a dope fiend, an ex-convict, a wife-beater, and a non-provider. She had been told it was wrong to get a divorce. I explained to her that marriage is of the heart. If two hearts blend harmoniously, lovingly, and sincerely, that is the ideal marriage. The pure action of the heart is love.

Following this explanation she knew what to do. She knew in her heart that there is no divine law which compelled her to be browbeaten, intimidated, and beaten because someone said, "I pronounce you man and wife."

If you are in doubt as to what to do, ask for guidance, knowing that there is always an answer and you will receive it. Follow the *lead* that comes to you in the silence of your soul. It speaks to you in peace.

DRIFTING INTO DIVORCE

Recently a young couple, married for only a few months, were seeking a divorce. I discovered that the young man had a constant fear that his wife would leave him. He expected rejection, and he believed that she would be unfaithful. These thoughts haunted his mind, and became an obsession with him. His mental attitude was one of separation and suspicion. She felt unresponsive to him; it was his own feeling or atmosphere of loss and separation operating through them. This brought about a condition or action in accordance with the mental pattern behind it. There is a law of action and reaction, or cause and effect. The thought is the action, and the response of the subconscious mind is the reaction.

His wife left home and asked for a divorce, which is what he feared and believed she would do.

DIVORCE BEGINS IN THE MIND

Divorce takes place first in the mind; the legal proceedings follow after. These two young people were full of resentment, fear, suspicion, and anger. These attitudes weaken, exhaust, and debilitate the whole being. They learned that hate divides and that love unites. They began to realize what they had been doing with their minds. Neither one of them knew the law of mental action, and they were misusing their minds and bringing on chaos and misery. These two people went back together at my suggestion and experimented with prayer therapy.

They began to radiate love, peace, and good will to each other. Each one practiced radiating harmony, health, peace, and love to the other, and they alternated in the reading of the Psalms every night. Their marriage is growing more beautiful everyday.

THE NAGGING WIFE

Many times the reason the wife nags is because she gets no attention. Oftentimes, it is a craving for love and affection. Give your wife attention, and show your appreciation. Praise and exalt all her many good points. There is also the nagging type of woman who wants to make the man conform to her particular pattern. This is about the quickest way in the world to get rid of a man.

The wife and the husband must cease being scavengers—always looking at the petty faults or errors in each other. Let each give attention and praise for the constructive and wonderful qualities in the other.

THE BROODING HUSBAND

If a man begins to brood, grows morbid against his wife because of the things she said or did, he is, psychologically speaking, committing adultery. One of the meanings of adultery is idolatry, i.e., giving attention to or uniting mentally with that which is negative and destructive. When a man is silently resenting his wife and is full of hostility toward her, he is unfaithful. He is not faithful to his marriage vows, which are to love, cherish, and honor her all the days of his life.

The man who is brooding, bitter, and resentful can swallow his sharp remarks, abate his anger, and he can go to great lengths to be considerate, kind, and courteous. He can deftly skirt the differences. Through praise and mental effort, he can get out of the habit of antagonism. Then, he will be able to get along better, not only with his wife, but with business associates also. Assume the harmonious state, and eventually you will find peace and harmony.

THE GREAT MISTAKE

A great mistake is to discuss your marital problems or difficulties with neighbors and relatives. Suppose, for example, a wife says to the neighbor, "John never gives me any money. He treats my mother abominably, drinks to excess, and is constantly abusive and insulting."

Now, this wife is degrading and belittling her husband in the eyes of all the neighbors and relatives. He no longer appears as the ideal husband to them. Never discuss your marital problems with anyone except a trained counselor. Why cause numerous people to think negatively of your marriage? Moreover, as you discuss and dwell upon these shortcomings of your husband, you are actually creating these states within yourself. Who is thinking and feeling it? You are! As you think and feel, so are you.

Relatives will usually give you the wrong advice. It is usually biased and prejudiced because it is not given in an impersonal way. Any advice you receive which violates the Golden Rule, which is a cosmic law, is not good or sound.

It is well to remember that no two human beings ever lived beneath the same roof without clashes of temperament, periods of hurts and strain. Never display the unhappy side of your marriage to your friends. Keep your quarrels to yourself. Refrain from criticism and condemnation of your partner.

DON'T TRY TO MAKE YOUR WIFE OVER

A husband must not try to make his wife over into a second edition of himself. The tactless attempt to change her in many ways is foreign to her nature. These attempts are always foolish, and many times result in a dissolution of the marriage. These attempts to alter her destroy her pride and self-esteem, and arouse a spirit of contrariness and resentment that proves fatal to the marriage bond.

Adjustments are needed, of course, but if you have a good look inside your own mind, and study your character and behavior, you will find so many shortcomings, they will keep you busy the rest of your life. If you say, "I will make him over into what I want," you are looking for trouble and the divorce court. You are asking for misery. You will have to learn the hard way that there is no one to change but yourself.

PRAY TOGETHER AND STAY TOGETHER
THROUGH STEPS IN PRAYER

The first step: Never carry over from one day to another accumulated irritations arising from little disappointments. Be sure to forgive each other for any sharpness before you retire at night. The moment you awaken in the morning, claim infinite intelligence is guiding you in all your ways. Send out loving thoughts of peace, harmony, and love to your marriage partner, to all members of the family, and to the whole world.

The second step: Say grace at breakfast. Give thanks for the wonderful food, for your abundance, and for all your blessings. Make sure that no problems, worries, or arguments shall enter into the table conversation; the same applies at dinner time. Say to your wife or husband, "I appreciate all you are doing, and I radiate love and good will to you all day long."

The third step: The husband and wife should alternate in praying each night. Do not take your marriage partner for granted. Show your appreciation and love. Think appreciation and good will, rather than condemnation, criticism, and nagging. The way to build a peaceful home and a happy marriage is to use a foundation of love, beauty, harmony, mutual respect, faith in God, and all things good. Read the 23rd, 27th, and 91st Psalms, the 11th chapter of Hebrews, the 13th chapter of I Corinthians, and other great texts of the Bible before going to sleep. As you practice these truths, your marriage will grow more and more blessed through the years.

REVIEW YOUR ACTIONS

1. Ignorance of mental and spiritual laws is the cause of all marital unhappiness. By praying scientifically together, you stay together.

2. The best time to prevent divorce is before marriage. If you learn how to pray in the right way, you will attract the right mate for you.

3. Marriage is the union of a man and woman who are bound together by love. Their hearts beat as one, and they move onward, upward, and Godward.

4. Marriage does not bequeath happiness. People find happiness by dwelling on the eternal Truths of God and the spiritual values of life. Then, the man and woman can contribute to each other's happiness and joy.

5. You attract the right mate by dwelling on the qualities and characteristics you admire in a woman or a man, and then your subconscious mind will bring you together in divine order.

6. You must build into your mentality the mental equivalent of what you want in a marriage partner. If you want to attract an honest, sincere, and loving partner in life, you must be honest, sincere, and loving yourself.

7. You do not have to repeat mistakes in marriage. When you really believe you can have the type man or woman you idealize, it is done unto you as you believe. To believe is to accept something as true. Accept your ideal companion now mentally.

8. Do not wonder how, why, or where you will meet the mate you are praying for. Trust implicitly the wisdom of your subconscious mind. It has the "know-how," and you don't have to assist it.

9. You are mentally divorced when you indulge in peeves, grudges, ill will, and hostility toward your marriage partner. You are mentally dwelling with error in the bed of your mind. Adhere to your marriage vows, "I promise to cherish, love, and honor him (or her) all the days of my life."

10. Cease projecting fear patterns to your marriage partner. Project love, peace, harmony, and good will, and your marriage will grow more beautiful and more wonderful through the years.

11. Radiate love, peace, and good will to each other. These vibrations are picked up by the subconscious mind resulting in mutual trust, affection, and respect.

12. A nagging wife is usually seeking attention and appreciation. She is craving for love and affection. Praise and exalt her many good points. Show her that you love her and appreciate her.

13. A man who loves his wife does not do anything unloving or unkind in word, manner, or action. Love is what love does.

14. In marital problems, always seek expert advice. You would not go to a carpenter to pull a tooth; neither should you discuss your marriage problems with relatives or friends. You should go to a trained person for counsel.

15. Never try to make your wife or husband over. These attempts are always foolish and tend to destroy the pride and self-esteem of the other. Moreover, it arouses a spirit of resentment that proves fatal to the marriage bond. Cease trying to make the other a second edition of yourself.

16. Pray together and you will stay together. Scientific prayer solves all problems. Mentally picture your wife as she ought to be, joyous, happy, healthy, and beautiful. See your husband as he ought to be, strong, powerful, loving, harmonious, and kind. Maintain this mental picture, and you will experience the marriage made in heaven, which is harmony and peace.

15

YOUR SUBCONSCIOUS MIND AND YOUR HAPPINESS

William James, father of American psychology, said that the greatest discovery of the nineteenth century was not in the realm of physical science. The greatest discovery was the power of the subconscious touched by faith. In every human being is that limitless reservoir of power, which can overcome any problem in the world.

True and lasting happiness will come into your life the day you get the clear realization that you can overcome any weakness—the day you realize that your subconscious can solve your problems, heal your body, and prosper you beyond your fondest dream.

You might have felt very happy when your child was born, when you got married, when you graduated from college, or when you won a great victory or a prize. You might have been very happy when you became engaged to the loveliest girl or the most handsome man. You could go on and list innumerable experiences, which have made you happy. However, no matter how marvelous these experiences are, they do not give real lasting happiness—they are transitory.

The Book of Proverbs gives the answer: *Whosoever trusteth in the Lord, happy is he.* When you trust in the Lord (the power and wisdom of your subconscious mind) to lead, guide, govern, and direct all your ways, you will become poised, serene, and relaxed. As you radiate love, peace, and good will to all, you are really building a superstructure of happiness for all the days of your life.

YOU MUST CHOOSE HAPPINESS

Happiness is a state of mind. There is a phrase in the Bible which says, *Choose ye this day whom ye will serve.* You have the freedom to choose happiness. This may seem extraordinarily simple, and it is. Perhaps this is why people stumble over the way to happiness; they do not see the simplicity of the key to happiness. The great things of life are simple, dynamic, and creative. They produce well-being and happiness.

St. Paul reveals to you how you can think your way into a life of dynamic power and happiness in these words: *Finally, brethren, whatsoever things are true, whatsoever things are honest, whatsoever things are just, whatsoever things are pure, whatsoever things are lovely, whatsoever things are of good report; if there be any virtue, and if there be any praise, think on these things.* PHILIPPIANS 4:8.

HOW TO CHOOSE HAPPINESS

Begin now to choose happiness. This is how you do it: When you open your eyes in the morning, say to yourself, "Divine order takes charge of my life today and every day. All things work together for good for me today. This is a new and wonderful day for me. There will never be another day like this one. I am divinely guided all day long, and whatever I do will prosper. Divine love surrounds me, enfolds me, and enwraps me, and I go forth in peace. Whenever my attention wanders away from that which is good and constructive, I will immediately bring it back to the contemplation of that which is lovely and of good report. I am a spiritual and mental magnet attracting to myself all things, which bless and prosper me. I am going to be a wonderful success in all my undertakings today. I am definitely going to be happy all day long."

Start each day in this manner; then you will be choosing happiness, and you will be a radiant joyous person.

HE MADE IT A HABIT TO BE HAPPY

A number of years ago, I stayed for about a week in a farmer's house in Connemarra on the west coast of Ireland. He seemed to be always singing and whistling and was full of humor. I asked him the secret of his happiness, and his reply was: "It is a habit of mine to be happy. Every morning when I awaken and every night before I go to sleep, I bless my family, the crops, the cattle, and I thank God for the wonderful harvest."

This farmer had made a practice of this for over forty years. As you know, thoughts repeated regularly and systematically sink into the subconscious mind and become habitual. He discovered that happiness is a habit.

YOU MUST DESIRE TO BE HAPPY

There is one very important point about being happy. You must sincerely *desire* to be happy. There are people who have been depressed, dejected, and unhappy so long that were they suddenly made happy by some wonderful, good, joyous news, they would actually be like the woman who said to me, "It is wrong to be so happy!" They have been so accustomed to the old mental patterns that they do not feel at home being happy! They long for the former, depressed, unhappy state.

I knew a woman in England who had rheumatism for many years. She would pat herself on the knee and say, "My rheumatism is bad today. I cannot go out. My rheumatism keeps me miserable."

This dear elderly lady got a lot of attention from her son, daughter, and the neighbors. She really wanted her rheumatism. She enjoyed her "misery" as she called it. This woman did not really want to be happy.

I suggested a curative procedure to her. I wrote down some biblical verses and told her that if she gave attention to these truths, her mental attitude would undoubtedly change and would result in her faith and confidence in being restored to health. She was not interested. There seems to be a peculiar, mental, morbid streak in many people, whereby they seem to enjoy being miserable and sad.

WHY CHOOSE UNHAPPINESS?

Many people choose unhappiness by entertaining these ideas: "Today is a black day; everything is going to go wrong." "I am not going to succeed." "Everyone is against me." "Business is bad, and it is going to get worse." "I'm always late." "I never get the breaks." "He can, but I can't." If you have this attitude of mind the first thing in the morning, you will attract all these experiences to you, and you will be very unhappy.

Begin to realize that the world you live in is determined largely by what goes on in your mind. Marcus Aurelius, the great Roman philosopher and sage, said, "A man's life is what his thoughts make of it." Emerson, America's foremost philosopher, said, "A man is what he thinks all day long." The thoughts you habitually entertain in your mind have the tendency to actualize themselves in physical conditions.

Make certain you do not indulge in negative thoughts, defeatist thoughts, or unkind, depressing thoughts. Recall frequently to your mind that you can experience nothing outside your own mentality.

IF I HAD A MILLION DOLLARS, I WOULD BE HAPPY

I have visited many men in mental institutions who were millionaires, but they insisted they were penniless and destitute. They were incarcerated because of psychotic, paranoic, and manic-depressive tendencies. Wealth in and of itself will not make you happy. On the other hand, it is not a deterrent to happiness. Today, there are many people trying to buy happiness through the purchase of radios, television sets, automobiles, a home in the country, a private yacht, and a swimming pool, but happiness cannot be purchased or procured in that way.

The kingdom of happiness is in your thought and feeling. Too many people have the idea that it takes something artificial to produce happiness. Some say, "If I were elected mayor, made president of the organization, promoted to general manager of the corporation, I would be happy."

The truth is that happiness is a mental and spiritual state.

None of these positions mentioned will necessarily bequeath happiness. Your strength, joy, and happiness consist in finding out the law of divine order and right action lodged in your subconscious mind and by applying these principles in all phases of your life.

HE FOUND HAPPINESS TO BE
THE HARVEST OF A QUIET MIND

Lecturing in San Francisco some years ago, I interviewed a man who was very unhappy and dejected over the way his business was going. He was the general manager. His heart was filled with resentment toward the vice president and the president of the organization. He claimed that they opposed him. Because of this internal strife, business was declining; he was receiving no dividends or stock bonuses.

This is how he solved his business problem: The first thing in the morning he affirmed quietly as follows, "All those working in our corporation are honest, sincere, cooperative, faithful, and full of good will to all. They are mental and spiritual links in the chain of this corporation's growth, welfare, and prosperity. I radiate love, peace, and good will in my thoughts, words, and deeds to my two associates and to all those in the company. The president and the vice president of our company are divinely guided in all their undertakings. The infinite intelligence of my subconscious mind makes all decisions through me. There is only right action in all our business transactions and in our relationship with each other. I send the messengers of peace, love, and good will before me to the office. Peace and harmony reign supreme in the minds and hearts of all those in the company including myself. I now go forth into a new day, full of faith, confidence, and trust."

This business executive repeated the above meditation slowly three times in the morning, feeling the truth of what he affirmed. When fearful or angry thoughts came into his mind during the day, he would say to himself, "Peace, harmony, and poise govern my mind at all times."

As he continued disciplining his mind in this manner, all the harmful thoughts ceased to come, and peace came into his mind. He reaped the harvest.

Subsequently, he wrote me to the effect that at the end of about two weeks of reordering his mind, the president and the vice president called him into the office, praised his operations and his new constructive ideas, and remarked how fortunate they were in having him as general manager. He was very happy in discovering that man finds happiness within himself.

THE BLOCK OR STUMP IS NOT REALLY THERE

I read a newspaper article some years ago, which told about a horse who had shied when he came to a stump on the road. Subsequently, every time the horse came to that same stump, he shied. The farmer dug the stump out, burned it, and leveled the old road. Yet, for twenty-five years, every time the horse passed the place where the former stump was, he shied. The horse was shying at the memory of a stump.

There is no block to your happiness save in your own thought life and mental imagery. Are fear or worry holding you back? Fear is a thought in your mind. You can dig it up this very moment by supplanting it with faith in success, achievement, and victory over all problems.

I knew a man who failed in business. He said to me, "I made mistakes. I've learned a lot. I am going back into business, and I will be a tremendous success." He faced up to that stump in his mind. He did not whine or complain, but he tore up the stump of failure, and through believing in his inner powers to back him up, he banished all fear thoughts and old depressions. Believe in yourself, and you will succeed and be happy.

THE HAPPIEST PEOPLE

The happiest man is he who constantly brings forth and practices what is best in him. Happiness and virtue complement each other. The best are not only the happiest, but the happiest are usually the best in the art of living life successfully. God is the highest and best in you. Express more of God's love, light, truth, and beauty, and you will become one of the happiest persons in the world today.

Epictetus, the Greek Stoic philosopher, said, "There is but one way to tranquility of mind and happiness; let this, therefore, be always ready at hand with thee, both when thou wakest early in the morning, and all the day long, and when thou goest late to sleep, to account no external things thine own, but commit all these to God."

SUMMARY OF STEPS TO HAPPINESS

1. William James said that the greatest discovery of the nineteenth century was the power of the subconscious mind touched by faith.
2. There is tremendous power within you. Happiness will come to you when you acquire a sublime confidence in this power. Then, you will make your dreams come true.
3. You can rise victorious over any defeat and realize the cherished desires of your heart through the marvelous power of your subconscious mind. This is the meaning

of *Whosoever trusteth in the Lord* [spiritual laws of the subconscious mind], *happy is he.*

4. You must choose happiness. Happiness is a habit. It is a good habit to ponder often on *Whatsoever things are true, whatsoever things are honest, whatsoever things are just, whatsoever things are pure, whatsoever things are lovely, whatsoever things are of good report; if there be any virtue, and if there be any praise, think on these things.* PHILIPPIANS 4:8.

5. When you open your eyes in the morning, say to yourself, I choose happiness today. I choose success today. I choose right action today. I choose love and good will for all today. I choose peace today. Pour life, love, and interest into this affirmation, and you have chosen happiness.

6. Give thanks for all your blessings several times a day. Furthermore, pray for the peace, happiness, and prosperity of all members of your family, your associates, and all people everywhere.

7. You must sincerely desire to be happy. Nothing is accomplished without desire. Desire is a wish with wings of imagination and faith. Imagine the fulfillment of your desire, and feel its reality, and it will come to pass. Happiness comes in answered prayer.

8. By constantly dwelling on thoughts of fear, worry, anger, hate, and failure, you will become very depressed and unhappy. Remember, your life is what your thoughts make of it.

9. You cannot buy happiness with all the money in the world. Some millionaires are very happy, some are very unhappy. Many people with very little worldly goods are very happy, and some are very unhappy. Some married people are happy, and some very unhappy. Some single people are

happy, and some are very unhappy. The kingdom of happiness is in your thought and feeling.

10. Happiness is the harvest of a quiet mind. Anchor your thoughts on peace, poise, security, and divine guidance, and your mind will be productive of happiness.

11. There is no block to your happiness. External things are not causative, these are effects, not cause. Take your cue from the only creative principle within you. Your thought is cause, and a new cause produces a new effect. Choose happiness.

12. The happiest man is he who brings forth the highest and the best in him. God is the highest and the best in him, for the kingdom of God is within.

16

YOUR SUBCONSCIOUS MIND AND HARMONIOUS HUMAN RELATIONS

In studying this book, you learn that your subconscious mind is a recording machine, which faithfully reproduces whatever you impress upon it. This is one of the reasons for the application of the Golden Rule in human relations.

MATTHEW 7:12 says, *All things whatsoever ye would that men should do unto you, do ye even so to them.* This quotation has outer and inner meanings. You are interested in its inner meaning from the standpoint of your subconscious mind, which is: As you would that men should *think* about you, think you about them in like manner. As you would that men should *feel* about you, feel you also about them in like manner. As you would want men to *act* toward you, act you toward them in like manner.

For example, you may be polite and courteous to someone in your office, but when his back is turned, you are very critical and resentful toward him in your mind. Such negative thoughts are highly destructive to you. It is like taking poison. You are actually taking mental poisons, which rob you of vitality, enthusiasm, strength, guidance, and good will. These negative thoughts and emotions sink down into your subconscious, and cause all kinds of difficulties and maladies in your life.

THE MASTER KEY TO HAPPY RELATIONSHIPS WITH OTHERS

Judge not, that ye be not judged. For with what judgment ye judge, ye shall be judged: and with what measure ye mete, it shall be measured to you again. MATTHEW 7:1–2.

A study of these verses and the application of the inner truths therein contained represent the real key to harmonious relations. To judge is to think, to arrive at a mental verdict or conclusion in your mind. The thought you have about the other person is your thought, because you are thinking it. Your thoughts are creative, therefore, you actually create in your own experience what you think and feel about the other person. It is also true that the suggestion you give to another, you give to yourself because your mind is the creative medium.

This is why it is said, *For with what judgment ye judge, ye shall be judged.* When you know this law and the way your subconscious mind works, you are careful to think, feel, and act right toward the other. These verses teach you about the emancipation of man and reveal to you the solution to your individual problems.

AND WITH WHAT MEASURE YE METE,
IT SHALL BE MEASURED TO YOU AGAIN

The good you do for others comes back to you in like measure; and the evil you do returns to you by the law of your own mind. If a man cheats and deceives another, he is actually cheating and deceiving himself. His sense of guilt and mood of loss inevitably will attract loss to him in some way, at some time. His subconscious records his mental act and reacts according to the mental intention or motivation.

Your subconscious mind is impersonal and unchanging, neither considering persons nor respecting religious affiliations or institutions of any kind. It is neither compassionate nor vindictive. The way you think, feel, and act toward others returns at last upon yourself.

THE DAILY HEADLINES MADE HIM SICK

Begin now to observe yourself. Observe your reactions to people, conditions, and circumstances. How do you respond to the events and news of the day? It makes no difference if all the other people were wrong and you alone were right. If the news disturbs you, it is your evil because your negative emotions robbed you of peace and harmony.

A woman wrote me about her husband, saying that he goes into a rage when he reads what certain newspaper columnists write in the newspaper. She added that this constant reaction of anger and suppressed rage on his part brought on bleeding ulcers, and his physician recommended an emotional reconditioning.

I invited this man to see me and I explained to him the way his mind functions indicating how emotionally immature it

was to get angry when others write articles with which he dis-
approves or disagrees.

He began to realize that he should give the newspaperman
freedom to express himself even though the latter disagreed
with him politically, religiously, or in any other way. In the same
manner, the newspaperman would give him freedom to write
a letter to the newspaper disagreeing with his published statements. He learned that he could disagree without being disagreeable. He awakened to the simple truth that it is never what
a person says or does that affects him, it is his reaction to what
is said or done that matters.

This explanation was the cure for this man, and he realized
that with a little practice he could master his morning tantrums.
His wife told me, subsequently, that he laughed at himself and
also at what the columnists say. They no longer have power to
disturb, annoy, and irritate him. His ulcers have disappeared
due to his emotional poise and serenity.

I HATE WOMEN, BUT I LIKE MEN

A private secretary was very bitter toward some of the girls in
her office because they were gossiping about her, and as she
said, spreading vicious lies about her. She admitted that she did
not like women. She said, "I hate women, but I like men." I discovered also that she spoke to the girls who were under her in
the office in a very haughty, imperious, and irritable tone of
voice. She pointed out that they took a delight in making things
difficult for her. There was a certain pomposity in her way of
speaking, and I could see where her tone of voice would affect
some people unpleasantly.

If all the people in the office or factory annoy you, isn't it a possibility that the vibration, annoyance, and turmoil may be due to some subconscious pattern or mental projection from you? We know that a dog will react ferociously if you hate or fear dogs. Animals pick up your subconscious vibrations and react accordingly. Many undisciplined human beings are just as sensitive as dogs, cats, and other animals.

I suggested a process of prayer to this private secretary who hated women, explaining to her that when she began to identify herself with spiritual values and commenced to affirm the truths of life, her voice, mannerisms, and hatred of women would completely disappear. She was surprised to know that the emotion of hatred shows up in a person's speech, actions, in his writings, and in all phases of his life. She ceased reacting in the typical resentful and angry way. She established a pattern of prayer, which she practiced regularly, systematically, and conscientiously in the office.

The prayer was as follows: "I think, speak, and act lovingly, quietly, and peacefully. I now radiate love, peace, tolerance, and kindliness to all the girls who criticized me and gossiped about me. I anchor my thoughts on peace, harmony, and good will to all. Whenever I am about to react negatively, I say firmly to myself, 'I am going to think, speak, and act from the standpoint of the principle of harmony, health, and peace within myself.' Creative intelligence leads, rules, and guides me in all my ways."

The practice of this prayer transformed her life, and she found that all criticism and annoyance ceased. The girls became coworkers and friends along life's journey. She discovered that *there is no one to change but myself.*

HIS INNER SPEECH HELD BACK HIS PROMOTION

One day a salesman came to see me and described his difficulties in working with the sales manager of his organization. He had been with the company ten years and had received no promotion or recognition of any kind. He showed me his sales figures, which were greater proportionately than the other men in the territory. He said that the sales manager did not like him, that he was unjustly treated, and that at conferences the manager was rude to him, and at times ridiculed his suggestions.

I explained that undoubtedly the cause was to a great degree within himself, and that his concept and belief about his superior bore witness to the reaction of this man. *The measure we mete, shall be measured to us again.* His mental measure or concept of the sales manager was that he was mean and cantankerous. He was filled with bitterness and hostility toward the executive. On his way to work he conducted a vigorous conversation with himself filled with criticism, mental arguments, recriminations, and denunciations of his sales manager.

What he gave out mentally, he was inevitably bound to get back. This salesman realized that his inner speech was highly destructive because the intensity and force of his silent thoughts and emotions, and personally conducted mental condemnation and vilification of the sales manager, entered into his own subconscious mind. This brought about the negative response from his boss as well as creating many other personal, physical, and emotional disorders.

He began to pray frequently as follows: "I am the only thinker in my universe. I am responsible for what I think about my boss. My sales manager is not responsible for the way I think about him. I refuse to give power to any person, place, or thing to annoy me or disturb me. I wish health, success, peace of mind, and happiness for my boss. I sincerely wish him well, and I know he is divinely guided in all his ways."

He repeated this prayer out loud slowly, quietly, and feelingly, knowing that his mind is like a garden, and that whatever he plants in the garden will come forth like seeds after their kind.

I also taught him to practice mental imagery prior to sleep in this way: He imagined that his sales manager was congratulating him on his fine work, on his zeal and enthusiasm, and on his wonderful response from customers. He felt the reality of all this, felt his handshake, heard the tone of his voice, and saw him smile. He made a real mental movie, dramatizing it to the best of his ability. Night after night he conducted this mental movie, knowing that his subconscious mind was the receptive plate on which his conscious imagery would be impressed.

Gradually by a process of what may be termed mental and spiritual osmosis, the impression was made on his subconscious mind, and the expression automatically came forth. The sales manager subsequently called him up to San Francisco, congratulated him, and gave him a new assignment as Division Sales Manager over one hundred men with a big increase in salary. He changed his concept and estimate of his boss, and the latter responded accordingly.

BECOMING EMOTIONALLY MATURE

What the other person says or does cannot really annoy or irritate you except you permit him to disturb you. The only way he can annoy you is through your own thought. For example, if you get angry, you have to go through four stages in your mind: You begin to think about what he said. You decide to get angry and generate an emotion of rage. Then, you decide to act. Perhaps, you talk back and react in kind. You see that the thought, emotion, reaction, and action all take place in your mind.

When you become emotionally mature, you do not respond negatively to the criticism and resentment of others. To do so would mean that you had descended to that state of low mental vibration and become one with the negative atmosphere of the other. Identify yourself with your aim in life, and do not permit any person, place, or thing to deflect you from your inner sense of peace, tranquility, and radiant health.

THE MEANING OF LOVE IN HARMONIOUS HUMAN RELATIONS

Sigmund Freud, the Austrian founder of psychoanalysis, said that unless the personality has love, it sickens and dies. Love includes understanding, good will, and respect for the divinity in the other person. The more love and good will you emanate and exude, the more comes back to you.

If you puncture the other fellow's ego and wound his estimate of himself, you cannot gain his good will. Recognize that every man wants to be loved and appreciated, and made to feel important in the world. Realize that the other man is conscious of his true worth, and that, like yourself, he feels the dignity of being an expression of the One Life Principle animating all men. As you do this consciously and knowingly, you build the other person up, and he returns your love and good will.

HE HATED AUDIENCES

An actor told me that the audience booed and hissed him on his first appearance on the stage. He added that the play was badly written and that undoubtedly he did not play a good role. He admitted openly to me that for months afterward he hated audiences. He called them dopes, dummies, stupid, ignorant, gullible, etc. He quit the stage in disgust and went to work in a drugstore for a year.

One day a friend invited him to hear a lecture in Town Hall, New York City, on "How to Get Along With Ourselves." This lecture changed his life. He went back to the stage and began to pray sincerely for the audience and himself. He poured out love and good will every night before appearing on the stage. He made it a habit to claim that the peace of God filled the hearts of all present, and that all present were lifted up and inspired. During each performance he sent out love vibrations to the audience. Today, he is a great actor, and he loves and respects people. His good will and esteem are transmitted to others and are felt by them.

HANDLING DIFFICULT PEOPLE

There are difficult people in the world who are twisted and distorted mentally. They are malconditioned. Many are mental delinquents, argumentative, uncooperative, cantankerous, cynical, and sour on life. They are sick psychologically. Many people have deformed and distorted minds, probably warped during childhood. Many have congenital deformities. You would not condemn a person who had tuberculosis, nor should you condemn a person who is mentally ill. No one, for example, hates or resents a hunchback; there are many mental hunchbacks. You should have compassion and understanding. *To understand all is to forgive all.*

MISERY LOVES COMPANY

The hateful, frustrated, distorted, and twisted personality is out of tune with the Infinite. He resents those who are peaceful, happy, and joyous. Usually he criticizes, condemns, and vilifies those who have been very good and kind to him. His attitude is this: Why should they be so happy when he is so miserable? He wants to drag them down to his own level. Misery loves company. When you understand this you remain unmoved, calm, and dispassionate.

THE PRACTICE OF EMPATHY IN
HUMAN RELATIONS

A girl visited me recently stating that she hated another girl in her office. She gave as her reason that the other girl was prettier, happier, and wealthier than she, and, in addition, was engaged to the boss of the company where they worked. One day after the marriage had taken place, the crippled daughter (by a former marriage) of the woman whom she hated came into the office. The child put her arms around her mother and said, "Mommy, Mommy, I love my new daddy! Look what he gave me!" She showed her mother a wonderful new toy.

She said to me, "My heart went out to that little girl, and I knew how happy she must feel. I got a vision of how happy this woman was. All of a sudden I felt love for her, and I went into the office and wished her all the happiness in the world, and I meant it."

In psychological circles today, this is called empathy, which simply means the imaginative projection of your mental attitude into that of another. She projected her mental mood or the feeling of her heart into that of the other woman, and began to think and look out through the other woman's brain. She was actually thinking and feeling as the other woman, and also as the child, because she likewise had projected herself into the mind of the child. She was looking out from that vantage point on the child's mother.

If tempted to injure or think ill of another, project yourself

mentally into the mind of Moses and think from the standpoint
of the Ten Commandments. If you are prone to be envious, jealous, or angry, project yourself into the mind of Jesus and think
from that standpoint, and you will feel the truth of the words
Love ye one another.

APPEASEMENT NEVER WINS

Do not permit people to take advantage of you and gain their
point by temper tantrums, crying jags, or so-called heart attacks.
These people are dictators who try to enslave you and make you
do their bidding. Be firm but kind, and refuse to yield. Appeasement never wins. Refuse to contribute to their delinquency, selfishness, and possessiveness. Remember, do that which is right.
You are here to fulfill your ideal and remain true to the eternal
verities and spiritual values of life which are eternal.

Give no one in all the world the power to deflect you from
your goal, your aim in life, which is to express your hidden talents to the world, to serve humanity, and to reveal more and
more of God's wisdom, truth, and beauty to all people in the
world. Remain true to your ideal. Know definitely and absolutely that whatever contributes to your peace, happiness, and
fulfillment must of necessity bless all men who walk the earth.
The harmony of the part is the harmony of the whole, for the
whole is in the part, and the part is in the whole. All you owe
the other, as Paul says, is love, and love is the fulfilling of the
law of health, happiness, and peace of mind.

PROFITABLE POINTERS IN HUMAN RELATIONS

1. Your subconscious mind is a recording machine, which
   reproduces your habitual thinking. Think good of the
   other, and you are actually thinking good about yourself.

2. A hateful or resentful thought is a mental poison. Do not think ill of another for to do so is to think ill of yourself. You are the only thinker in your universe, and your thoughts are creative.

3. Your mind is a creative medium; therefore, what you think and feel about the other, you are bringing to pass in your own experience. This is the psychological meaning of the Golden Rule. As you would that man should think about you, think you about them in the same manner.

4. To cheat, rob, or defraud another brings lack, loss, and limitation to yourself. Your subconscious mind records your inner motivations, thoughts, and feelings. These being of a negative nature, loss, limitation, and trouble come to you in countless ways. Actually, what you do to the other, you are doing to yourself.

5. The good you do, the kindness proffered, the love and good will you send forth, will all come back to you multiplied in many ways.

6. You are the only thinker in your world. You are responsible for the way you think about the other. Remember, the other person is not responsible for the way you think about him. Your thoughts are reproduced. What are you thinking now about the other fellow?

7. Become emotionally mature and permit other people to differ from you. They have a perfect right to disagree with you, and you have the same freedom to disagree with them. You can disagree without being disagreeable.

8. Animals pick up your fear vibrations and snap at you. If you love animals, they will never attack you. Many undisciplined human beings are just as sensitive as dogs, cats, and other animals.

9. Your inner speech, representing your silent thoughts and feelings, is experienced in the reactions of others toward you.

10. Wish for the other what you wish for yourself. This is the key to harmonious human relations.

11. Change your concept and estimate of your employer. Feel and know he is practicing the Golden Rule and the Law of Love, and he will respond accordingly.

12. The other person cannot annoy you or irritate you except you permit him. Your thought is creative; you can bless him. If someone calls you a skunk, you have the freedom to say to the other, "God's peace fills your soul."

13. Love is the answer to getting along with others. Love is understanding, good will, and respecting the divinity of the other.

14. You would not hate a hunchback or cripple. You would have compassion. Have compassion and understanding for mental hunchbacks who have been conditioned negatively. To understand all is to forgive all.

15. Rejoice in the success, promotion, and good fortune of the other. In doing so, you attract good fortune to yourself.

16. Never yield to emotional scenes and tantrums of others. Appeasement never wins. Do not be a doormat. Adhere to that which is right. Stick to your ideal, knowing that the mental outlook, which gives you peace, happiness, and joy is right, good, and true. What blesses you, blesses all.

17. All you owe any person in the world is love, and love is wishing for everyone what you wish for yourself—health, happiness, and all the blessings of life.

17

HOW TO USE YOUR SUBCONSCIOUS MIND FOR FORGIVENESS

Life plays no favorites. God is Life, and this Life Principle is flowing through you this moment. God loves to express Himself as harmony, peace, beauty, joy, and abundance through you. This is called the will of God or the tendency of Life.

If you set up resistance in your mind to the flow of Life through you, this emotional congestion will get snarled up in your subconscious mind and cause all kinds of negative conditions. God has nothing to do with unhappy or chaotic conditions in the world. All these conditions are brought about by man's negative and destructive thinking. Therefore, it is silly to blame God for your trouble or sickness.

Many persons habitually set up mental resistance to the flow of Life by accusing and reproaching God for the sin, sickness, and suffering of mankind. Others cast the blame on God for their pains, aches, loss of loved ones, personal tragedies, and accidents. They are angry at God, and they believe He is responsible for their misery.

As long as people entertain such negative concepts about God, they will experience the automatic negative reactions from their subconscious minds. Actually, such people do not know that they are punishing themselves. They must see the truth, find release, and give up all condemnation, resentment, and anger against anyone or any power outside themselves. Otherwise, they cannot go forward into a healthy, happy, or creative activity. The minute these people entertain a God of love in their minds and hearts, and when they believe that God is their Loving Father who watches over them, cares for them, guides them, sustains and strengthens them, this concept and belief about God or the Life Principle will be accepted by their subconscious mind, and they will find themselves blessed in countless ways.

LIFE ALWAYS FORGIVES YOU

Life forgives you when you cut your finger. The subconscious intelligence within you sets about immediately to repair it. New cells build bridges over the cut. Should you take some tainted food by error, Life forgives you and causes you to regurgitate it in order to preserve you. If you burn your hand, the Life Principle reduces the edema and congestion, and gives you new skin, tissue, and cells. Life holds no grudges against you, and it is always forgiving you. Life brings you back to health, vitality, harmony, and peace, if you cooperate by thinking in harmony with nature. Negative, hurtful memories, bitterness, and ill will clutter up and impede the free flow of the Life Principle in you.

HOW HE BANISHED THAT FEELING OF GUILT

I knew a man who worked every night until about one o'clock in the morning. He paid no attention to his two boys or his wife. He was always too busy working hard. He thought people should pat him on the back because he was working so arduously and persistently past midnight every night. He had a blood pressure of over two hundred and was full of guilt. Unconsciously, he proceeded to punish himself by hard work and he completely ignored his children. A normal man does not do that. He is interested in his boys and in their development. He does not shut his wife out of his world.

I explained to him why he was working so arduously, "There is something eating you inside, otherwise, you would not act this way. You are punishing yourself, and you have to learn to forgive yourself." He did have a deep sense of guilt. It was toward a brother.

I explained to him that God was not punishing him, but that he was punishing himself. For example, if you misuse the laws of life, you will suffer accordingly. If you put your hand on a naked charged wire, you will get burned. The forces of nature are not evil; it is your use of them that determines whether they have a good or evil effect. Electricity is not evil; it depends on how you use it, whether to burn down a structure or light up a home. The only sin is ignorance of the law, and the only punishment is the automatic reaction of man's misuse of the law.

If you misuse the principle of chemistry, you may blow up the office or the factory. If you strike your hand on a board, you may cause your hand to bleed. The board is not for that purpose. Its purpose may be to lean upon or to support your feet.

This man realized that God does not condemn or punish anyone, and that all his suffering was due to the reaction of his subconscious mind to his own negative and destructive thinking. He had cheated his brother at one time, and the brother had now passed on. Still, he was full of remorse and guilt.

I asked him, "Would you cheat your brother now?"

He said, "No."

"Did you feel you were justified at the time?"

His reply was, "Yes."

"But, you would not do it now?"

He added, "No, I am helping others to know how to live."

I added the following comment, "You have a greater reason and understanding now. Forgiveness is to forgive yourself. Forgiveness is getting your thoughts in line with the divine law of harmony. Self-condemnation is called hell (bondage and restriction); forgiveness is called heaven (harmony and peace)."

The burden of guilt and self-condemnation was lifted from his mind, and he had a complete healing. The doctor tested his blood pressure, and it had become normal. The explanation was the cure.

A MURDERER LEARNED TO FORGIVE HIMSELF

A man who murdered his brother in Europe visited me many years ago. He was suffering from great mental anguish and torture believing that God must punish him. He explained that his brother had been having an affair with his wife, and that he had shot him on the spur of the moment. This had happened about fifteen years previous to his interview with me. In the meantime, this man had married an American girl and had been blessed with three lovely children. He was in a position where he helped many people, and he was a transformed man.

My explanation to him was that physically and psychologically he was not the same man who shot his brother, since scientists inform us that every cell of our bodies changes every eleven months. Moreover, mentally and spiritually he was a new man. He was now full of love and good will for humanity. The "old" man who committed the crime fifteen years before was mentally and spiritually dead. Actually, he was condemning an innocent man!

This explanation had a profound effect upon him, and he said it was as if a great weight had been lifted from his mind. He realized the significance of the following truth in the Bible: *Come now, let us reason together, saith the Lord: though your sins be as scarlet, they shall be as white as snow; though they be red like crimson, they shall be as wool.* ISAIAH 1:18.

CRITICISM CANNOT HURT YOU WITHOUT YOUR CONSENT

A schoolteacher told me that one of her associates criticized a speech she had given, saying to her that she spoke too fast, she swallowed some of her words, she couldn't be heard, her diction was poor, and her speech ineffective. This teacher was furious and full of resentment toward her critic.

She admitted to me that the criticisms were just. Her first reaction was really childish, and she agreed that the letter was really a blessing and a marvelous corrective. She proceeded immediately to supplement her deficiencies in her speech by enrolling in a course in public speaking at City College. She wrote and thanked the writer of the note for her interest, expressing appreciation for her conclusions and findings, which enabled the teacher to correct the matter at once.

HOW TO BE COMPASSIONATE

Suppose none of the things mentioned in the letter had been true of the teacher. The latter would have realized that her class material had upset the prejudices, superstitions, or narrow sectarian beliefs of the writer of the note, and that a psychologically ill person was simply pouring forth her resentment because a psychological boil had been hurt.

To understand this fact is to be compassionate. The next logical step would be to pray for the other person's peace, harmony, and understanding. You cannot be hurt when you know that you are master of your thoughts, reactions, and emotions. Emotions follow thoughts, and you have the power to reject all thoughts, which may disturb or upset you.

LEFT AT THE ALTAR

Some years ago I visited a church to perform a marriage ceremony. The young man did not appear, and at the end of two hours, the bride-to-be shed a few tears, and then said to me, "I prayed for divine guidance. This might be the answer for He never faileth."

That was her reaction—faith in God and all things good. She had no bitterness in her heart because as she said, "It must not have been right action because my prayer was for right action for both of us." Someone else having a similar experience would have gone into a tantrum, have had an emotional fit, required sedation, and perhaps needed hospitalization.

Tune in with the infinite intelligence within your subconscious depths, trusting the answer in the same way that you trusted your mother when she held you in her arms. This is how you can acquire poise and mental and emotional health.

IT IS WRONG TO MARRY. SEX IS EVIL
AND I AM EVIL

Some time ago I talked to a young lady aged twenty-two. She was taught that it was a sin to dance, to play cards, to swim, and to go out with men. She was threatened by her mother who told her she would burn eternally in hell-fire if she disobeyed her will and her religious teachings. This girl wore a black dress and black stockings. She wore no rouge, lipstick, or any form of makeup because her mother said that these things were sinful. Her mother told her that all men were evil, and that sex was of the devil and simply diabolic debauchery.

This girl had to learn how to forgive herself as she was full of guilt. To forgive means to give for. She had to give up all these false beliefs for the truths of life and a new estimate of herself. When she went out with young men in the office where she worked, she had a deep sense of guilt and thought that God would punish her. Several eligible young men proposed to her, but she said to me, "It is wrong to marry. Sex is evil and I am evil." This was her conscience or early conditioning speaking.

She came to me once weekly for about ten weeks, and I taught her the workings of the conscious and subconscious mind as set forth in this book. This young girl gradually came to see that she had been completely brainwashed, mesmerized, and conditioned by an ignorant, superstitious, bigoted, and frustrated mother. She broke away completely from her family and started to live a wonderful life.

At my suggestion she dressed up and had her hair attended

to. She took lessons in dancing from a *man,* and she also took driving lessons. She learned to swim, play cards, and had a number of dates. She began to love life. She prayed for a divine companion by claiming that Infinite Spirit would attract to her a man who harmonized with her thoroughly. Eventually this came to pass. As she left my office one evening, there was a man waiting to see me and I casually introduced them. They are now married and harmonize with each other perfectly.

FORGIVENESS IS NECESSARY FOR HEALING

And when ye stand praying, forgive, if ye have ought against any . . .
—MARK 11:25

Forgiveness of others is essential to mental peace and radiant health. You must forgive everyone who has ever hurt you if you want perfect health and happiness. Forgive yourself by getting your thoughts in harmony with divine law and order. You cannot really forgive yourself completely until you have forgiven others first. To refuse to forgive yourself is nothing more or less than spiritual pride or ignorance.

In the psychosomatic field of medicine today, it is being constantly stressed that resentment, condemnation of others, remorse, and hostility are behind a host of maladies ranging from arthritis to cardiac disease. They point out that these sick people, who were hurt, mistreated, deceived, or injured, were full of resentment and hatred for those who hurt them. This caused inflamed and festering wounds in their subconscious minds. There is only one remedy. They have to cut out and discard their hurts, and the one and only sure way is by forgiveness.

FORGIVENESS IS LOVE IN ACTION

The essential ingredient in the art of forgiveness is the willingness to forgive. If you sincerely desire to forgive the other, you are fifty-one percent over the hurdle. I feel sure you know that to forgive the other does not necessarily mean that you like him or want to associate with him. You cannot be compelled to like someone, neither can a government legislate good will, love, peace, or tolerance. It is quite impossible to like people because someone in Washington issues an edict to that effect. We can, however, love people without liking them.

The Bible says, *Love ye one another.* This, anyone can do who really wants to do it. Love means that you wish for the other health, happiness, peace, joy, and all the blessings of life. There is only one prerequisite, and that is sincerity. You are not being magnanimous when you forgive, you are really being selfish, because what you wish for the other, you are actually wishing for yourself. The reason is that you are thinking it and you are feeling it. As you think and feel, so are you. Could anything be simpler than that?

TECHNIQUE OF FORGIVENESS

The following is a simple method, which works wonders in your life as you practice it: Quiet your mind, relax, and let go. Think of God and His love for you, and then affirm, "I fully and freely forgive (mention the name of the offender); I release him mentally and spiritually. I completely forgive everything connected with the matter in question. I am free, and he/she is free. It is a marvelous feeling. It is my day of general amnesty. I release anybody and everybody who has ever hurt me, and I wish for each and everyone health, happiness, peace, and all the blessings of life. I do this freely, joyously, and lovingly, and whenever I think of the person or persons who hurt me, I say, 'I have released you, and all the blessings of life are yours.' I am free and you are free. It is wonderful!"

The great secret of true forgiveness is that once you have forgiven the person, it is unnecessary to repeat the prayer. Whenever the person comes to your mind, or the particular hurt happens to enter your mind, wish the delinquent well, and say, "Peace be to you." Do this as often as the thought enters your mind. You will find that after a few days the thought of the person or experience will return less and less often, until it fades into nothingness.

THE ACID TEST FOR FORGIVENESS

There is an acid test for gold. There is also an acid test for forgiveness. If I should tell you something wonderful about someone who has wronged you, cheated you, or defrauded you, and you sizzled at hearing the good news about this person, the roots of hatred would still be in your subconscious mind, playing havoc with you.

Let us suppose you had a painful abscess on your jaw a year ago, and you told me about it. I would casually ask you if you had any pain now. You would automatically say, "Of course not, I have a memory of it but no pain." That is the whole story. You may have a memory of the incident but no sting or hurt anymore. This is the acid test, and you must meet it psychologically and spiritually, otherwise, you are simply deceiving yourself and not practicing the true art of forgiveness.

TO UNDERSTAND ALL IS TO FORGIVE ALL

When man understands the creative law of his own mind, he ceases to blame other people and conditions for making or marring his life. He knows that his own thoughts and feelings create his destiny. Furthermore, he is aware that externals are not the causes and conditioners of his life and his experiences. To think that others can mar your happiness, that you are the football of a cruel fate, that you must oppose and fight others for a living—all these and others like them are untenable when you understand that thoughts are things. The Bible says the same thing. *For as a man thinketh in his heart, so is he.* PROVERBS 23:7.

SUMMARY OF YOUR AIDS TO FORGIVENESS

1. God, or Life, is no respecter of persons. Life plays no favorites. Life, or God, seems to favor you when you align yourself with the principle of harmony, health, joy, and peace.

2. God, or Life, never sends disease, sickness, accident, or suffering. We bring these things on ourselves by our own negative destructive thinking based upon the law *as we sow, so shall we reap.*

3. Your concept of God is the most important thing in your life. If you really believe in a God of love, your subconscious mind will respond in countless blessings to you. Believe in a God of love.

4. Life, or God, holds no grudge against you. Life never condemns you. Life heals a severe cut on your hand. Life forgives you if you burn your finger. It reduces the edema and restores the part to wholeness and perfection.

5. Your guilt complex is a false concept of God and Life. God, or Life, does not punish or judge you. You do this to yourself by your false beliefs, negative thinking, and self-condemnation.

6. God, or Life, does not condemn or punish you. The forces of nature are not evil. The effect of their use depends on

how you use the power within you. You can use electricity to kill someone or to light the house. You can use water to drown a child, or quench his thirst. Good and evil come right back to the thought and purpose in man's own mind.

7. God, or life, never punishes. Man punishes himself by his false concepts of God, Life, and the Universe. His thoughts are creative, and he creates his own misery.

8. If another criticizes you, and these faults are within you, rejoice, give thanks, and appreciate the comments. This gives you the opportunity to correct the particular fault.

9. You cannot be hurt by criticism when you know that you are master of your thoughts, reactions, and emotions. This gives you the opportunity to pray and bless the other, thereby blessing yourself.

10. When you pray for guidance and right action, take what comes. Realize it is good and very good. Then there is no cause for self-pity, criticism, or hatred.

11. There is nothing good or bad, but thinking makes it so. There is no evil in sex, the desire for food, wealth, or true expression. It depends on how you use these urges, desires, or aspirations. Your desire for food can be met without killing someone for a loaf of bread.

12. Resentment, hatred, ill will, and hostility are behind a host of maladies. Forgive yourself and everybody else by pouring out love, life, joy, and good will to all those who have hurt you. Continue until such time as you meet them in your mind and you are at peace with them.

13. To forgive is to *give something for*. Give love, peace, joy, wisdom, and all the blessings of life to the other, until there is no sting left in your mind. This is really the acid test of forgiveness.

14. Let us suppose you had an abscess in your jaw about a year ago. It was very painful. Ask yourself if it is painful now. The answer is in the negative. Likewise, if someone has hurt you, lied about and vilified you, and said all manner of evil about you, is your thought of that person negative? Do you sizzle when he or she comes into your mind? If so, the roots of hatred are still there, playing havoc with you and your good. The only way is to wither them with love by wishing for the person all the blessings of life, until you can meet the person in your mind, and you can sincerely react with a benediction of peace and good will. This is the meaning of *forgive until seventy times seven.*

18

HOW YOUR SUBCONSCIOUS REMOVES MENTAL BLOCKS

The solution lies within the problem. The answer is in every question. If you are presented with a difficult situation and you cannot see your way clear, the best procedure is to assume that infinite intelligence within your subconscious mind knows all and sees all, has the answer, and is revealing it to you now. Your new mental attitude that the creative intelligence is bringing about a happy solution will enable you to find the answer. Rest assured that such an attitude of mind will bring order, peace, and meaning to all your undertakings.

HOW TO BREAK OR BUILD A HABIT

You are a creature of habit. Habit is the function of your subconscious mind. You learned to swim, ride a bicycle, dance, and drive a car by consciously doing these things over and over again until they established tracks in your subconscious mind. Then, the automatic habit action of your subconscious mind took over. This is sometimes called second nature, which is a reaction of your subconscious mind to your thinking and acting.

You are free to choose a good habit or a bad habit. If you repeat a negative thought or act over a period of time, you will be under the compulsion of a habit. The law of your subconscious is compulsion.

HOW HE BROKE A BAD HABIT

Mr. Jones said to me, "An uncontrollable urge to drink seizes me, and I remain drunk for two weeks at a time. I can't give up this terrible habit."

Time and time again these experiences had occurred to this unfortunate man. He had grown into the habit of drinking to excess. Although he had started drinking of his own initiative, he also began to realize that he could change the habit and establish a new one. He said that while through his willpower he was able to suppress his desires temporarily, his continued efforts to suppress the many urges only made matters worse. His repeated failures convinced him that he was hopeless and powerless to control his urge or obsession. This idea of being powerless operated as a powerful suggestion to his subconscious mind and aggravated his weakness, making his life a succession of failures.

I taught him to harmonize the functions of the conscious and subconscious mind. When these two cooperate, the idea or desire implanted in the subconscious mind is realized. His reasoning mind agreed that if the old habit path or track had carried him into trouble, he could consciously form a new path to freedom, sobriety, and peace of mind. He knew that his destructive habit was automatic, but since it was acquired through his conscious choice, he realized that if he had been conditioned negatively, he also could be conditioned positively. As a result, he ceased thinking of the fact that he was powerless to overcome the habit. Moreover, he understood clearly that there was no obstacle to his healing other than his own thought. Therefore, there was no occasion for great mental effort or mental coercion.

THE POWER OF HIS MENTAL PICTURE

This man acquired a practice of relaxing his body and getting into a relaxed, drowsy, meditative state. Then he filled his mind with the picture of the desired end, knowing his subconscious mind could bring it about the easiest way. He imagined his daughter congratulating him on his freedom, and saying to him, "Daddy, it's wonderful to have you home!" He had lost his family through drink. He was not allowed to visit them, and his wife would not speak to him.

Regularly, systematically, he used to sit down and meditate in the way outlined. When his attention wandered, he made it a habit to immediately recall the mental picture of his daughter with her smile and the scene of his home enlivened by her cheerful voice. All this brought about a reconditioning of his mind. It was a gradual process. He kept it up. He persevered knowing that sooner or later he would establish a new habit pattern in his subconscious mind.

I told him that he could liken his conscious mind to a camera, that his subconscious mind was the sensitive plate on which he registered and impressed the picture. This made a profound impression on him, and his whole aim was to firmly impress the picture on his mind and develop it there. Films are developed in the dark; likewise, mental pictures are developed in the darkroom of the subconscious mind.

FOCUSED ATTENTION

Realizing that his conscious mind was simply a camera, he used no effort. There was no mental struggle. He quietly adjusted his thoughts and focused his attention on the scene before him until he gradually became identified with the picture. He became absorbed in the mental atmosphere, repeating the mental movie frequently. There was no room for doubt that a healing would follow. When there was any temptation to drink, he would switch his imagination from any reveries of drinking bouts to the feeling of being at home with his family. He was successful because he confidently expected to experience the picture he was developing in his mind. Today he is president of a multimillion-dollar concern and is radiantly happy.

HE SAID A JINX WAS FOLLOWING HIM

Mr. Block said that he had been making an annual income of $20,000, but for the past three months all doors seemed to jam tightly. He brought clients up to the point where they were about to sign on the dotted line, and then at the eleventh hour the door closed. He added that perhaps a jinx was following him.

In discussing the matter with Mr. Block, I discovered that three months previously he had become very irritated, annoyed, and resentful toward a dentist who, after he had promised to sign a contract, had withdrawn at the last moment. He began to live in the unconscious fear that other clients would do the same, thereby setting up a history of frustration, hostility, and obstacles. He gradually built up in his mind a belief in obstruction and last minute cancellations until a vicious circle had been estab-lished. *What I fear most has come upon me.* Mr. Block realized that the trouble was in his own mind, and that it was essential to change his mental attitude.

His run of so-called misfortune was broken in the follow-ing way: "I realize I am one with the infinite intelligence of my subconscious mind which knows no obstacle, difficulty, or de-lay. I live in the joyous expectancy of the best. My deeper mind responds to my thoughts. I know that the work of the infinite power of my subconscious cannot be hindered. Infinite intelli-gence always finishes successfully whatever it begins. Creative wisdom works through me bringing all my plans and purposes to completion. Whatever I start, I bring to a successful conclu-sion. My aim in life is to give wonderful service, and all those whom I contact are blessed by what I have to offer. All my work comes to full fruition in divine order."

He repeated this prayer every morning before going to call on his customers, and he also prayed each night prior to sleep. In a short time he had established a new habit pattern in his sub-conscious mind, and he was back in his old accustomed stride as a successful salesman.

HOW MUCH DO YOU WANT WHAT YOU WANT?

A young man asked Socrates how he could get wisdom. Socrates replied, "Come with me." He took the lad to a river, pushed the boy's head under the water, held it there until the boy was gasping for air, then relaxed and released his head. When the boy regained his composure, he asked him, "What did you desire most when you were under water?"

"I wanted air," said the boy.

Socrates said to him, "When you want wisdom as much as

you wanted air when you were immersed in the water, you will receive it."

Likewise, when you really have an intense desire to overcome any block in your life, and you come to a clear-cut decision that there is a way out, and that is the course you wish to follow, then victory and triumph are assured.

If you really want peace of mind and inner calm, you will get it. Regardless of how unjustly you have been treated, or how unfair the boss has been, or what a mean scoundrel someone has proved to be, all this makes no difference to you when you awaken to your mental and spiritual powers. You know what you want, and you will definitely refuse to let the thieves (thoughts) of hatred, anger, hostility, and ill will rob you of peace, harmony, health, and happiness. You cease to become upset by people, conditions, news, and events by identifying your thoughts immediately with your aim in life. Your aim is peace, health, inspiration, harmony, and abundance. Feel a river of peace flowing through you now. Your thought is the immaterial and invisible power, and you choose to let it bless, inspire, and give you peace.

WHY HE COULD NOT BE HEALED

This is a case history of a married man with four children who was supporting and secretly living with another woman during his business trips. He was ill, nervous, irritable, and cantankerous, and he could not sleep without drugs. The doctor's medicine failed to bring down his high blood pressure of over two hundred. He had pains in numerous organs of his body, which doctors could not diagnose or relieve. To make matters worse, he was drinking heavily.

The cause of all this was a deep unconscious sense of guilt. He had violated the marriage vows, and this troubled him. The religious creed he was brought up on was deeply lodged in his subconscious mind, and he drank excessively to heal the wound of guilt. Some invalids take morphine and codeine for severe pains; he was taking alcohol for the pain or wound in his mind. It was the old story of adding fuel to the fire.

THE EXPLANATION AND THE CURE

He listened to the explanation of how his mind worked. He faced his problem, looked at it, and gave up his dual role. He knew that his drinking was an unconscious attempt to escape. The hidden cause lodged in his subconscious mind had to be eradicated; then the healing would follow.

He began to impress his subconscious mind three or four times a day by using the following prayer: "My mind is full of peace, poise, balance, and equilibrium. The infinite lies stretched in smiling repose within me. I am not afraid of anything in the past, the present, or the future. The infinite intelligence of my subconscious mind leads, guides, and directs me in all ways. I now meet every situation with faith, poise, calmness, and confidence. I am now completely free from the habit. My mind is full of inner peace, freedom, and joy. I forgive myself; then I am forgiven. Peace, sobriety, and confidence reign supreme in my mind."

He repeated this prayer frequently as outlined, being fully aware of what he was doing and why he was doing it. Knowing what he was doing gave him the necessary faith and confidence. I explained to him that as he spoke these statements out loud, slowly, lovingly, and meaningfully, they would gradually sink down into his subconscious mind. Like seeds, they would grow after their kind. These truths, on which he concentrated, went in through his eyes, his ears heard the sound, and the healing vibrations of these words reached his subconscious mind and obliterated all the negative mental patterns which caused all the trouble. Light dispels darkness. The constructive thought destroys the negative thought. He became a transformed man within a month.

REFUSING TO ADMIT IT

If you are an alcoholic or drug addict; admit it. Do not dodge the issue. Many people remain alcoholics because they refuse to admit it.

Your disease is an instability, an inner fear. You are refusing to face life, and so you try to escape your responsibilities through the bottle. As an alcoholic you have no free will, although you think you have, and you may even boast about your willpower. If you are a habitual drunkard and say bravely, "I will not touch it anymore," you have no power to make this assertion come true, because you do not know where to locate the power.

You are living in a psychological prison of your own making, and you are bound by your beliefs, opinions, training, and environmental influences. Like most people, you are a creature of habit. You are conditioned to react the way you do.

BUILDING IN THE IDEA OF FREEDOM

You can build the idea of freedom and peace of mind into your mentality so that it reaches your subconscious depths. The latter, being all-powerful, will free you from all desire for alcohol. Then, you will have the new understanding of how your mind works, and you can truly back up your statement and prove the truth to yourself.

FIFTY-ONE PERCENT HEALED

If you have a keen desire to free yourself from any destructive habit, you are fifty-one percent healed already. When you have a greater desire to give up the bad habit than to continue it, you will not experience too much difficulty in gaining complete freedom.

Whatever thought you anchor the mind upon, the latter magnifies. If you engage the mind on the concept of freedom (freedom from the habit) and peace of mind, and if you keep it focused on this new direction of attention, you generate feelings and emotions, which gradually emotionalize the concept of freedom and peace. Whatever idea you emotionalize is accepted by your subconscious and brought to pass.

THE LAW OF SUBSTITUTION

Realize that something good can come out of your suffering. You have not suffered in vain. However, it is foolish to continue to suffer.

If you continue as an alcoholic, it will bring about mental and physical deterioration and decay. Realize that the power in your subconscious is backing you up. Even though you may be seized with melancholia, you should begin to imagine the joy of freedom that is in store for you. This is the law of substitution. Your imagination took you to the bottle; let it take you now to freedom and peace of mind. You will suffer a little bit, but it is for a constructive purpose. You will bear it like a mother in the pangs of childbirth, and you will, likewise, bring forth a child of the mind. Your subconscious will give birth to sobriety.

CAUSE OF ALCOHOLISM

The real cause of alcoholism is negative and destructive thinking; for as a man thinketh, so is he. The alcoholic has a deep sense of inferiority, inadequacy, defeat, and frustration, usually accompanied by a deep inner hostility. He has countless alibis as to his reason for drinking, but the sole reason is in his *thought life*.

THREE MAGIC STEPS

The first step: Get still; quiet the wheels of the mind. Enter into a sleepy, drowsy state. In this relaxed, peaceful, receptive state, you are preparing for the second step.

The second step: Take a brief phrase, which can readily be graven on the memory, and repeat it over and over as a lullaby. Use the phrase, "Sobriety and peace of mind are mine now, and I give thanks." To prevent the mind from wandering, repeat it aloud or sketch its pronunciation with the lips and tongue as you say it mentally. This helps its entry into the subconscious mind. Do this for five minutes or more. You will find a deep emotional response.

The third step: Just before going to sleep, practice what Johann von Goethe, German author, used to do. Imagine a friend, a loved one in front of you. Your eyes are closed, you are relaxed and at peace. The loved one or friend is subjectively present, and is saying to you, "Congratulations!" You see the smile; you hear the voice. You mentally touch the hand; it is all real and vivid. The word *congratulations* implies complete freedom. Hear it over and over again until you get the subconscious reaction, which satisfies.

KEEP ON KEEPING ON

When fear knocks at the door of your mind, or when worry, anxiety, and doubt cross your mind, behold your vision, your goal. Think of the infinite power within your subconscious mind, which you can generate by your thinking and imagining, and this will give you confidence, power, and courage. Keep on, persevere, *until the day breaks, and the shadows flee away.*

REVIEW YOUR THOUGHT POWER

1. The solution lies within the problem. The answer is in every question. Infinite intelligence responds to you as you call upon it with faith and confidence.
2. Habit is the function of your subconscious mind. There is no greater evidence of the marvelous power of your subconscious than the force and sway habit holds in your life. You are a creature of habit.
3. You form habit patterns in your subconscious mind by repeating a thought and act over and over again until it establishes tracks in the subconscious mind and becomes automatic, such as swimming, dancing, typing, walking, driving your car, etc.
4. You have freedom to choose. You can choose a good habit or a bad habit. Prayer is a good habit.
5. Whatever mental picture, backed by faith, you behold in your conscious mind, your subconscious mind will bring to pass.
6. The only obstacle to your success and achievement is your own thought or mental image.
7. When your attention wanders, bring it back to the contemplation of your good or goal. Make a habit of this. This is called disciplining the mind.
8. Your conscious mind is the camera, and your subconscious

mind is the sensitive plate on which you register or impress the picture.

9. The only jinx that follows anyone is a fear thought repeated over and over in the mind. Break the jinx by knowing that whatever you start you will bring to a conclusion in divine order. Picture the happy ending and sustain it with confidence.

10. To form a new habit, you must be convinced that it is desirable. When your desire to give up the bad habit is greater than your desire to continue, you are fifty-one percent healed already.

11. The statements of others cannot hurt you except through your own thoughts and mental participation. Identify yourself with your aim, which is peace, harmony, and joy. You are the only thinker in your universe.

12. Excessive drinking is an unconscious desire to escape. The cause of alcoholism is negative and destructive thinking. The cure is to think of freedom, sobriety, and perfection, and to feel the thrill of accomplishment.

13. Many people remain alcoholics because they refuse to admit it.

14. The law of your subconscious mind, which held you in bondage and inhibited your freedom of action, will give you freedom and happiness. It depends on how you use it.

15. Your imagination took you to the bottle; let it take you to freedom by imagining you are free.

16. The real cause of alcoholism is negative and destructive thinking. *As a man thinketh in his heart* [subconscious mind], *so is he*.

17. When fear knocks at the door of your mind, let faith in God and all things good open the door.

19

HOW TO USE YOUR SUBCONSCIOUS MIND TO REMOVE FEAR

One of our students told me that he was invited to speak at a banquet. He said he was panic stricken at the thought of speaking before a thousand people. He overcame his fear this way: For several nights he sat down in an armchair for about five minutes and said to himself slowly, quietly, and positively, "I am going to master this fear. I am overcoming it now. I speak with poise and confidence. I am relaxed and at ease." He operated a definite law of mind and overcame his fear.

The subconscious mind is amenable to suggestion and is controlled by suggestion. When you still your mind and relax, the thoughts of your conscious mind sink down into the subconscious through a process similar to osmosis, whereby fluids separated by a porous membrane intermingle. As these positive seeds, or thoughts, sink into the subconscious area, they grow after their kind, and you become poised, serene, and calm.

MAN'S GREATEST ENEMY

It is said that fear is man's greatest enemy. Fear is behind failure, sickness, and poor human relations. Millions of people are afraid of the past, the future, old age, insanity, and death. Fear is a thought in your mind, and you are afraid of your own thoughts.

A little boy can be paralyzed with fear when he is told there is a boogie man under his bed who is going to take him away. When his father turns on the light and shows him there is no boogie man, he is freed from fear. The fear in the mind of the boy was as real as if there really was a boogie man there. He was healed of a false thought in his mind. The thing he feared did not exist. Likewise, most of your fears have no reality. They are merely a conglomeration of sinister shadows, and shadows have no reality.

DO THE THING YOU FEAR

Ralph Waldo Emerson, philosopher and poet, said, "Do the thing you are afraid to do, and the death of fear is certain."

There was a time when the writer of this chapter was filled with unutterable fear when standing before an audience. The way I overcame it was to stand before the audience, do the thing I was afraid to do, and the death of fear was certain.

When you affirm positively that you are going to master your fears, and you come to a definite decision in your conscious mind, you release the power of the subconscious, which flows in response to the nature of your thought.

BANISHING STAGE FRIGHT

A young lady was invited to an audition. She had been looking forward to the interview. However, on three previous occasions, she had failed miserably due to stage fright.

She possessed a very good voice, but she was certain that when the time came for her to sing, she would be seized with stage fright. The subconscious mind takes your fears as a request, proceeds to manifest them, and brings them into your experience. On three previous auditions she sang wrong notes, and she finally broke down and cried. The cause, as previously outlined, was an involuntary autosuggestion, i.e., a silent fear thought emotionalized and subjectified.

She overcame it by the following technique: Three times a day she isolated herself in a room. She sat down comfortably in an armchair, relaxed her body, and closed her eyes. She stilled her mind and body to the best of her ability. Physical inertia favors passivity and renders the mind more receptive to suggestion. She counteracted the fear suggestion by its converse, saying to herself, "I sing beautifully. I am poised, serene, confident, and calm."

She repeated the words slowly, quietly, and with feeling from five to ten times at each sitting. She had three such "sittings" every day and one immediately prior to sleep at night. At the end of a week she was completely poised and confident, and gave a definitely outstanding audition. Carry out the above procedure, and the death of fear is certain.

FEAR OF FAILURE

Occasionally young men from the local university come to see me, as well as schoolteachers, who often seem to suffer from suggestive amnesia at examinations. The complaint is always the same: "I know the answers after the examination is over, but I can't remember the answers during the examination."

The idea, which realizes itself, is the one to which we invariably give concentrated attention. I find that each one is obsessed with the idea of failure. Fear is behind the temporary amnesia, and it is the cause of the whole experience.

One young medical student was the most brilliant person in his class, yet he found himself failing to answer simple questions at the time of written or oral examinations. I explained to him that the reason was he had been worrying and was fearful for several days previous to the examination. These negative thoughts became charged with fear.

Thoughts enveloped in the powerful emotion of fear are realized in the subconscious mind. In other words, this young man was requesting his subconscious mind to see to it that he failed, and that is exactly what it did. On the day of the examination he found himself stricken with what is called, in psychological circles, suggestive amnesia.

HOW HE OVERCAME THE FEAR

He learned that his subconscious mind was the storehouse of memory, and that it had a perfect record of all he had heard and read during his medical training. Moreover, he learned that the subconscious mind was responsive and reciprocal. The way to be *en rapport* with it was to be relaxed, peaceful, and confident.

Every night and morning he began to imagine his mother congratulating him on his wonderful record. He would hold an imaginary letter from her in his hand. As he began to contemplate the happy result, he called forth a corresponding or reciprocal response or reaction in himself. The all-wise and omnipotent power of the subconscious took over, dictated, and directed his conscious mind accordingly. He imagined the end, thereby willing the means to the realization of the end. Following this procedure, he had no trouble passing subsequent examinations. In other words, the subjective wisdom took over, compelling him to give an excellent account of himself.

FEAR OF WATER, MOUNTAINS, CLOSED PLACES, ETC.

There are many people who are afraid to go into an elevator, climb mountains, or even swim in the water. It may well be that the individual had unpleasant experiences in the water in his youth, such as having been thrown forcibly into the water without being able to swim. He might have been forcibly detained in an elevator, which failed to function properly, causing resultant fear of closed places.

I had an experience when I was about ten years of age. I accidentally fell into a pool and went down three times. I can still remember the dark water engulfing my head, and my gasping for air until another boy pulled me out at the last moment. This experience sank into my subconscious mind, and for years I feared the water.

An elderly psychologist said to me, "Go down to the swimming pool, look at the water, and say out loud in strong tones, 'I am going to master you. I can dominate you.' Then go into the water, take lessons, and overcome it." This I did, and I mastered the water. Do not permit water to master you. Remember, you are the master of the water.

When I assumed a new attitude of mind, the omnipotent power of the subconscious responded, giving me strength, faith, and confidence, and enabling me to overcome my fear.

MASTER TECHNIQUE FOR OVERCOMING
ANY PARTICULAR FEAR

The following is a process and technique for overcoming fear, which I teach from the platform. It works like a charm. Try it!

Suppose you are afraid of the water, a mountain, an interview, an audition, or you fear closed places. If you are afraid of swimming, begin now to sit still for five or ten minutes three or four times a day, and imagine you are swimming. Actually, you are swimming in your mind. It is a subjective experience. Mentally you have projected yourself into the water. You feel the chill of the water and the movement of your arms and legs. It is all real, vivid, and a joyous activity of the mind. It is not idle daydreaming, for you know that what you are experiencing in your imagination will be developed in your subconscious mind. Then you will be compelled to express the image and likeness of the picture you impressed on your deeper mind. This is the law of the subconscious.

You could apply the same technique if you are afraid of mountains or high places. Imagine you are climbing the mountain, feel the reality of it all, enjoy the scenery, knowing that as you continue to do this mentally, you will do it physically with ease and comfort.

HE BLESSED THE ELEVATOR

I knew an executive of a large corporation who was terrified to ride in an elevator. He would walk up five flights of stairs to his office every morning. He said that he began to bless the elevator every night and several times a day. He finally overcame his fear. This was how he blessed the elevator: "The elevator in our building is a wonderful idea. It came out of the universal mind. It is a boon and a blessing to all our employees. It gives wonderful service. It operates in divine order. I ride in it in peace and joy. I remain silent now while the currents of life, love, and understanding flow through the patterns of my thought. In my imagination I am now in the elevator, and I step out into my office. The elevator is full of our employees. I talk to them, and they are friendly, joyous, and free. It is a wonderful experience of freedom, faith, and confidence. I give thanks."

He continued this prayer for about ten days, and on the eleventh day, he walked into the elevator with other members of the organization and felt completely free.

NORMAL AND ABNORMAL FEAR

Man is born only with two fears, the fear of falling and the fear of noise. These are a sort of alarm system given you by nature as a means of self-preservation. Normal fear is good. You hear an automobile coming down the road, and you step aside to survive. The momentary fear of being run over is overcome by your action. All other fears were given to you by parents, relatives, teachers, and all those who influenced your early years.

ABNORMAL FEAR

Abnormal fear takes place when man lets his imagination run riot. I knew a woman who was invited to go on a trip around the world by plane. She began to cut out of the newspapers all reports of airplane catastrophes. She pictured herself going down in the ocean, being drowned, etc. This is abnormal fear. Had she persisted in this, she would undoubtedly have attracted what she feared most.

Another example of abnormal fear is that of a businessman in New York, who was very prosperous and successful. He had his own private mental motion picture of which he was the director. He would run this mental movie of failure, bank-ruptcy, empty shelves, and no bank balance until he sank into a deep depression. He refused to stop this morbid imagery and kept reminding his wife that "this can't last," "there will be a recession," "I feel sure we will go bankrupt," etc.

His wife told me that he finally did go into bankruptcy, and all the things he imagined and feared came to pass. The things he feared did not exist, but he brought them to pass by con-stantly fearing, believing, and expecting financial disaster. *Job said, the thing I feared has come upon me.*

There are people who are afraid that something terrible will happen to their children, and that some dread catastrophe will befall them. When they read about an epidemic or rare disease, they live in fear that they will catch it, and some imagine they have the disease already. All this is abnormal fear.

THE ANSWER TO ABNORMAL FEAR

Move mentally to the opposite. To stay at the extreme of fear is stagnation plus mental and physical deterioration. When fear arises, there immediately comes with it a desire for something opposite to the thing feared. Place your attention on the thing immediately desired. Get absorbed and engrossed in your de-sire, knowing that the subjective always overturns the objective. This attitude will give you confidence and lift your spirits. The infinite power of your subconscious mind is moving on your behalf, and it cannot fail. Therefore, peace and assurance are yours.

EXAMINE YOUR FEARS

The president of a large organization told me that when he was a salesman he used to walk around the block five or six times before he called on a customer. The sales manager came along one day and said to him, "Don't be afraid of the boogie man behind the door. There is no boogie man. It is a false belief."

The manager told him that whenever he looked at his own fears he stared them in the face and stood up to them, looking them straight in the eye. Then they faded and shrank into insignificance.

HE LANDED IN THE JUNGLE

A chaplain told me of his experiences in the Second World War. He had to parachute from a damaged plane and land in the jungle. He said he was frightened, but he knew there were two kinds of fear, normal and abnormal, which we have previously pointed out.

He decided to do something about the fear immediately, and began to talk to himself saying, "John, you can't surrender to your fear. Your fear is a desire for safety and security, and a way out."

He began to claim, "Infinite intelligence which guides the planets in their courses is now leading and guiding me out of this jungle."

He kept saying this out loud to himself for ten minutes or more. "Then," he added, "something began to stir inside me. A mood of confidence began to seize me, and I began to walk. After a few days, I miraculously came out of the jungle, and was picked up by a rescue plane."

His changed mental attitude saved him. His confidence and trust in the subjective wisdom and power within him was the solution to his problem.

He said, "Had I begun to bemoan my fate and indulge my

fears, I would have succumbed to the monster fear, and probably would have died of fear and starvation."

HE DISMISSED HIMSELF

The general manager of an organization told me that for three years he feared he would lose his position. He was always imagining failure. The thing he feared did not exist, save as a morbid anxious thought in his own mind. His vivid imagination dramatized the loss of his job until he became nervous and neurotic. Finally he was asked to resign.

Actually, he dismissed himself. His constant negative imagery and fear suggestions to his subconscious mind caused the latter to respond and react accordingly. It caused him to make mistakes and foolish decisions, which resulted in his failure as a general manager. His dismissal would never have happened, if he had immediately moved to the opposite in his mind.

THEY PLOTTED AGAINST HIM

During a recent world lecture tour, I had a two-hour conversation with a prominent government official. He had a deep sense of inner peace and serenity. He said that all the abuse he receives politically from newspapers and the opposition party never disturb him. His practice is to sit still for fifteen minutes in the morning and realize that in the center of himself is a deep still ocean of peace. Meditating in this way, he generates tremendous power, which overcomes all manner of difficulties and fears.

Some time previously, a colleague called him at midnight and told him a group of people were plotting against him. This is what he said to his colleague: "I am going to sleep now in perfect peace. You can discuss it with me at 10:00 A.M. tomorrow."

He said to me, "I know that no negative thought can ever manifest except I emotionalize the thought and accept it mentally. I refuse to entertain their suggestion of fear. Therefore, no harm can come to me."

Notice how calm he was, how cool, how peaceful! He did not start getting excited, tearing his hair, or wringing his hands. At his center he found the still water, an inner peace, and there was a great calm.

DELIVER YOURSELF FROM ALL YOUR FEARS

Use this perfect formula for casting out fear. *I sought the Lord, and he heard me, and delivered me from all my fears.* PSALMS 34:4. The *Lord* is an ancient word meaning *law*—the power of your subconscious mind.

Learn the wonders of your subconscious, and how it works and functions. Master the techniques given to you in this chapter. Put them into practice now, today! Your subconscious will respond, and you will be free of all fears. *I sought the Lord, and he heard me, and delivered me from all my fears.*

STEP THIS WAY TO FREEDOM FROM FEAR

1. Do the thing you are afraid to do, and the death of fear is certain. Say to yourself and mean it, "I am going to master this fear," and you will.

2. Fear is a negative thought in your mind. Supplant it with a constructive thought. Fear has killed millions. Confidence is greater than fear. Nothing is more powerful than faith in God and the good.

3. Fear is man's greatest enemy. It is behind failure, sickness, and bad human relations. Love casts out fear. Love is an emotional attachment to the good things of life. Fall in love

with honesty, integrity, justice, good will, and success. Live in the joyous expectancy of the best, and invariably the best will come to you.

4. Counteract the fear suggestions with the opposite, such as "I sing beautifully; I am poised, serene, and calm." It will pay fabulous dividends.

5. Fear is behind amnesia at oral and written examination time. You can overcome this by affirming frequently, "I have a perfect memory for everything I need to know," or you can imagine a friend congratulating you on your brilliant success on the examination. Persevere and you will win.

6. If you are afraid to cross water, swim. In your imagination swim freely, joyously. Project yourself into the water mentally. Feel the chill and thrill of swimming across the pool. Make it vivid. As you do this subjectively, you will be compelled to go into the water and conquer it. This is the law of your mind.

7. If you are afraid of closed places, such as elevators, lecture halls, etc., mentally ride in an elevator blessing all its parts and functions. You will be amazed how quickly the fear will be dissipated.

8. You were born with only two fears, the fear of falling and the fear of noise. All your other fears were acquired. Get rid of them.

9. Normal fear is good. Abnormal fear is very bad and destructive. To constantly indulge in fear thoughts results in abnormal fear, obsessions, and complexes. To fear something persistently causes a sense of panic and terror.

10. You can overcome abnormal fear when you know the power of your subconscious mind can change conditions and bring to pass the cherished desires of your heart. Give

your immediate attention and devotion to your desire which is the opposite of your fear. This is the love that casts out fear.

11. If you are afraid of failure, give attention to success. If you are afraid of sickness, dwell on your perfect health. If you are afraid of an accident, dwell on the guidance and protection of God. If you are afraid of death, dwell on Eternal Life. God is Life, and that is your life now.

12. The great law of substitution is the answer to fear. Whatever you fear has its solution in the form of your desire. If you are sick, you desire health. If you are in the prison of fear, you desire freedom. Expect the good. Mentally concentrate on the good, and know that your subconscious mind answers you always. It never fails.

13. The things you fear do not really exist except as thoughts in your mind. Thoughts are creative. This is why Job said, *The thing I feared has come upon me*. Think good and good follows.

14. Look at your fears; hold them up to the light of reason. Learn to laugh at your fears. That is the best medicine.

15. Nothing can disturb you but your own thought. The suggestions, statements, or threats of other persons have no power. The power is within you, and when your thoughts are focused on that which is good, then God's power is with your thoughts of good. There is only one Creative Power, and It moves as harmony. There are no divisions of quarrels in it. Its source is Love. This is why God's power is with your thoughts of good.

20

HOW TO STAY YOUNG
IN SPIRIT FOREVER

Your subconscious mind never grows old. It is timeless, ageless, and endless. It is a part of the universal mind of God, which was never born, and it will never die.

Fatigue or old age cannot be predicated on any spiritual quality or power. Patience, kindness, veracity, humility, good will, peace, harmony, and brotherly love are attributes and qualities, which never grow old. If you continue to generate these qualities here on this plane of life, you will always remain young in spirit.

I remember reading an article in one of our magazines some years ago, which stated that a group of eminent medical men at the De Courcy Clinic, in Cincinnati, Ohio, reported that years alone are not responsible for bringing about degenerative disorders. These same physicians stated that it is the fear of time, not time itself, that has a harmful aging effect on our minds and bodies, and that the neurotic fear of the effects of time may well be the cause of premature aging.

During the many years of my public life, I have had occasion to study the biographies of the famous men and women who have continued their productive activities into the years well beyond the normal span of life. Some of them achieve their greatness in old age. At the same time, it has been my privilege to meet and to know countless individuals of no prominence who, in their lesser sphere, belonged to those hardy mortals who have proved that old age of itself does not destroy the creative powers of the mind and body.

HE HAD GROWN OLD IN HIS THOUGHT LIFE

A few years ago I called on an old friend in London, England. He was over 80 years of age, very ill, and obviously was yielding to his advancing years. Our conversation revealed his physical weakness, his sense of frustration, and a general deterioration almost approaching lifelessness. His cry was that he was useless and that no one wanted him. With an expression of hopelessness he betrayed his false philosophy, "We are born, grow up, become old, good for nothing, and that's the end."

This mental attitude of futility and worthlessness was the chief reason for his sickness. He was looking forward only to senescence, and after that—nothing. Indeed, he had grown old in his thought life, and his subconscious mind brought about all the evidence of his habitual thinking.

AGE IS THE DAWN OF WISDOM

Unfortunately, many people have the same attitude as this unhappy man. They are afraid of what they term "old age," the end, and extinction, which really means that they are afraid of life. Yet, life is endless. Age is not the flight of years, but the dawn of wisdom.

Wisdom is an awareness of the tremendous spiritual powers in your subconscious mind and the knowledge of how to apply these powers to lead a full and happy life. Get it out of your head once and for all that 65, 75, or 85 years of age is synonymous with the end for you or anybody else. It can be the beginning of a glorious, fruitful, active, and most productive life pattern, better than you have ever experienced. Believe this, expect it, and your subconscious will bring it to pass.

WELCOME THE CHANGE

Old age is not a tragic occurrence. What we call the aging process is really change. It is to be welcomed joyfully and gladly as each phase of human life is a step forward on the path, which has no end. Man has powers, which transcend his bodily powers. He has senses, which transcend his five physical senses.

Scientists today are finding positive indisputable evidence that something conscious in man can leave his present body and travel thousands of miles to see, hear, touch, and speak to people even though his physical body never leaves the couch on which it reclines.

Man's life is spiritual and eternal. He need never grow old for Life, or God, cannot grow old. The Bible says that God is Life. Life is self-renewing, eternal, indestructible, and is the reality of all men.

EVIDENCE FOR SURVIVAL

The evidence gathered by the psychical research societies both in Great Britain and America is overwhelming. You may go into any large metropolitan library and get volumes on *The*

Proceedings of the Psychical Research Society based on findings of distinguished scientists on survival following so-called death. You will find a startling report on scientific experiments establishing the reality of life after death in *The Case for Psychic Survival* by Hereward Carrington, Director of the American Psychical Institute.

LIFE IS

A woman asked Thomas Edison, the electrical wizard, "Mr. Edison, what is electricity?"

He replied, "Madame, electricity is. Use it."

Electricity is a name we give an invisible power which we do not fully comprehend, but we learn all we can about the principle of electricity and its uses. We use it in countless ways.

The scientist cannot see an electron with his eyes, yet he accepts it as a scientific fact, because it is the only valid conclusion, which coincides with his other experimental evidence. We cannot see life. However, we know we are alive. Life is, and we are here to express it in all its beauty and glory.

MIND AND SPIRIT DO NOT GROW OLD

The Bible says, *And this is life eternal, that they might know thee the only true God.* JOHN 17:3.

The man who thinks or believes that the earthly cycle of birth, adolescence, youth, maturity, and old age is all there is to life, is indeed to be pitied. Such a man has no anchor, no hope, no vision, and to him life has no meaning.

This type of belief brings frustration, stagnation, cynicism, and a sense of hopelessness resulting in neurosis and mental aberrations of all kinds. If you cannot play a fast game of tennis, or swim as fast as your son, or if your body has slowed down, or you walk with a slow step, remember life is always clothing itself anew. What men call death is but a journey to a new city in another dimension of Life.

I say to men and women in my lectures that they should accept what we call old age gracefully. Age has its own glory, beauty, and wisdom, which belong to it. Peace, love, joy, beauty, happiness, wisdom, good will, and understanding are qualities, which never grow old or die.

Ralph Waldo Emerson, poet and philosopher, said, "We do not count a man's years until he has nothing else to count."

Your character, the quality of your mind, your faith, and your convictions are not subject to decay.

YOU ARE AS YOUNG AS YOU THINK YOU ARE

I give public lectures in Caxton Hall, London, England, every few years, and following one of these lectures, a surgeon said to me, "I am 84 years of age. I operate every morning, visit patients in the afternoons, and I write for medical and other scientific journals in the evening."

His attitude was that he was as useful as he believed himself to be, and that he was as young as his thoughts. He said to me, "It's true what you said, 'Man is as strong as he thinks he is, and as valuable as he thinks he is.'"

This surgeon has not surrendered to advancing years. He knows that he is immortal. His final comment to me was, "If I should pass on tomorrow, I would be operating on people in the next dimension, not with a surgeon's scalpel, but with mental and spiritual surgery."

YOUR GRAY HAIRS ARE AN ASSET

Don't ever quit a job and say, "I am retired; I am old; I am finished." That would be stagnation, death, and you would be finished. Some men are old at 30, while others are young at 80. The mind is the master weaver, the architect, the designer, and the sculptor. George Bernard Shaw was active at 90, and the artistic quality of his mind had not relaxed from active duty.

I meet men and women who tell me that some employers almost slam the door in their faces when they say they are over 40. This attitude on the part of the employers is to be considered cold, callous, evil, and completely void of compassion and understanding. The total emphasis seems to be on youth, i.e., you must be under 35 years of age to receive consideration. The reasoning behind this is certainly very shallow. If the employer would stop and think, he would realize that the man or woman was not selling his age or gray hair, rather, he was willing to give of his talents, his experience, and his wisdom gathered through years of experience in the marketplace of life.

AGE IS AN ASSET

Your age should be a distinct asset to any organization, because of your practice and application through the years of the principles of the Golden Rule and the law of love and good will. Your gray hair, if you have any, should stand for greater wisdom, skill, and understanding. Your emotional and spiritual maturity should be a tremendous blessing to any organization.

A man should not be asked to resign when he is 65 years of age. That is the time of life when he could be most useful in handling personnel problems, making plans for the future, making decisions, and guiding others in the realm of creative ideas based on his experience and insight into the nature of the business.

BE YOUR AGE

A motion-picture writer in Hollywood told me that he had to write scripts, which would cater to the twelve-year-old mind. This is a tragic state of affairs if the great masses of people are expected to become emotionally and spiritually mature. It means that the emphasis is placed on youth in spite of the fact that youth stands for inexperience, lack of discernment, and hasty judgment.

I CAN KEEP UP WITH THE BEST OF THEM

I am now thinking of a man 65 years of age who is trying frantically to keep young. He swims with young men every Sunday, goes on long hikes, plays tennis, and boasts of his prowess and physical powers, saying, "Look, I can keep up with the best of them!"

He should remember the great truth: *As a man thinketh in his heart, so is he.* PROVERBS 23:7.

Diets, exercises, and games of all kinds will not keep this man young. It is necessary for him to observe that he grows old or remains young in accordance with his processes of thinking. Your subconscious mind is conditioned by your thoughts. If your thoughts are constantly on the beautiful, the noble, and the good, you will remain young regardless of the chronological years.

FEAR OF OLD AGE

Job said, *The thing which I greatly feared is come upon me.* There are many people who fear old age and are uncertain about the future, because they anticipate mental and physical deterioration as the years advance. What they think and feel comes to pass.

You grow old when you lose interest in life, when you cease to dream, to hunger after new truths, and to search for new worlds to conquer. When your mind is open to new ideas, new interests, and when you raise the curtain and let in the sunshine and inspiration of new truths of life and the universe, you will be young and vital.

YOU HAVE MUCH TO GIVE

If you are 65 or 95 years of age, realize you have much to give. You can help stabilize, advise, and direct the younger generation. You can give the benefit of your knowledge, your experience, and your wisdom. You can always look ahead for at all times you are gazing into infinite life. You will find that you can never cease to unveil the glories and wonders of life. Try to learn something new every moment of the day, and you will find your mind will always be young.

ONE HUNDRED AND TEN YEARS OLD

Some years ago while lecturing in Bombay, India, I was introduced to a man who said he was 110 years old. He had the most beautiful face I have ever seen. He seemed transfigured by the radiance of an inner light. There was a rare beauty in his eyes indicating he had grown old in years with gladness and with no indication that his mind had dimmed its lights.

RETIREMENT—A NEW VENTURE

Be sure that your mind never retires. It must be like a parachute, which is no good unless it opens up. Be open and receptive to new ideas. I have seen men of 65 and 70 retire. They seemed to rot away, and in a few months passed on. They obviously felt that life was at an end.

Retirement can be a new venture, a new challenge, a new path, the beginning of the fulfillment of a long dream. It is inexpressibly depressing to hear a man say, "What shall I do now that I am retired?" He is saying in effect, "I am mentally and physically dead. My mind is bankrupt of ideas."

All this is a false picture. The real truth is that you can accomplish more at 90 than you did at 60, because each day you are growing in wisdom and understanding of life and the universe through your new studies and interest.

HE GRADUATED TO A BETTER JOB

An executive, who lives near me, was forced to retire a few months ago because he had reached the age of 65. He said to me, "I look upon my retirement as promotion from kindergarten to the first grade." He philosophized in this manner: He said that when he left high school, he went up the ladder by going to college. He realized this was a step forward in his education and understanding of life in general. Likewise, he added, now he could do the things he had always wanted to do, and therefore, his retirement was still another step forward on the ladder of life and wisdom.

He came to the wise conclusion that he was no longer going to concentrate on making a living. Now he was going to give all his attention to living life. He is an amateur photographer, and he took additional courses on the subject. He took a trip around the world and took movies of famous places. He now lectures before various groups, lodges, and clubs, and is in popular demand.

There are countless ways of taking an interest in something worthwhile outside yourself. Become enthusiastic over new creative ideas, make spiritual progress, and continue to learn and to grow. In this manner you remain young in heart, because you are hungering and thirsting after new truths, and your body will reflect your thinking at all times.

YOU MUST BE A PRODUCER AND NOT A
PRISONER OF SOCIETY

The newspapers are taking cognizance of the fact that the voting population of the elderly in California elections is increasing by leaps and bounds. This means that their voices will be heard in the legislature of the state and also in the halls of Congress. I believe there will be enacted a federal law prohibiting employers from discrimination against men and women because of age.

A man of 65 years may be younger mentally, physically, and physiologically than many men at 30. It is stupid and ridiculous to tell a man he cannot be hired because he is over 40. It is like saying to him that he is ready for the scrap heap or the junk pile.

What is a man of 40 or over to do? Must he bury his talents and hide his light under a bushel? Men who are deprived and prevented from working because of age must be sustained by government treasuries at county, state, and federal levels. The many organizations who refuse to hire them and benefit from their wisdom and experience will be taxed to support them. This is a form of financial suicide.

Man is here to enjoy the fruit of his labor, and he is here to be a producer and not a prisoner of society, which compels him to idleness.

Man's body slows down gradually as he advances through

the years, but his conscious mind can be made much more active, alert, alive, and quickened by the inspiration from his subconscious mind. His mind, in reality, never grows old. Job said,
*Oh that I were as in months past, as in the days when God preserved
me; When his candle shined upon my head, and when by his light I
walked through darkness; As I was in the days of my youth, when the
secret of God was upon my tabernacle.* JOB 29:2–4.

SECRET OF YOUTH

To recapture the days of your youth, feel the miraculous, healing, self-renewing power of your subconscious mind moving
through your whole being. Know and feel that you are inspired,
lifted up, rejuvenated, revitalized, and recharged spiritually.
You can bubble over with enthusiasm and joy, as in the days of
your youth, for the simple reason that you can always mentally
and emotionally recapture the joyous state.

The candle, which shines upon your head, is divine intelligence, and reveals to you everything you need to know; it enables you to affirm the presence of your good, regardless of
appearances. You walk by the guidance of your subconscious
mind, because you know that the dawn appears and the shadows flee away.

GET A VISION

Instead of saying, "I am old," say, "I am wise in the way of the
Divine Life." Don't let the corporation, newspapers, or statistics
hold a picture before you of old age, declining years, decrepi-
tude, senility, and uselessness. Reject it, for it is a lie. Refuse to
be hypnotized by such propaganda. Affirm life—not death. Get
a vision of yourself as happy, radiant, successful, serene, and
powerful.

YOUR MIND DOES NOT GROW OLD

Former President Herbert Hoover, now 88 years old, is very active and is performing monumental work. I interviewed him a few years ago in his suite at the Waldorf-Astoria, New York City. I found him healthy, happy, vigorous, and full of life and enthusiasm. He was keeping several secretaries busy handling his correspondence and was himself writing books of a political and historical nature. Like all great men, I found him affable, genial, amiable, loving, and most understanding.

His mental acumen and sagacity gave me the thrill of a lifetime. He is a deeply religious man, and is full of faith in God and in the triumph of the eternal truth of life. He was subjected to a barrage of criticism and condemnation in the years of the Great Depression, but he weathered the storm and did not grow old in hatred, resentment, ill will, and bitterness. On the contrary, he went into the silence of his soul, and communing with the Divine Presence within him, he found the peace, which is the power at the heart of God.

HIS MIND ACTIVE AT NINETY-NINE

My father learned the French language at 65 years of age, and became an authority on it at 70. He made a study of Gaelic when he was over 60, and became an acknowledged and famous teacher of the subject. He assisted my sister in a school of higher learning and continued to do so until he passed away at 99. His mind was as clear at 99 as it was when he was 20. Moreover, his handwriting and his reasoning powers had improved with age. Truly, you are as old as you think and feel.

WE NEED OUR SENIOR CITIZENS

Marcus Porcius Cato, the Roman patriot, learned Greek at 80. Madame Ernestine Schumann-Heink, the great German-American contralto, reached the pinnacle of her musical success after she became a grandmother. It is wonderful to behold the accomplishments of the oldsters. General Douglas MacArthur, Harry S. Truman, General Dwight David Eisenhower, and American financier Bernard Baruch are interesting, active, and contributing their talents and wisdom to the world.

The Greek philosopher Socrates learned to play musical instruments when he was 80 years old. Michelangelo was painting his greatest canvases at 80. At 80, Cios Simonides won the prize for poetry, Johann von Goethe finished *Faust*, and Leopold von Ranke commenced his *History of the World*, which he finished at 92.

Alfred Tennyson wrote a magnificent poem, "Crossing the Bar," at 83. Isaac Newton was hard at work close to 85. At 88 John Wesley was directing, preaching, and guiding Methodism. We have several men of 95 years who come to my lectures, and they tell me they are in better health now than they were at 20.

Let us place our senior citizens in high places and give them every opportunity to bring forth the flowers of Paradise.

If you are retired, get interested in the laws of life and the wonders of your subconscious mind. Do something you have always wanted to do. Study new subjects, and investigate new ideas.

Pray as follows: *As the hart panteth after the water brooks, so panteth my soul after thee, O God.* PSALMS 42:1.

THE FRUITS OF OLD AGE

His flesh shall be fresher than a child's: he shall return to the days of his youth.

—Job 33:25

Old age really means the contemplation of the Truths of God from the highest standpoint. Realize that you are on an endless journey, a series of important steps in the ceaseless, tireless, endless ocean of life. Then, with the Psalmist you will say, *They shall still bring forth fruit in old age; they shall be fat and flourishing.* Psalms 92:14.

But the fruit of the Spirit is love, joy, peace, longsuffering, gentleness, goodness, faith, meekness, temperance; against such there is no law. Galatians 5:22–23.

You are a son of Infinite Life, which knows no end, and you are a child of Eternity.

PROFITABLE POINTERS

1. Patience, kindness, love, good will, joy, happiness, wisdom, and understanding are qualities, which never grow old. Cultivate them and express them, and remain young in mind and body.
2. Some research physicians say that the neurotic fear of the effects of time may well be the cause of premature aging.
3. Age is not the flight of years; it is the dawn of wisdom in the mind of man.
4. The most productive years of your life can be from 65 to 95.
5. Welcome the advancing years. It means you are moving higher on the path of life, which has no end.
6. God is Life, and that is your life now. Life is self-renewing,

eternal, and indestructible, and is the reality of all men. You live forever, because your life is God's life.

7. Evidence of survival after death is overwhelming. Study *Proceedings of Psychical Research Society of Great Britain and America* in your library. The work is based on the scientific research by outstanding scientists for over 75 years.

8. You cannot see your mind, but you know you have a mind. You cannot see spirit, but you know that the spirit of the game, the spirit of the artist, the spirit of the musician, and the spirit of the speaker is real. Likewise, the spirit of goodness, truth, and beauty moving in your mind and heart are real. You cannot see life, but you know you are alive.

9. Old age may be called the contemplation of the Truths of God from the highest standpoint. The joys of old age are greater than those of youth. Your mind is engaged in spiritual and mental athletics. Nature slows down your body so that you may have the opportunity to meditate on things divine.

10. We do not count a man's years until he has nothing else to count. Your faith and convictions are not subject to decay.

11. You are as young as you think you are. You are as strong as you think you are. You are as useful as you think you are. You are as young as your thoughts.

12. Your gray hairs are an asset. You are not selling your gray hairs. You are selling your talent, abilities, and wisdom, which you have garnered through the years.

13. Diets and exercises won't keep you young. *As a man thinketh, so is he.*

14. Fear of old age can bring about physical and mental deterioration. *The thing I greatly feared has come upon me.*

15. You grow old when you cease to dream, and when you lose

interest in life. You grow old if you are irritable, crotchety, petulant, and cantankerous. Fill your mind with the Truths of God and radiate the sunshine of His love—this is youth.

16. Look ahead, for at all times you are gazing into infinite life.

17. Your retirement is a new venture. Take up new studies and new interests. You can now do the things you always wanted to do when you were so busy making a living. Give your attention to living life.

18. Become a producer and not a prisoner of society. Don't hide your light under a bushel.

19. The secret of youth is love, joy, inner peace, and laughter. *In Him there is fullness of joy. In Him there is no darkness at all.*

20. You are needed. Some of the great philosophers, artists, scientists, writers, and others accomplished their greatest work after they were 80 years old.

21. The fruits of old age are love, joy, peace, patience, gentleness, goodness, faith, meekness, and temperance.

22. You are a son of Infinite Life which knows no end. You are a child of Eternity. You are wonderful!

YOU CAN CHANGE YOUR WHOLE LIFE

"These will I wear today!"
So putteth by the Spirit
Lightly its garb of flesh,
And passeth to inherit
A residence afresh.
—THE SONG CELESTIAL

CONTENTS

1

BANISH THAT FEELING OF GUILT

But if the wicked will turn from all his sins that he hath committed, and keep all my statutes, and do that which is lawful and right, he shall surely live, he shall not die. All his transgressions that he hath committed, they shall not be mentioned unto him: in his righteousness that he hath done he shall live.

—Ezekiel 19:21–22

The wicked are the bewitched and means anyone who thinks negatively and destructively. Life holds no grudge against any living being in the world. God is Life, and this Life Principle is moving in you now animating, sustaining, and strengthening you. If you are wondering where God is, the Life Principle in you is God. You are alive with the life of God.

Life is forever forgiving us. We must let the scales of superstition fall from our eyes and become aware of simple truths which were always known. Truth has been distorted, twisted, and prostituted beyond recognition. This is why guilt is universal. In all ages people have been told to banish this sense of guilt, and they employed various ceremonies and rituals for this purpose. In olden days they sacrificed their bullocks and doves to propitiate the gods of wrath. When storms came, crops ruined, or a great drought prevailed, the people believed the gods were angry. The jungle priest had to give the people an answer. If he did not give the people an explanation, they killed him. Therefore, the jungle priests gave answers which satisfied the superstitious imaginings of these people.

In remote parts of the world, people have sacrificed their children to appease the so-called angry gods of flood, fire, and famine. This is somewhat like paying a gangster, giving him tribute every week so he will not throw a bomb into your store in order to curry favor with him.

If you burn your hand, life forgives you, reducing the edema, giving you new skin, tissue, and cells. Life does not hold a grudge against you. If you injure your hand, cutting it severely, life forgives you. New cells build bridges over the cut. Life is always forgiving you. Life is givingness and forgiveness. If you take some bad food, life forgives you, too, and causes you to expel and regurgitate it. Life has no ill will against you.

We must learn to use the Life Principle the right way and cease going against the stream of life. When a child is born, it is Universal Life individualizing Itself and appearing in your home; rejoice! The child has no discrimination nor discernment; it has not begun to use its reason as yet; therefore it is subject to the mood of parents. Every child wants to follow its own inner inherent drives, and it thinks nothing evil about these things, but the father or mother who does not understand says, "You little brat, you are a sinner. You are a naughty boy. God is going to punish you. You are going to suffer for this." The child is baffled; he cannot reason out what is wrong as he lacks discernment. He, therefore, feels cut off from love, protection, and security for that is what the mother represents to him. He feels that his mother is angry, and he reacts perhaps by micturating at night, indicating the child wants to drown his mother in resentment. The child may also react in this way by becoming timid, weak, and inferior, showing a deep sense of rejection.

A young boy might react to a cruel tyrannical father by becoming hostile, belligerent, and resentful. He knows his father is a big man, so he suppresses his anger. His rage is suppressed and it becomes a festering sore. Later on he finds himself opposed to authority because he has been against his father all his young life. He gets in trouble with the policeman, the professor at school, and other symbols of authority. He is always fighting his father, and he does not know it because no one has ever taught him how his mind works.

The President of the United States is subject to authority. Congress has power over him. We have to live and adjust to authority. Wherever we go, there is authority. We must learn to establish control over our thoughts, feelings, and responses. We must take charge of our own minds. When we do take charge of this motley crew in our minds and say to them, "I am the master, I am going to order my thoughts around and tell them what to give attention to," we will be like an employer ordering his employees to execute his instructions.

Man must take charge of his own mind and not permit others to govern it for him. Creed, dogma, tradition, superstition, fear, and ignorance rule the mind of the average man. The average man does not own his own mind. It does not belong to him. It is often ruled over and governed by the rank superstitions of others.

We must realize that a great sense of guilt comes from what is called conscience. A great number of people think that the voice of conscience is that of God. It is not. Conscience is your inner feeling and the voice of someone else. Often it is the voice of fear, superstition, and weird concepts of God. I knew a boy who feared that he would be punished by God because he did not go to church on Sunday. This is the inner voice of superstition and false belief implanted in his subconscious by his parents or teachers. This belief on the part of the boy gave him a sense of guilt, and he felt that he must be punished.

When you were young, you were given taboos, restrictions, homilies, and a series of don'ts. You were perhaps told that you were evil, a sinner, and that God would punish you. Perhaps you were told of a lake of fire waiting for you, if you did not behave and believe in a particular creed. The minds of children are contaminated and polluted with all kinds of strange notions and false doctrines.

A young boy said to me, "If I ride my bicycle without lights, I would feel that I must be punished, that I must fall because my mother said, 'You will fall. You are going to be hurt. You are naughty. You are going to be punished.'"

What a disastrous thing to tell a child. It would be so much better to tell him that he should not ride a bicycle at night without lights. Mother and father should explain thoroughly to the boy that the instructions are for his own good, for his own self-preservation. It is much better to tell a boy that God's Love will always take care of him rather than frighten him with dreadful, hypnotic suggestions of danger.

Children should never be told that they were born in iniquity and conceived in sin. They should be taught that they are children of God, that God is their real Father, and that God is Love. They also should be taught that Love cannot do anything unloving. Of course, there is the good conscience where the boy is taught the Golden Rule, love of others, and that honesty is the best policy. When a boy is about to steal, there is that within him which tells him, "No, you shouldn't do that."

The mother and father are there to teach the child the difference between rat poison and butter, the difference between the skunk and the cat, the difference between what is right and what is wrong. The child has to go to school. He must learn manners; be indoctrinated properly. He learns what is right, true, noble, and God-like. Yet how many are taught these qualities today?

Everyone wants self-esteem, wants to feel worthy, wants to be recognized by his neighbors as honest, sincere, and good. You want your children and your wife to love you. You want the respect of the community. When a man falls short of expressing himself in doing the right thing, he feels a sense of guilt and proceeds to punish himself.

I knew a man who worked every night until about one o'clock in the morning. He paid no attention to his two boys or his wife. He was always too busy working hard. He thought people should pat him on the back because he was working so arduously and persistently past midnight every night. He had a blood pressure of over two hundred and was full of guilt. Unconsciously, he proceeded to punish himself by hard work and completely ignored his children. A normal man does not do that. He is interested in his boys, etc. He does not shut his wife out of his world.

I explained to him why he was working so arduously, "There

is something eating you inside, otherwise, you would not act that way. You are punishing yourself." He did have a sense of guilt. It was toward a brother. Then he realized what he had been doing to himself.

I explained to him that God was not punishing him. If we misused the laws of life, we would suffer accordingly. If a man puts his hand on a naked wire, he will get burned. Electricity itself is not evil. The only sin is ignorance of the law, and the only punishment is the automatic reaction of man's misuse of the law.

If a man misuses the principle of chemistry, he may blow up the office or the factory. If he strikes his hand on a board, he may cause his hand to bleed. The board is not for that purpose. Its purpose may be to lean upon or to support your feet.

This man realized that God does not condemn or punish anyone, and that all his suffering was due to the reaction of his subconscious mind and to his own negative and destructive thinking. He had cheated his brother at one time, and the brother had now passed on. Still he was full of remorse and guilt.

I asked him, "Would you do that now?"

He said, "No."

"You felt that it was the right thing to do at that time?"

His reply was, "Yes."

"But you would not do it now?"

He added, "No. I am helping others to know how to live."

I added the following comment, "You have a greater reason and understanding now. The past is dead, nothing lives but this moment. As you change this moment, you change your destiny. Forgiveness is to forgive yourself. You cannot forgive another without first forgiving yourself. Forgiveness is getting your thoughts in line with the Divine Presence and the Divine Law of Harmony. Self-condemnation is hell, forgiveness is heaven." This man was completely healed and became free.

Self-condemnation is one of the most destructive of all mental poisons sending psychic pus all over your system. It destroys your vitality, enthusiasm, energy, and may affect all the organs of your body.

If you have a glass of dirty water, you may condemn, resent, and curse it indefinitely, but you will not get clean water. However, if you continually pour clean water into the glass, you will have clean water.

A man who murdered his brother in Europe came to see me in Los Angeles some years ago. He was suffering from great mental anguish and torture believing that God must punish him. He explained that his brother was having an affair with his wife and that he shot him on the spur of the moment. This had happened about fifteen years ago. In the meantime, this man had married an American girl and had three lovely children. He was in a position where he helped many people and was a transformed man.

My explanation to him was to the point that physically and psychologically he was not the same man who shot his brother, as they say every cell of our bodies changes every year. Moreover, mentally and spiritually he was a new man. He was full of love and good will for humanity. The old man who committed the crime was dead and gone. Actually he was condemning an innocent man!

This man understood and realized that death and resurrection are constantly taking place in our lives. Man must die to that which he is before he can live to that which he wants to be. This man realized the significance of the following Truths in the Bible: *Come now, and let us reason together, saith the Lord; though your sins shall be as scarlet, they shall be as white as snow; though they be red like crimson, they shall be as wool.* ISAIAH 1:18. *And their sins and iniquities will I remember no more.* HEBREWS 10:17. *I, even I, am he that blotteth out thy transgressions for mine own sake, and will not remember thy sins.* ISAIAH 43:25. *Behold, I make all things new.* REV. 21:5. *And the Spirit of the Lord will come upon thee, and thou . . . shalt be turned into another man.* I. SAMUEL 10:6.

Let us suppose that a man misused the law of his mind for fifty years. By trial and error and study he learns how to use his mind by giving constructive imagery, life-giving patterns, and God-like ideas to his subconscious mind. This process would be analogous to pure water flowing into dirty water. By filling his mind with the Truths of God, he would be giving life-giving thoughts to his deeper mind. Then the past mistakes are changed, wiped out, obliterated, and remembered no more.

Begin with God and you end with God. Begin with Love and you end with Love. A new beginning is a new end. Begin now to use your subconscious the right way, and you will no longer experience the negations of the past because the subconscious is changed through prayer. The Healing Presence of God is within you. Let it flow through you and become a channel for His Love, Truth, and Beauty.

To teach children that they are born with the stain of original sin, because Adam and Eve sinned is ecclesiastical verbiage and out of place altogether in the modern interpretation of the Bible. Original sin really means that man has forgotten his Divine Origin and takes the commandments and superstitions of men for the Truths of God. Every child in the world is born into the race mind and all that his environment represents— that is also one of the meanings of original sin.

When you learn the laws of your mind, and your own divinity, you are no longer subject to the taboos, restrictions, false beliefs, and the corrupt indoctrination you received in your youth. If you want to cleanse your children's minds, practice the Presence of God in the home. Think God-like thoughts, then the home will be saturated with a lovely mood or atmosphere. You will see the child grow in the image and likeness of the dominant mood of the home. This is the real meaning of baptism.

Jesus said to the woman caught in adultery, "Woman, where are thine accusers? hath no man condemned thee? Neither do I condemn thee; go, and sin no more."

Truth does not condemn. When we cease accusing ourselves, we are free. God has always forgiven man, but man must forgive himself. Cease mentally stoning and flagellating yourself. Focus your attention on your ideal and with faith in God move forward in the Light.

I will restore to you the years that the locust hath eaten.

The locust represents grief or some other negative state of mind which irritates and annoys you inside. The negative emotion is called the meal of the locust.

Many people are full of guilt because they failed to visit their father or mother prior to their transition to the next dimension. Their statements are somewhat as follows: "Oh, I mistreated my mother before she passed on." "My husband died, and I was out at the time." "I did not forgive my father, and now he is dead and gone." "Etc."

The Bible gives you the answer and teaches you how to forgive yourself and others. The first thing you must realize is that there is no time or space in the Mind Principle. This very moment you can relax mentally and think of your mother whom you believe you wronged in some way. Imagine that you are talking to her, tell her how lovely and beautiful she is and how much you love her. Exalt her in your mind and realize the Presence of God is there and that His Love, Light, Truth, and Beauty are flowing through her. Realize also that she is alive with the Life of God. Live in this imaginary scene until you get the fragrant reaction which fills your soul with joy. Continue to dramatize this mental scene, and the reaction will come, and you will feel free; your mother also will be free. The action of God has taken place, your mother will forget all about the incident, and so will you. A complete healing will follow this procedure.

If you made a recording of your talk on a tape machine, you could erase it. In the same manner you can erase these psychic traumas from your subconscious mind by impressing on your subconscious the spiritual Truths of God. The new vibratory tone of your thoughts erase the old negative patterns of thought lodged in your subconscious.

A man said to me recently, "My conscience is my guide." He was writing vitriolic articles attacking a certain religious group. I explained to him the working of his deeper mind. He realized that his biases, hatreds, and superstitious patterns were planted in his subconscious mind when he was young and that his mental conditioning was the reason for his resentment, hostility, and antagonism to other religious groups.

Many people have become victims of ruthless superstition and ignorant biases. Following the voice of conscience has ruined the lives of many people. One man I knew said, "I hear a voice inside me urging me to kill my mother-in-law." The voice he heard was real enough, like the voices and scenes you hear in your dreams. The subconscious mind is always dramatizing the impressions we make upon it. It is our Book of Life which keeps a record of all our thoughts, feelings, and beliefs. I explained to him that his constant hatred and resentment of his mother-in-law was murder in his own heart and that his evil and destructive thoughts were constantly sinking down into his mind and would eventually saturate the subconscious with the idea of murder. The subconscious acts by reacting, and the law of the subconscious is one of compulsion; therefore, he would eventually commit the murder. The voices he heard were those of his own subconscious talking back to him. My explanation was the cure. He blessed and prayed for his mother-in-law; they became good friends, and she calls him "my son."

Those who put thousands of Protestants to death in the days of the Spanish Inquisition did so in the name of conscience. This conscience represented religious hatred and bigotry. Research scholars and archaeologists have definite evidence that parents in ancient Babylon stoned children to death because of some minor infraction of certain laws and rules which they promulgated.

Many people walking the streets of Los Angeles are victims of a neurotic conscience. The patterns of conscience vary with different religions, racial and social influences. You must learn to differentiate between what you call conscience and the voice of God. God always speaks in peace and never in confusion. The voice of God is always constructive, harmonious, and peaceful. The voice and intimations of the Divine are always lifeward, tending toward the life more abundant. Whenever you have an urge to go against the laws of life such as the Golden Rule, the Ten Commandments, or Paul's Love Epistle in the thirteenth chapter of Corinthians, you know very well it cannot be the voice of Truth or God.

Some time ago I talked to a young lady aged twenty-two. She was taught it was a sin to dance, to play cards, to swim, and to go out with men. She was threatened by her mother who told her she would burn eternally in hell-fire if she disobeyed her will and her religious teachings. This girl wore a black dress, black stockings. She wore no rouge, lip-stick, or any form of makeup because her mother said that these things were sinful. Her mother told her that all men were evil and that sex was of the devil, simply diabolic debauchery.

This girl was full of guilt. When she went out with young men in the office where she worked, she had a deep sense of guilt and thought that God would punish her. Several eligible young men proposed to her but she said to me, "It is wrong to marry. Sex is evil and I am evil." This was her conscience or early conditioning speaking. Actually it was not her own feeling but the voice of her mother lodged in her subconscious depths.

She came to me once weekly for about ten weeks, and I taught her the workings of the conscious and subconscious mind. I gave her my book *The Miracles of Your Mind* and also *Love Is Freedom* which deals with marriage and divorce. She studied these books carefully and systematically. This young girl realized that she had been completely brainwashed, mesmerized, and conditioned by an ignorant, superstitious, bigoted, and frustrated mother. She broke away completely from her family and started to live a wonderful life.

At my suggestion she dressed up, had her hair attended to. She took lessons in driving from a *man*, and she also took dancing lessons. She learned to swim, play cards, and had a number of dates. She began to love life. She prayed for a divine companion by claiming that Infinite Spirit would attract to her a man who harmonized with her thoroughly. This came to pass. As she left my office one Monday evening, there was a man waiting to see me and I casually introduced them, which is something I rarely do in my office. She said to me on leaving, "I saw that man in my dreams; I know we will get married," and they did. They harmonize with each other perfectly.

My experience with people of all religious persuasions is that conscience, as it is usually found, has been the curse of curses in thousands of lives. What about your conscience? Do you think it is a sin to smoke, to take a glass of wine, to dance, or to go to the movies? Do you think it is a sin to laugh and enjoy yourself? If so, you are very sick psychologically and are a victim of brainwashing. The young child is indoctrinated with father's and mother's ideas and in addition perhaps the weird and superstitious concepts of uncles and aunts, teachers and others who do not always instill and inculcate the Truths of God.

It is shocking and diabolical to inculcate into the minds of children that there is a hell-fire waiting for them if they sin, that there is a devil tempting them, that God will punish them, and that they are here to suffer. It is no wonder that the offices of psychiatrists are full of so-called religious people.

A young girl came to see me stating that she had to wash her hands about one hundred times a day and that she was always afraid of some infection. This girl was a Catholic and her husband was of the Jewish faith. They were quite happy together until she began receiving letters from her mother that she had done great evil and added religious threats plus moral condemnation. I explained to this girl that Love knows no creed, race, or sectarian group. Love transcends all creeds. Furthermore, she realized that no one could break up her marriage when Love reigned supreme. She learned to laugh at herself for being so upset. She understood why her mother wrote these foolish letters. She realized that her mother was brainwashed with religious taboos, prejudices, and strictures of all kinds, and that she was writing from the standpoint of superstition, bias, and ignorance, and not from the standpoint of God or Truth. In God there is no Greek or Jew, no bond or free, no Catholic or Protestant, Hindu or atheist. God has no religion and knows nothing about creeds, dogmas, and man-made opinions. This young lady learned to pray and imagined that she had a letter from her mother which was full of love, kindness, and good will.

I told her the story of Orage, a disciple of Ouspensky, who taught his students as follows: "Compose a letter written as from your friend to yourself which would completely satisfy you if you received it. Put into exact words what you would like your friend to write or say to you."

Every night she would embrace her mother in her imagination and radiate love, peace, and joy to her, and then she would read the imaginary letter from her mother which filled her soul with joy. She continued to do this for about three weeks every night, and at the end of that time, she received a letter from her mother apologizing for her previous letters and containing almost the exact words which she had been picturing, feeling, and rejoicing in each night.

In many parts of the world men have several wives; this is their religious custom or tradition. Our Bible teaches that love is an at—one—ment or a union of two souls seeking their way back to the heart of reality. If an American or Englishman had several wives, his conscience might destroy him because of his sense of guilt. A woman in this country would not want to be one of several wives; she would feel guilty and probably get seriously ill mentally and physically.

Howbeit in vain do they worship me, teaching for doctrines the commandments of men. For laying aside the commandment of God, ye hold the traditions of men . . .

In these few verses tersely put, we have the answer to the guilt complexes of millions of supposedly religious and intelligent people. Do the dead thoughts and doctrinal wrappings and trappings of your parents and grandparents rule and govern you, or are you controlled by God and His Spiritual Truths? Learn the great Law of Life. God is Life, and this Life seeks expression through you as beauty, harmony, joy, love, order, rhythm, and abundance. The Kingdom of God is within you. Infinite Intelligence will lead and guide you in all your ways when you turn to It and call upon It.

You can be inspired from On High by claiming that "God thinks, speaks, and acts through me now, and I feel the influx of the Holy Spirit animating and sustaining me in all my ways." Life cannot wish death. God is Love, and Love cannot wish anything unloving. God is Peace, and Peace cannot wish pain. The will of God for you is always something wonderful, magnificent, and glorious. It is something transcending your fondest dreams. Life feels Itself to be beauty, joy, peace, love, wisdom, intelligence, and harmony. It seeks to express all these qualities through you. These are the murmurings and whisperings of your heart-strings. This is the true voice of conscience which urges you to rise higher, to move to higher levels of awareness.

The Center of Divine Inspiration which inspired the illumined seers who wrote the Bible, speaks through the great poets, artists, and writers, and it is within you and can be contacted at the Divine Center in your own mind. Your conscience should be guided by the great Truths of God, the spiritual values of life by an understanding of the principles and laws of life. Get acquainted with the Indwelling Presence. *Acquaint now thyself with Him, and be at peace, therefore good shall come unto thee.*

It was the voice of conscience which caused the people two

thousand years ago to say to Jesus that he should not heal on the Sabbath. These thoughts, traditional beliefs are contrary to the laws of life and are definitely evil and destructive. Do you say to your children: "Your parents have the only truth, you must believe what we say. You must never think for yourself. You must accept our dogma." This is disastrous and utterly dicta-torial and a totalitarian attitude. It may well be the case that everything you are teaching them is a lie, and they will grow up so conditioned that when they violate any of these foolish and grotesque taboos which you gave them, they will have a guilt complex and be seized with fear, and then proceed to punish themselves.

The morals of people vary throughout the world and are of a geographical nature. These are based on the mores and tra-ditional concepts of the particular country or race. The moral standards of the various cultures are true only when they con-form to the Principle of Life which is forever seeking to express Itself through us as harmony, health, peace, joy, love, symme-try, and the life more abundant.

There are women and men who live in hatred of one another and who are hopelessly incompatible because they are afraid to get a divorce due to religious beliefs. They are full of guilt and believe that God would punish them. They are victims of early training and superstitious dogma implanted in their minds by the bigoted propensities of parents and others. They would rather live the lie than have the decency to break up the lie. They say, "Whom God hath joined together, let no man put asunder." God is Love, and if the heart is the chamber of God's Presence and if Love does not unite the two hearts of the man and woman, the marriage is a mockery, a farce, a sham, and a masquerade.

Many people are full of guilt because they accept as right that which is actually wrong. God condemns no one. God has already forgiven you. Forgive yourself. Change your thought and keep it changed. Think on whatsoever things are true, just, lovely, noble, and of good report. Think from the standpoint of the Golden Rule and the Law of Love. Would you think of disobeying the principles of chemistry, physics, mathematics, and engineering? Would you build a wheel off center? Are you believing in antiquated, dead, grotesque, ignorant superstitions and prejudices in the name of religious beliefs, or have you made a serious inquiry into the workings of your subconscious and conscious mind? The modern scientist has to conform to natural law; he cannot change it. Your religion must also conform to natural law. The result is conscience *with knowing*. The Law of Life is the law of health, happiness, peace, order, beauty, right action, and abundance. Divine Order is Heaven's First Law.

Remember ye not the former things, neither consider the things of old. ISAIAH 43:18.

Forgetting those things which are behind, and reaching forth unto those things which are before, press toward the mark for the prize. PHILIPPIANS 3:13–14. And enter into the glorious liberty of the sons of God.

2

YOUR WILL AND
GOD'S WILL

Nevertheless, not my will, but thy will be done.

Is this resignation or blind fatalism? It is not! Every man wants to experience God's will because God's will for him is always something wonderful, glorious, magnificent, and joyous.

. . . And his name shall be called Wonderful, Counselor, The Mighty God, The Everlasting Father, The Prince of Peace. ISAIAH 9:6.

The name of God means the nature of God. God is Love, and therefore God cannot wish for you anything unloving. God is Absolute Peace, and He cannot wish for you discord, chaos, and confusion. God is Life, and Life cannot wish death; that would be a contradiction of its own nature. God is Absolute Joy and cannot wish grief or sorrow. God is Absolute and Unalloyed Harmony and cannot wish sickness or disease. God is

Infinite Riches of All Kinds and cannot wish poverty; to think so would be a form of insanity.

God's will for you is something transcending your fondest dreams. The will of God, as Judge Troward, author of *Edinburgh Lectures* and other works on Mental Science, so eloquently puts it, is the tendency of God, and God being Life cannot wish anything detrimental to Itself. Life feels Itself to be Love, Joy, Peace, Beauty, and Its tendency is to express Its own nature which is the same yesterday, today, and forever. When a man says, "I am poor; I am sick; I am weak; I am tired; I am broke; etc.," he brings these conditions on himself by his negative destructive statements.

The name of God is given as I AM in the third chapter of Exodus. I AM is a nameless name. It means Existence, Being, Life, Awareness, Unconditioned Consciousness. It is the Only Presence, the Only Power, and the Cause of All. God creates all things by first imagining Himself to be these things, and then He feels Himself to be that which He imagined Himself to be— this is the way all things are made. Man creates the same way God creates, but he should follow God's pattern of harmony, health, peace, wholeness, beauty, order, symmetry, and right action. Whatever man imagines and feels to be true is brought forth in his life. This is why man should imagine only whatsoever things are lovely and of good report. Whatever man attaches to the I AM within him, he becomes. Therefore man should never say, "I am inferior; I am a failure; etc." To do so is to manifest such states.

The Life Principle as it flows through you takes the shape of the mental mold which you prepare for It. Let us take the analogy of water, which will take the shape of any vessel into which it is poured, yet it ever remains the same H_2O, regardless of the shape and size of the container. Your thoughts, imagery, and mental patterns mold, fashion, and shape your life.

You are here to grow, expand, and unfold, and if all your faculties were fully developed when you were born, you would never discover yourself. If, for example, you were compelled to love your husband or wife, you would have no free will. This is why you say, "I choose . . . . from all the women in the world to be my lawful wedded wife." You are not an automaton, you have freedom to give love or retain it. You have the capacity to choose, select, and arrive at a decision through your capacity to reason. In the beginning, man looks out at the three-dimensional world and is governed by appearances and conditions until he awakens to the fact that, through the medium of his own thought and feeling, he can control and direct his life. Gradually man awakens to the Truth that circumstances and conditions are effects and not causes. All outer conditions are subject to change. As man changes his mind he changes his body, environment, and conditions.

Thy will be done on earth as it is in Heaven.

A wonderful prayer! Realize that God's will is always being expressed through you at all times. Make a habit of affirming that God's will is being expressed in all departments of your life, making certain, of course, that you know what you mean when you say, "God's will be done."

God is Boundless Love, absolute bliss, indescribable beauty, Infinite Intelligence, absolute harmony, omnipotent, supreme, and absolute peace. There are no divisions or quarrels in the absolute. God is Infinitely Good, Perfect, and the Author only of Perfect Good. Pray aright in this way, "God's will is being made manifest in my life as harmony, perfect health, happiness, peace, joy, abundance, love, and perfect divine expression. It is wonderful!"

If you meditate on the above prayer regularly, your present environment and circumstances will magically change and be transformed into the likeness of what you are contemplating. Now, when you say, "God's will is operating in my life," it has a magnificent and beautiful significance full of spiritual precious stones. When you say, "God's plan is made manifest in my life," that, too, has a new and wonderful meaning. God's plan is God's will, and His plan can only be beauty, order, symmetry, love, health, and all the good things of life. God's plan for you could only be to express more of Himself through you moving ever onward, upward, and Godward. *Jesus said, As thou has believed, so be it done unto thee.*

It is a magnificent prayer and superb spiritual strategy to say, "God's will be done," particularly when you understand the spiritual significance of these words. If you enthrone in your mind the definite idea that God's will is operating in all your affairs, this constructive belief in your mind will govern your life and cause you to act and express yourself as you believe. Your dominant conviction dictates, governs, and controls your entire life. It is a wonderful thing to know, as Quimby expressed it, that "man is belief expressed." When you know that the Light and Love of God are guiding and governing you in all your ways, you are automatically protected from making errors in judgment, unwise decisions, and wasting your time and efforts along useless lines of endeavor.

A British pilgrim to Lourdes, who was staying with his boy in the hotel where I was said, "If it is God's will, my boy will be healed." I said to him, "God's will for the boy must, by the nature of God, be perfect health for the boy." *I am come that they*

might have life, and that they might have it more abundantly. JOHN
10:10. *Therefore I say unto you, what things soever you desire, when
ye pray, believe that ye receive them, and ye shall have them.* MARK
11:24. And notice, *whatsoever* is the word. It does not designate
anything limited. This marvelous promise of the Bible says,
*Whatsoever things you desire, believe you have received them, and you
shall have them.*

This man seemed to think that God's will for his boy must
be something unpleasant or evil. What a monstrous concept of
God! When you say, "If," it means you are full of doubt, fear,
and anxiety. There is no "if" in prayer. Cross it out! Never, never say,
"If it is God's will," or "If it is right for me." What isn't right for
you? Do you have two Gods or one? When you pray for right
action, there is only right action. If you are thinking wrong action, you have two powers, God and a devil. Begin to place the
true God back on the throne of His glory in your mind.

This father realized immediately what prayer really meant
and he said, "I now know what God's will for my boy is, and I am
going to claim it, feel it, and believe it until it becomes a part of my
consciousness. When I reach a conviction in my mind, my will or
desire becomes God's will or the conviction that 'It is done.'"

A remarkable change took place in the boy as the father
began to pray meaningfully and with deep understanding,
"God's Healing Power is made manifest in the mind and body
of my son, and God walks and talks in him."

I have heard this expression frequently, "I want it if God
wants me to have it." If you really believe that God is the Divine
Presence or Life within you and is Infinite Intelligence and All
Powerful, and is Boundless Love, why should you think that
God did not want you to have it, whether it is health, peace, joy,
true place, abundance, new home, marriage, or what not?

Many people utter another superstitious phrase, "Maybe it isn't good for me." When people use such an expression, they are living in a world of duality, of two powers. They have God and a devil, they are double-minded. Isn't happiness good for you? Surely, you must agree that God wants you to be happy. If you pray for right action, why would you begin to think of wrong action? There is only a principle of right action in the world. There is no principle of wrong action. There is a Principle of Joy, none of sadness. There is a Principle of Love, none of hatred. There is a Principle of Truth, and none of error. There is a Principle of Harmony, and none of discord.

What kind of a God would you have that did not want you to be joyous, free, radiant, and illumined? You are here to reproduce all the qualities, attributes, potencies, and aspects of God and to move from glory to glory.

And he said unto him, Son, thou are ever with me, and all that I have is thine. LUKE 15:31.

If you have a desire for healing, for true expression, for greater wisdom and spiritual understanding, or for greater wealth and expression to do the things you want to do, surely there is not a doubt in your mind but that God wants you to have all these things. If you think that God wants you to be sick or is testing you in some strange way, or if you think that God could create sickness, such a God is not worthy of your consideration and attention, and the belief is only a false, superstitious concept in your mind.

God wants you to be prosperous as well as healthy. Many people, because of false theological beliefs implanted in their subconscious minds when they were young and impressionable, believe that there is some virtue in lack and limitation. You must eradicate that false belief from your subconscious mind and realize that the Infinite Riches of God are all around you. You cannot count the sands on the seashore or the stars in the heavens above. Did you ever try to count the flowers by the wayside as you drive along the road? Everywhere you look you see a profusion of God's wealth. God's ideas are infinite, and you can have an idea now that could put a million men to work. Ideas are wealth. An invention is an idea in the mind, so is a book, a new business venture, a new real estate project. Men today are proving that they can look at a vast desert and make it rejoice and blossom as the rose. Nature is lavish, extravagant, and bountiful. Man in his greed and lust creates an artificial shortage, but there is no shortage of God's wisdom or creative ideas in the mind of man, if he will become open and receptive to the Divine Influx, which is always ready and available.

Believe that your supply is from God and that He supplies all your needs at every moment of time and point of space. The external world, economic conditions, stock market fluctuation, inflation or deflation, or opinions of man cannot touch you when you are lifted up in consciousness—that dimension of spiritual awareness, where you believe in your heart that your supply is truly and literally from God and nowhere else. The channels through which you receive your wealth are not the source, and you should not confuse the two. You should be completely free in your economic living and prospered in all your ways.

You are not glorifying God when sick, frustrated, neurotic, unhappy, and poverty stricken. You are here to dramatize, portray, and express in your life that which is true of God. To believe in a God of Love is to express love, and to believe in a God of Abundance is to express the abundant life. *According to your belief is it done unto you.* If you have a desire to write a play, write a novel, build a new house, would it not be extremely foolish for you to think that God did not want you to write the play or novel, or build the house? God is within you and your desire to express is from God. God gave you your brain, your mind, the hands to write, also the urge to achieve and express, plus the intelligence and capacity to do all these things.

Imagine saying, "If God wants me to write a play, He will let me know." This would be the quintessence of absurdity. *It is the Father within, He doeth the works.* Your idea or desire must be appropriated in consciousness and felt as true, and when it is accepted subconsciously, then the subconscious will bring it to pass. Your conscious wish or desire has now passed from mere wishing and desiring to a subconscious conviction. The law of the subconscious is one of compulsion, and the will of the subconscious comes to pass. *Not my will* (idea, desire, plan), *but Thy will be done* (my conviction or consciousness) which automatically comes to pass. Our subconscious convictions and beliefs dictate and control all our conscious actions. The subconscious is the power that moves the world.

The dictionary defines will as choice, intention, inclination, determination, tendency, and in order to make it the will of Omnipotence you must animate it, make it alive within you by enthusiasm, feeling, and animation until it becomes embodied in the subconscious mind. When man learns to choose wisely, he will choose happiness, peace, security, joy, health, abundance, and all the blessings of life. He will enthrone the spiritual values and Truths of God in his mind and busy his mind with these eternal verities until they become a part of his consciousness in the same manner as an apple becomes a part of his blood stream.

Choose Divine Guidance, Right Action, Divine Order, and Divine Success in your life. What is true of God is true of you for

God indwells you. God is always successful, whether making a star, planet, tree, or cosmos. Therefore you were born to succeed as the Infinite cannot fail. The worldly minded man who is a victim of the race mind unconsciously chooses sickness, misfortune, lack, and limitation of all kinds. He fails to realize that thoughts are things, that what he imagines, he becomes, and what he feels he attracts. If man does not do his own thinking, the newspapers, the neighbors, and the race mind will do his thinking for him, and his life will be a mess.

Choose ye this day, whom ye will serve. JOSHUA 14:15.

Choose Life, Love, Truth, and Beauty. Choose Wisdom, and you will find that all Its ways are pleasantness, and all Its paths are peace. You can misuse and misapply any law. You can misuse electricity, chemistry, or any force in nature. The good and evil you experience are the movements and actions of your own mind relative to the Life Principle, which is forever pure and perfect in Itself.

A man came to see me some time ago. He was an alcoholic and said that if he took one drink he should be compelled to keep on drinking until he fell unconscious on the floor. In other words, he had lost control and was compelled by the law of his subconscious mind to drink. His story was a familiar one. His wife divorced him because of his infidelity. He resented her action and hated her because she refused to take him back. Then he turned to drink to relieve the psychic pain in the same way you might take aspirin for a headache. He repeated this act over and over again, and each time he took a drink to bolster up his spirits, he was rejecting the Power of God within him and suggesting weakness and inferiority to his subconscious mind.

Habits are formed by repeating certain thought patterns or

actions over and over again until they establish patterns in the subconscious mind, where they grow until they reach the point of saturation. He now has a psychic bartender established in his subconscious mind that reminds him repeatedly, "You need a drink." When he takes one, he is off to the races; in other words, he has lost control. His wish or conscious will is not to drink, but the will of the subconscious now takes over and says, "You must drink." He has lost control. His choice to drink, which he repeated over and over again until it became an established habit pattern, is now in control.

He can reverse the pattern and be free by the use of the same law which made him a compulsive drinker. Regularly and systematically he contemplates freedom and peace of mind, claiming that his food and drink are God's ideas, which constantly unfold within him, bringing him harmony, health, and peace. He runs a movie in his mind several times daily by imagining himself free, happy, and joyous. He pictures himself doing what he longs to do and hears a friend congratulate him on his freedom and sobriety. Whenever he is tempted, he flashes the movie in his mind and knows that the Power of the Almighty is flowing through his mental movie, and that by a process of mental and spiritual osmosis the mental image is sinking down into his subconscious, where it is being developed in the dark room of his mind. Impressions are made in the subconscious by repetition, faith, and expectancy, and as he continues faithfully imagining his freedom and peace of mind, the day breaks and the shadows flee away. His will (desire for complete freedom from the destructive habit) has become God's will (his deep abiding conviction lodged in the subconscious mind), and he is compelled to express freedom, for the Law of the subconscious is compulsion. The law which held him in bondage is the same law which freed him, enabling him to enter into the glorious liberty of the sons of God.

Thy will be done on earth as it is in Heaven is a wonderful prayer as you now realize. *Heaven* means your own mind or mental and spiritual awareness. What you feel as true in the heavens of your own mind, you shall experience on earth or the objective plane (body, world, environment, circumstances).

Your *will* is your capacity to define your objectives, to choose your goal, ideal, or plan. Live with it mentally by loving it, nursing it, giving it your attention and whole-souled devotion. Finally, it becomes jelled within you and *your will has become God's will,* or the joy of the answered prayer. It is wonderful!

3

THE LOVE THAT CASTS OUT FEAR

We are told in the Book of Proverbs that *The fear of the Lord is the beginning of wisdom.*

When you learn the laws of electricity, you are very careful how you apply them because you know the consequences. You know if you put your hand on a naked wire or cause a short circuit what will happen. You learn the theories about insulation and conductivity resulting in a healthy respect and reverence for these laws, and you will follow the nature of the principles.

Likewise, when you learn the principles of chemistry, you have a very healthy respect for the combination of chemicals, their atomic weight, etc., because you also know the disastrous consequences of mixing things together when you do not know the results. For instance, if you mix nitric acid and glycerine together, you will have a powerful explosive.

Fear is a reverence, a healthy respect. You have a healthy respect for the law when you learn the consequences of misusing it. You have a healthy respect for fire, so you do not put your finger into it. Similarly, when men know that their mind is a principle, like the principle of chemistry and physics, they have a very healthy respect for the subconscious mind. They learn that they can use it two ways.

A principle is the way a thing works. We realize that God also is principle. Principle does not change. God is Boundless Love, Infinite Intelligence, and has all the elements of personality. Nevertheless, God works by Law; therefore, we have to work by Law. This Law never changes.

Water runs down hill. It expands when frozen, taking the shape of any vessel into which it is poured. These, and many other characteristics, determine the principle by which water operates. Therefore, we learn that it runs down hill. Your mind operates in the same way. If you think good, good follows. If you think evil, evil follows. If you say, "God can heal me now, God can help me out of this situation," your words betray you. You should say and know, "God is helping and solving my problem now." You would never make the former statement if you knew the way God works.

Man sometimes uses his mind to oppose his good. He has a vivid imagination of things that he does not want. Oftentimes man is looking at obstacles, delays, and difficulties in his mind and he is vividly picturing these things. Then he turns around and says, "God can help me out of this problem." It does not work that way.

Pray this way, "God is helping me now, for God is the solution." Creative Intelligence is the Way, the Truth, and the Life.

If you say to me, "God can heal me," what are you saying?

You are saying, "I am now identified with sickness, pains, and aches," and the pain goes on for years. Instead say, "God is healing me now, this very moment. The Creative Intelligence which made me is healing me now."

You must have a healthy respect for the Law and realize that if you say, "I can't do this," you have faith in failure. Faith is an attitude of mind. Faith is the use you make of your mind. Many people have faith in a devil, that he is going to tempt them and bring harm to them. Others have faith in a hell and in a lake of fire that is waiting for them. This is an attitude of mind, an expectancy, a belief of the mind. How can a man believe in a good future if he fears death, torture, and torment? He cannot. If a man thinks that God is cruel, that God is punishing him, and God has created a hell waiting for him because he has sinned or erred (when he could not help himself anyway, since he has to err for that is the way he grows), that man cannot love God, or the Good. It is impossible because he is fearing the future and after-life. He has a God of fear, but God is a God of Love. Such a man cannot banish fear out of his mind, since he must come back to the unity of the One Power.

Basil King, who wrote *Conquest of Fear*, tells that he was going blind. He took a trip to France. He was a young man, depressed, dejected, feared the future, blindness, old age, and all the rest of it. He said he recalled something that a teacher said years previously: "The Life Principle is indestructible, invulnerable, and eternal. It always brings about the expedient which is an answer to the particular need of any man." He used to think that nature was cruel and raw, and that evil abounded in the world. He had strange concepts of God.

This man said a woman asked him, "What do you think God is?"

He replied in his naïveté, simplicity, and immaturity, "There are three supernal beings in the sky and three thrones." She laughed at him.

"I knew," he said, "that moment, I had a wrong concept." Then he began to think the Life Principle within him had overcome every obstacle in the world, whether it was a flood, volcanic eruption, war and destruction of all kinds. The Life Principle goes on invulnerable, eternal. Nothing can destroy it. The Life Principle gives fur to the animals in the North. In the South, in the Temperate Zone, it gives them hair, covers others with shells to preserve them. Others are given a poisonous fluid which they emit when attacked. It takes care of all forms of life, such as those that came out of the sea. It gave them legs, made them stand upright, etc., and gave some wings to fly in the air. Always, the Life Principle met the particular need. When primitive man met the tiger, he was frozen with fear. Gradually there came to his aid the dawn of reason, imagination, and memory. (There was a time when man had no memory). Later, man began to think, and this Power within him responded to his thought.

Basil King, in meditating and musing on the Power within, discovered that the Natural Principle, or Life, or Nature is not cruel, but when he combined or united with this Principle in thought, mighty forces came to his aid. He no longer believed in three supernal beings sitting on a throne, but he perceived that God was the Life Principle in him. The average man has pigeon-holed God and brings him out on Sundays, holidays, in cases of death, birth, and marriage, but the rest of the time He is put away in a corner. Some men are afraid to use the term "God." Others look askance when God is mentioned as they begin to think of God in terms of religious connotations because each has a different concept of God, like the blind men of old describing an elephant.

Basil King discarded all the sentimental, preternatural connotations associated with the name of God, and began to realize that God was the Life Principle within him, operating through him, and when he united with this Presence, mighty forces came to his aid. He found God the answer to every problem. He said, "This realization was the beginning of the process of casting out fear which was blinding me and paralyzing me." No man can conquer fear until he comes back to the fact that there is only One Power.

If you want to conquer fear, you have to come back to the Truth that there is One Power, indivisible, and Its source is Love. It has no opposition. It is the Life Principle that has overcome every opposition in this world and goes on conquering and to conquer. There is nothing to oppose It, for It is omnipotent.

Realize you are one with this God Power. You are aligned with It now, and mighty forces will come to your aid. You are one with God, with life, and with all things. *Thou shalt compass me about with songs of deliverance. I will fear no evil for Thou art with me. Thy rod and Thy staff, they comfort me.*

When we are fearful or indulge in negative thoughts, we are vibrating at a very low level. When you meditate on a psalm and say, *The Lord is my shepherd, I shall not want,* or "The Presence of God is right here where I am," or "I will fear no evil for God is with me," or "I dwell in the Secret Place of the Most High," and "God is guiding me now, the Presence of God is with me," you are thinking spiritually.

These spiritual thoughts are of a very high frequency and are of a very high vibration. What happens to the evil negative thoughts of fear, destruction, and disaster? These are destroyed and neutralized. You are now vibrating at a higher level. You are vibrating at a spiritual frequency, and just like you put your finger on a tuning fork, that is the end of the negative vibration. That is the end of the evil because evil is a false belief about God and His Infinite Goodness.

When we are full of fear, we have greater faith in evil than in God; this is shocking, but it is true. Fear is God upside down. Fear is faith in the wrong thing. You have faith that the sun will rise in the morning. You have faith that you can drive your car. You have faith that you will get an answer to your prayer when you pray for guidance, but many people have faith in the wrong thing. There are people who are looking forward to misfortune. There are people working in offices who are afraid of their jobs, afraid they are going to lose their money, and of what is going to happen to them when they grow old, instead of realizing, "I am always in my true place, for God is my employer. I am working for Him and I live forever."

A pilot said to me, "I am never afraid when I navigate a plane, whether I go north, south, east, or west, for I am a pilot for God. I am flying for Him, and I am as safe in the sky as on the earth. Nothing can happen to me. It is impossible."

That man has faith in the Goodness of God, in the right action of God, in the guidance of God. He has faith in the Eternal Principle, and in the immutable, changeless Laws of God. Faith is your attitude of mind, what you expect, what you are focusing on, the things that you are vividly imagining.

Some people are afraid of old age, some are afraid of death, but that which they are afraid of does not exist. You are alive; you are alive with the Life of God. You are alive now. God is Life Eternal. Because God lives, you live. God cannot die; therefore, you cannot die.

Realize God is your employer. He is always taking care of you, loves you, and you are always in your true place. When someone makes negative statements about you, begin to dwell on the above Truths, and you will always be taken care of. "I will fear no evil for Thou art with me. Thy rod and Thy staff, they comfort me." "Perfect Love casteth out fear, for fear has a torment. He that feareth is not made perfect in love."

Dr. Brunt of Capetown, South Africa, told me about a frail woman about eighty years of age. A little granddaughter came to live with her. Her parents were killed out in the jungle somewhere. She said this woman loved this little child, and would go through fire and water for her because that is what you do when you are in love. There was a poisonous snake about to hypnotize the child (for that is what a snake does, it hypnotizes you), and this frail woman seized some branches of a tree and killed the snake. Her fear of the snake was swallowed up in victory and triumph. Love casts out fear. She had that all-embracing mood of love to save that child at all costs which cast out her fear.

Love is always outgoing. It is an emanation. Fear is turning within in morbid introspection, believing someone is going to hurt you or that evil spirits can possess you. When any person believes in external powers, he denies the one God. God is within you, and moves as a Unity. It is the Life Principle within you forever seeking to express Itself as Love, Peace, Bliss, Joy, and Right Action.

When we are fearful, we are very selfish in the wrong way. Fear is a morbid introspection. Cease building a wall around yourself saying, "I am going to get hurt. These people are against me. God is against me." Many people are over-concerned with themselves. To say, "I won't go anywhere, I might get hurt" is morbid selfishness.

Love is always outgoing. Love must have an object. You can fall in love with music, art, a great project, etc. You can fall deeply in love with the Truths of the Bible. You can become absorbed and engrossed in science and many other things.

Einstein loved the principle of mathematics. He said, "It reveals to me all its secrets." That is what love does. You can fall in love with astronomy, and it will reveal to you all its secrets.

You can readily see, therefore, what love is. It is an outgoing. It must have an object. How much do you want what you want? Do you want to leave your old self with your false concepts and old ideas? Are you willing to get new ideas, new imagery, new viewpoints? Are you open and receptive? Do you want good digestion? If you do, you must give up resentment. You must give up your grudges and peeves. To be made whole, release your fears and hates. You have to leave Los Angeles to go to Denver. Likewise, you have to leave your jealousies, hates, plus your false concepts of God in order to enter into the joy of health and happiness.

How much do you want what you want to be? How much do you love this new ideal? Emerson said, "Do the thing you are afraid to do, and the death of fear is certain." By example, if you are afraid to talk before an audience, get up and talk. After a while you will overcome that fear. Do it again, again, and again.

If you are afraid to swim, look at the water and say, "I am going to conquer you. God is love, and I am in charge of my own thoughts, my own feelings, and my own responses." You are a king; you are the master. Are the thoughts, ideas, and images in your mind going to master you, or are you going to master them? Are you the employer? Yes, you are. You can order your thoughts around and tell them to give attention to your ideal and the Truths of God which were always true.

Focus your attention on that which is good, that which is true, that which heals and blesses you. You can determine your own response to whatever happens, to the headlines in the newspapers, and to what people say. You are the master. You are a king in charge of your mind, responses, thoughts, ideas, and imagery. You are the absolute master. You are the God over your own realm. "I will make you God, to Pharaoh."

You mold and fashion your own destiny. There are no external forces. You are the absolute monarch over your own world, and you are in complete charge. You can enter into the glorious liberty of the sons of God, but you must know how. Where is the fear if you are a god in your own world, which you are?

The thing man fears does not exist. It exists only as a thought in his mind. An actor was saying to himself, "I am going to fail. I am going to strike the wrong note. I am going to say the wrong thing." His vivid imagination was on failure. He had to fall in love with a new concept of himself, and he became the great artist that he now is. He fell in love with the new concept, the new estimate, the new blueprint of himself. Fear means you are wrapped up in your own shortcomings and thinking too much about your inadequacies.

Think of the Greatness within you. All fear is based upon the fact that you are thinking from the standpoint of inferiority, weakness, and inadequacy, instead of thinking from the standpoint of the Infinite God within you which is the Power that moves in the world. When you are presented with an assignment, realize, "I do this through the Power of God which moves through me." Tremendous powers will come in response to that attitude. "Act as though I am, and I will be." Act as though you believe that this Power is here, and that It will come to your aid.

This actor had to fall in love with a new estimate of himself. Love is a fascination. You become entranced, fascinated, and absorbed; moreover, you become emotionally involved because love is an emotional attachment. Therefore, you become attached to the ideals and goals of life. You can fall in love with your goal, and all fear will go away. Fall in love with something now.

Fall in love with a nobler, sweeter, grander concept of yourself. Fall in love with the Greater Self within you. Dwell on Its tremendous potentialities and qualities. Let God's Power captivate your imagination. Let it thrill you through and through, for love causes you to unite with your ideal. You don't try to hold the ideal; it holds you entranced. That is love; then all fear goes away. Fear is swallowed up in love. Love and fear cannot dwell together. The reason people hate and are jealous is that they have a false concept of God. If anyone thinks that there is a lake of fire, and that God is judging him, or is punishing him, or that the stars are governing him, I want to say frankly, categorically, and incisively, such a concept is atheistic. It is the denial of the Presence, the Power, the Omnipotence, and the Love of God.

We know there is no power but God, and there are no divisions or quarrels in It; therefore, let us align ourselves with God. We do not try to change God. God is constant; God is invariable. Man is variable and inconstant. The Truths of God remain the same yesterday, today, and forever. "Who shall hurt you if you are a follower of that which is good?" "No evil shall befall the just." "If God be for you, who can be against you?" "There is no fear in love. Perfect love casteth out fear."

You are told over and over again in Genesis that *The Lord giveth the increase*, and whatever you give attention to, negative or positive, your subconscious mind magnifies and multiplies it beyond your imagination. Therefore, if you dwell on loss, loss comes to you. Perhaps it comes in loss of prestige, health, finances, family, or in business. And if you continue with this negative pattern, of course, what you fear most comes upon you. If your faith is in loss, that is inverted faith, isn't it? Do not have faith in the gloomy, morbid aspect of things instead, have faith in the real Truths of God.

Isn't it far more interesting, fascinating, alluring, and captivating to contemplate the things which are good? Eat the blessed bread of the Blessed God by imagining perfect health and happiness, and by contemplating the Truths of God which are also true of you. Practice the Love that casts out fear.

Fall in love. Love is a principle of life. When fear comes, move to the opposite. Fear is a signal to do something. When you are cold, you build a fire; therefore, do not stay frozen at this end of the pendulum. Affirm, "God is here. God is with me now." Realize His Presence, His rod—the Power, His staff—your authority, to wield this Power. It is right there with you.

A girl taking an examination in school said that her knees were shaking with fear. She decided to overcome the fear and said to herself, "The Lord is my shepherd. God is right here. God is my peace. The Peace of God flows through me. The Love of God is here, and there is right action. I am at peace. The poise and the harmony of God are here." She moved to the opposite. That is the Law of Substitution. Begin to think of the Eternal Verities. Impress them on your mind. You do it with feeling and with understanding; then the fear goes away. You have supplanted it; it is the Law of Substitution.

Probably you read about the soldier in the Korean War. He said bullets were falling all around him, and he was all alone. He was shaking with fright, and all he could remember were a few passages from the Psalms. *Under His wings shall I rest*, and *The Lord is my light and my salvation. The Lord is the strength of my life, of whom shall I be afraid?* As he dwelt on these Truths he said, "Faith and an inner sense of peace and poise came to me." He found his way to safety and back to his company. Had he remained frozen at that point of fear, he would have been doomed, paralyzed, and unable to flee; but he moved to the opposite.

When fear comes, it is the Divine Self in you telling you there is something wonderful waiting to come into your experience. It means the end of the old condition, and the birth of the new.

All parents should find out what their children are being taught, because they must not permit teachers to brainwash, mesmerize, and hypnotize their children with devils, demons, and falsehoods which bedevil them. They should be taught about a God of Love. They should be instructed to release the Imprisoned Splendor, that they are children of God, that God never deserts His creation, that He cares for them and loves them, that He is the Life Principle within them, and that God loves to manifest Himself through all men. That is why you have Divine impulses and the reason why you want to conquer, explore, sing, and dance, because it is God seeking to express beauty, harmony, rhythm, and wisdom through you.

Fear thoughts, worry thoughts, negative thoughts, thoughts of war, etc., will not hurt you unless you entertain them for a long period of time, and except you emotionalize them deeply; otherwise, they will not hurt you in the slightest. They are potential trouble for you, but they are not actualized. Remember that whatever idea you emotionalize becomes impressed in your subconscious, and the subconscious brings it to pass.

Wives sit at home and fear that they are going to lose their husbands. Husbands are afraid they are going to lose their wives. Mothers are afraid they are going to lose their sons, their jobs, and everything else under the sun. All these things do not exist. They are morbid pictures in the mind. There is no law on earth which compels people to think of these negative things. This negative imagining is a distorted, twisted, diabolical perversion of their God-given faculty of imagination.

Why should any mother in the world think evil of her own son? Why should she think because he is late getting home that he has been run over by a truck, that he is in the hospital being operated on, that he has fallen into a pool? Why not surround him with the Presence of God and say, "Where he is, God is, and God's Love surrounds him. Where God is, there is no accident or death; there is only Love, and the whole Armor of God is where he is." Nothing can ever happen to that child because his mother loved him.

Prayer is a realization of the Presence of God where the person is, and that is the Presence of Harmony, Peace, Love, Bliss, and Joy. You do not pray for protection, for if you do, you have a God of fear. I do not pray that a person is protected because if I do, it means that I have another power opposing God. I realize the Divine Presence is where the person is, and realize the Love of God is there.

If a man will sit down frequently and go back to the simple Truths that God is guiding him, that there is right action in his life, and that the Love of God is flowing through him, then the Wisdom of God will reveal to him what to do. The Healing Presence of God will be released in his body, and Infinite Intelligence will give him all the ideas necessary to handle the problems of the day. This is resting in God. He is asking for guidance and direction, and when he communes with the Divine Presence, Mighty Forces come to his aid. Man will no longer be anxious or disturbed when he thinks from the standpoint of the Infinite One, the Power that moves the world. Cease thinking from the superimposed standpoint of fear, ignorance, doubt, anxiety, and false concepts.

The answer to all fear is to realize that God is, that He is right where you are, that there is no power to challenge God, that one with God is a majority, and if God be for you, who can be against you? No one!

Realize that there are no enemies outside, that the universe is friendly, that God is friendly. When you are friendly with God and when you love the Source which created you, and when you are grateful, you can hate no man. Fall in love with the Truths of God, and you will find that the whole universe responds to you. Come back to the simple Truth which an ancient mystic discovered in silent meditation: "Let nothing disturb you. Everything in this world passes away, but God. God alone is sufficient."

4

REMOVING MENTAL STUMBLING BLOCKS

The solution lies within the problem. The answer is in every question. If you are presented with a difficult situation, and you cannot see your way clear, the best procedure is to assume that Infinite Intelligence which knows all and sees all has the answer and is revealing it to you now. Your new mental attitude that Creative Intelligence is bringing about a happy solution will enable you to find the answer. When you begin—God begins. Rest assured that such an attitude will bring order, plan, and meaning to all your undertakings.

The Bible says, *Behold I send an Angel before thee, to keep thee in the way, and to bring thee into the place which I have prepared.* EXODUS 23:20. This means that your mood of faith and confidence in an Almighty Power moving on your behalf goes before you to make straight, joyous, and perfect your way.

I will lift up mine eyes unto the hills, from whence cometh my help.

PSALMS 121:1. Cease whining, crying, complaining, and moaning; this attitude will only add to your misery, suffering, and lack. Instead, envision your good, the way that you want things to be. Rehearse your knowledge about the Great Truths of Life. Rise up mentally above the hardships and difficulties and think of God and His Wisdom. Then you will generate a tremendous liberating, healing force which will inspire you, open doors, reveal new ways, plans, and supply you with all your needs for the accomplishment of your goals.

You can change your whole life, if you really want to. You must give up resentment and ill will in order to have good digestion and perfect health. You must give up the lesser for the greater if you want to advance and move forward in life.

I knew a young lady who had a beautiful singing voice, but she was constantly demeaning, demoting, and criticizing herself by saying, "I do not have a chance. I am too old. I do not know the right people."

She had to cease condemning herself in order to get what she wanted. She decided to fall in love with a new concept of herself. She imagined that she was singing before an audience and she became entranced, fascinated, and absorbed in the joy of it all. A new door of expression opened for her because she gave up her old way of thinking and affirmed the Truth about herself.

How much do you really want to be a new person? Do you really want to change conditions, experiences, and your whole personality? The first requirement is that you must come to a clear-cut, definite decision in your mind that you are going to transform your life. You must desire to change with all your heart and cease being a propaganda machine idly repeating all the old stereotyped concepts, ideas, and beliefs implanted in your subconscious mind since birth.

A woman wrote me to the effect that she was about to divorce her husband because he was so tyrannical in the home and that her children were terrified of him. In talking to him, I discovered that he was the victim of long repressed fears. Moreover, his father was unduly harsh and strict with him. He resented his father very much even though the latter had long since passed on to the next dimension of life.

He understood my diagnosis which was that I believed he was unconsciously trying to retaliate with his own father by his despotic, tyrannical attitude toward his own children. The man had to desire to change himself in order to save his marriage.

He released his father through prayer by wishing for him peace, and all the blessings of life. He continued in this manner until all the roots of hatred were withered. He adopted a pattern of prayer by meditating at three specific periods—morning, afternoon, and evening. Finally, he discovered that prayer was a good habit. He changed his thoughts and kept them changed.. As a result, his home is peaceful and happy, and his children love him. It is possible to unwind that tangled skein and get at the significant core.

A husband started divorce proceedings against his wife. His main complaint was that she was too extravagant. In talking to her, I discovered that she had never received any appreciation, understanding, or approbation from her husband. She felt very insecure and was actually trying to purchase with money the deep inner sense of security which she had always lacked. They decided to become real partners. He shared a complete knowledge of his business assets with her and showed her that she was well provided for in case something should happen to him. They began to pray together every night for harmony, health, peace, God's guidance, right action, and all their difficulties were dissolved in the light of God's Love.

Let God's Love come into your thoughts, words, and actions, and your whole world will magically melt in the image and likeness of your inner contemplation. You will sometimes find that the seeming problems of gargantuan proportions can be reduced to a size so infinitesimal that it seems laughable.

There are alcoholics who do not want a healing; they do not want to give up their mental stumbling blocks, such as grudges, peeves, self-condemnation, resentments, and ill will. When an alcoholic admits to the fact that he is an alcoholic and has a strong, healthy desire for freedom and peace of mind, he is fifty-one percent healed. As he envisions his freedom state, his advancement, and enlargement in the right way, the Power of the Almighty will back him up; then the shakes and the cravings are automatically eliminated for the joy that is set before him.

All of us should begin to remove the old, accepted viewpoints, opinions, and false beliefs implanted in our minds when we were young and impressionable. The average man thinks and expresses the thoughts of dead men; the dead past seems to rule in the minds of millions of people. I talk to men who have not had a new idea or a new viewpoint in fifty years.

Are you a victim of propaganda, or do you think for yourself? A woman told me that she knows exactly how her husband is going to respond to headlines in the paper, to columnists, to certain politicians, and she can even repeat almost word for word his reactions to religious subjects. He is like the children in Red China who are conditioned to think, speak, act, and react according to a prescribed pattern. These children become like a phonograph which reproduces whatever is on the record. The recording machine is the subconscious mind which faithfully reproduces whatever is impressed upon it.

You are not born to be an automaton. You should think for yourself. Cease letting others think and speak in you and for you. Refuse to let others despoil and pollute your mind with thoughts of fear, sickness, and misfortune. If you have a ready ear and listen to the prejudices and fears of other people, you may contaminate yourself with the same.

The following is an instance where the "dead" spoke and acted through a young father. He was about to divorce his wife because she did not make the children kneel down and pray every night before retiring. His mental block was that he happened to be the son of an overly fastidious city-bred mother who was also somewhat of a religious fanatic. She had insisted on his kneeling down and repeating by rote certain prescribed prayers every night prior to sleep. As a boy he had resented this bedtime procedure and had repressed into his subconscious mind a rebellion against his mother's "punishment."

Psychologically speaking, this young father was trying to get even with his mother by imposing on his two boys the same religious ritual which he as a young boy was compelled to follow. His wife's custom was to teach the two boys a few simple prayers when they were in bed, emphasizing that God was a God of Love and that He would watch over them like a loving father.

I explained to the young father the reason for his resentment toward his wife, pointing out and elucidating on the facts that she had unwittingly frustrated his desire for revenge, thereby incurring his hostile feelings which were projected on her. He realized that the mental block to marital happiness was within himself, consequently he willingly accepted the interpretation.

Some years ago Lord Northcliffe who took over the London Times told about a man who came to the Times Building every Saturday afternoon, entered a certain room which was a bedroom, and remained there until the following Monday morning. Lord Northcliffe questioned the man and asked why he was there. He said that he brought twenty-five pounds of gold for the week-end in case the bank needed it. The amazing fact is that when Lord Northcliffe phoned the bank, they said that other men with the bag of gold had been occupying that room on week-ends for about one hundred years.

The reason for all this was due to an order issued by the owner of the Times during the battle of Waterloo, 1815, which happened to be on a Sunday. At that time the newspaper editor wanted to send men to cover the story and he could not raise sufficient money to cover the expedition. The following day he made an arrangement with a London Bank to send one thousand pounds in gold regularly to the Times Building when the bank closed on Saturday noon. This is an example of a thought of a dead man governing a big banking institution for one hundred years resulting in waste of time, money, and effort.

Are you repeating the same old patterns of thoughts, going through the same mental movements and reactions as you did thirty or forty years ago? Have you asked yourself about your prejudices, fears, biases, and jealousies? Why are they in your mind? Why have you not consulted someone about your abnormal fears? If you did, you would discover that they were a conglomeration of sinister shadows in your mind, and there is no power in a shadow.

Do you say that you have a personal saviour and that you

are saved by the blood of the lamb? Where did this weird concept come from? You should check into your religious beliefs and find out their source and origin. Make a definite decision now and that is: Believe nothing that you do not understand. Learn about your subconscious mind and the power of your own thought, and you will discover that the Saving Principle is within yourself.

You do not ride a mule to go to San Francisco like some of your grandfathers did; neither do you send a message to Chicago by pony express. In the same way, you should not permit the dead, superstitious, ignorant beliefs of antecedents to govern, rule, and manipulate your mind. There are many people who think that by the repetition of an incantation their circumstances can be changed without changing their mentality; consequently they are doomed to disappointment.

A businessman complained to me that he could not keep employees; therefore he had a constant turnover. I discovered that he had an atrociously bad temper which had driven all his clerks away. He realized that the stumbling block was within himself and he decided to change his thoughts and keep them changed.

He prayed that Infinite Intelligence would attract to him employees who would appreciate and love the work, and also feel that they were adequately compensated. He adopted a pattern of prayer whereby he prayed for the peace, prosperity, and happiness of each employee. He began to radiate love and good will to all his customers, his wife, and his children. He made a habit of this, for prayer is a habit. This man has no more trouble with his employees and close business associates.

A man wrote me saying that he had been praying for prosperity in his business for two years, but he had not achieved any results. He had had some glimmerings of spiritual truth, but his attitude of mind of deep-seated resentment toward a business associate who was very prosperous financially automatically and necessarily expressed itself in financial difficulties, sickness, and frustration.

I asked him how much he really wanted what he wanted. Did he desire it enough to give up his hostile attitude? There is no transaction without an exchange. He began to see that he could not attract wealth by condemning what he was praying for and resenting the affluence of his competitor. Frankly I inquired, "Do you prefer resentment and jealousy to prosperity and peace of mind?" Seeing the light, he began to pray for greater success and prosperity for his competitor. Prayer always prospers.

The stumbling block to our health, happiness, and achievement is always in our own mind, and spiritual understanding will cause our circumstances to improve in every respect. Per contra, a want of true spiritual understanding expresses itself in all sorts of difficulties in our life.

If there seems to be an undue delay in getting an answer to your prayer, it may be that the difficulty is deep-seated in your subconscious mind, requiring more prayer work; or you are not praying in the right way. In this case, ask Infinite Intelligence to reveal to you what you need to know.

When a man says that he must have a demonstration by Monday or Tuesday of next week, otherwise the judge will rule against him, or that he will lose his business unless there is an immediate answer, he must remember that God never fails, God is never late, and God is independent of time and space.

Time does not really matter, for prayer gets results irrespective of what the court said on a certain day. You trust God to put everything right regardless of what happened last Monday or Tuesday. You continue knowing that prayer always wins out irrespective and regardless of what may have happened.

"Great peace have they who love thy law and nothing shall offend them." As you love the law that your thought is creative and that the Spirit flows through the patterns of your thought is creative imagery, you will move away from all morbid introspection and negative concepts. When the impulse to despondency comes, it will stimulate you to think of true goals and ideals whereby you give your energy to your desires, aspirations, and ambitions rather than to conditions and circumstances.

Love your ideal until you are absorbed and engrossed in it. Let the old and worthless thoughts die. Love the new, the appealing, and elevating patterns of life. The outside world may argue with the inside world of your dreams and ideals. Remember the outside is effect, not cause. Be sure to see to it that the energy, vitality, and power of your belief run with the ideal you seek. Then you are on the way to spiritual maturity. In every adversity is the seed of opportunity.

Emerson said, "Whilst man sits on the cushion of advantages, he goes to sleep. When he is pushed, tormented, defeated, and harassed, he has a chance to learn something. He has been put on his wits, on his manhood. He has gained facts, learned of his ignorance, and is cured of his insanity of conceit."

Stand up to your problems, decide now with equanimity and faith in God to solve them. The door will open, and the way will be shown you.

I would like to mention an experience many seem to have. They start some desirable project, or they set out to accomplish an assignment for an employer, and they find that they are unable to complete it. They say something happens at the last minute, that the man who was to sign dropped dead, or he changed his mind at the eleventh hour. An actress said to me recently that everything went smoothly until she was called to sign the contract, and the producer had a heart attack one half hour previously, so the contract was postponed. Others complain that the sale falls through the moment they are about to sign.

The delay and block is in our own mind. What we fear, we attract. What we expect, we experience. Break the so-called jinx this way: Affirm boldly, "I and my Father are one. God thinks, speaks, and acts through me. There is only One Power, and that Power moves as a unit. No person, place, or thing can interfere with God's work, and my work is God's work, for God works through me. In Him I live, move, and have my being. In me God lives, moves, and expresses Himself fully. God's work cannot be delayed. God is always successful and completes all His undertakings. What is true of God is true of me. I bring all my undertakings to divine fulfillment and fruition in Divine Order through Divine Love."

You must want what you want with sufficient zeal and enthusiasm to take the trouble to learn how to think clearly, lucidly, and spiritually, since thought is the only cause.

Tune in with God, and you will rise triumphantly over all problems for, "He never faileth."

"I bore you on eagles' wings, and brought you unto myself."

5

TO BE, TO DO, AND TO HAVE

Whatsoever ye shall ask in my name, that I will do.

To be, to do, and to have—these are God's gifts to you. God is seeking to express Himself through you as your desire. Desire is the gift of God. As Browning said, "'Tis thou, God, who giveth, 'tis I who receive." Desire pushes man. It is the goad of action. It is behind all progress. Desire for health, happiness, true place, abundance, and security—all these are messengers of God, saying to each one of us, "Come on up higher!"

Desire is behind all progress. It is the push of the Life Principle. Desire causes us to jump out of the way of an oncoming bus. We do this because we have a basic desire to preserve our life. The farmer plants seed due to his desire to attain food for himself and his family. Man builds airplanes and space ships, due to his desire to collapse time and space and explore the world. Desire is an angel of God telling us of something which, if accepted by us, will make our life fuller and happier. The greater the expected benefit from the desire, the stronger is our desire. Where there is no expected benefit, gain, or advancement accruing, there is no desire; consequently, no action is found.

Failure to realize our desires to be, to do, and to have over a long period of time result in frustration and unhappiness. You are here to choose happiness, peace, prosperity, and all the blessings of Heaven. Your desire enables you to say, "This is good, therefore I choose it; however this is negative, so I reject it." All choice implies the perception of something preferable over what is rejected.

The idea which some schools of thought have of annihilating and suppressing desire is disastrous in its consequences. If man succeeded in this, good and evil would be alike to him, for nothing has any power to raise any desire in him. He would become dead to all feeling and to all motive of action. Your desire means you choose one thing in preference to another. Where desire is extinguished, no such capacity to choose can exist.

Troward, author of many mental and spiritual textbooks, points out that Indian devotees, who, in pursuance of their resolve to crush out all desire, both for good and evil alike, become attenuated human forms, hopeless wrecks of what were once living men. Troward points out that extinction of desire means apathy, no feeling, and no action. Desire is the cause of all feeling and action, and is the moving principle of the universe. Desire is the creative power and must be channeled and directed wisely. Desire and its fulfillment take place in your own mind.

There are no evil desires in the true sense. You may misdirect or misinterpret the desire which wells up within you. For example, if you are poor, you desire wealth. If you are sick, you desire health. If you are in prison, you want freedom. You may desire love, companionship, or perhaps true place. The man who desires wealth may, in his ignorance, fulfill his urge or desire by killing a banker or robbing a store. This is misdirection of his desire, and he finds himself in jail and charged with murder. Teach a man that there is an Infinite Intelligence within him which can fulfill his desires, and he overcomes his sense of opposition and frustration. Man's desire for food is legitimate and normal, but killing someone in order to get a loaf of bread breeds violence, opposition, guilt, and self-destruction.

There is a Power within man which will lift him up, set him on the high road to happiness, health, peace of mind, and the realization of his fondest dreams without depriving any other person of God's limitless blessings. A man who was broke, out of work, and frightfully frustrated came to one of our Sunday lectures some time ago and listened to the four steps of prayer. He went home and applied it. He had never heard a lecture on the mind, but he said, "This makes sense." He made a list of three things he wanted; you might call them material, but they were his needs. The items on the list were true place, an automobile, and all the money he needed.

He chose these concrete things to see if his thoughts were things. He wanted to prove to himself that the idea of the thing was the thing itself. I said in the lecture that the idea was the reality back of the form. He established a definite method of working and practiced it conscientiously every day, sticking to it long enough to give it a fair chance. This man knew that you do not learn to swim after one or two attempts.

He prayed for true place as follows: "I know Infinite Intelligence responds to me. It is now revealing my true place to me.

I am aware of my hidden talents. I am receiving a wonderful income. I know the idea of true place and its manifestation are one in Divine Mind. I follow the lead which comes."

Within two weeks from the day his experiment began he signed a contract for a job in San Francisco. He gave thanks and rejoiced in the Law of God. Then he went on to the next objective—a new car. He said to me, "I know I have the idea of a car. It is real, and I am going to remain faithful to it. It must manifest." He won a car in a raffle contest. Now he *knew* the secret of the subconscious that if he identified himself mentally and emotionally with the idea, the subconscious would bring it to pass. He was very thankful. The next request was more wealth. Each morning and evening during his prayer period he gave thanks for God's wealth circulating in his life claiming that his idea of wealth was fulfilled. He fell in love with a wealthy widow in San Francisco, and she financed his new business.

This man established a definite method of working, claiming each of his desires as already fulfilled. He claimed each one separately, but all at the same time during his morning and evening meditative period. If you pray like the above-mentioned man, and if no improvement at all shows itself within a couple of weeks, scrap that method and adopt a new one. Remember, there is an answer. That is as certain as the rising of the sun.

Cultivate simplicity and spontaneity, knowing that whatsoever ye shall ask in prayer, believing, ye shall receive. Decide now that you can do what you long to do and that you can be what you wish to be. No enlightened person today believes that a cruel fate condemns us to sickness, misery, or suffering. There is nothing holding us in mediocrity, in ill health, or in a miserable condition, but our own thoughts and false belief.

Come out of the prison of fear, want, and loneliness. Cease

thinking that God visits illness upon you for some strange reason, or that you must endure the sickness or be resigned to it. It is blasphemy to say that God is punishing you. It is also blasphemy to blame God for your sickness. Your mind and body are one. In the field of psychosomatic medicine they realize it is impossible to tell where the mind begins and the body ends. Research work today reveals that the hidden, underlying causes of physical maladies lie in the tangled depths of the mind, in frustrated rages, in baffled desires, in jealousies, and anxieties. Don't blame God for troubles we bring on ourselves by our own wrong thinking or our failure to think at all.

A girl said to me that all she desired was Wisdom. That is the overall desire of everyone, but our terminology is not the same. When you have Wisdom, you are expressing yourself fully here and now. An automobile is a spiritual idea in front of your door. A ham sandwich, when you are hungry, is an answer to your prayer and also is spiritual. If you sing well on the stage, it is just as spiritual as a man singing the 23rd Psalm in the choir. The man who repairs the roof of your house is performing spiritual labor just as well as a minister, priest, or rabbi who may be reading a text from the Bible or broadcasting a sermon.

Realize that the spirit and body are one. Cease looking down your nose at material things. Stop once and for all, separating the Spirit of God from the flesh and blood of the world. Every physical act, no matter how base you may consider it, is the Living Spirit within you animating material form. You are not degraded or bemeaned when you scrub a dirty floor or clean stables. If you are condemning anything in this world, you are demoting and depreciating yourself.

Good and bad are in your own thought, and you color

everything in the universe by the way you think and feel. Do not criticize, condemn, or despise your body or the world. Your body is the temple of the Living God, and the whole wide world is the body of God. The world is the Dance of God and the Song of God.

A man in Los Angeles had an ulcerated leg for five or six years. It would heal up for a time and then break out again. He said his father had the same thing, and that he supposed it was hereditary, and that he had resigned himself to it. He learned that was the wrong thing to do. He became aware of the fact that the Creative Intelligence which made his body never loses interest in that which It creates. He learned that the Healing Presence is within him and that the process of digestion, assimilation, and circulation are carried on by this Healing Presence. This man stopped fearing and expecting a relapse. For about five or ten minutes in the morning and evening he affirmed with deep understanding, "I have a Silent Partner, a Healing Presence who knows how to heal, and His Healing Presence is bringing about the beauty of wholeness now. I believe now that my Silent Partner is saturating my whole being with Its love, beauty, and perfection."

This slight alteration in his approach led him out of the lameness and pain into radiant health. God wants your best performance. Adopt a pragmatic standpoint and affirm boldly, "The Infinite Intelligence which created me knows the process of healing. It is healing me now in Divine Order. I believe, I accept, and I rejoice because my Silent Partner is responding now."

This attitude is sound, and it will work. We follow the desire which captivates and holds our attention. All of us find ourselves moving in the direction of the idea which dominates our mind for the time being. A burning desire to be and to do will start you off on the high road to success and achievement. John Bunyan had an intense desire to reveal the truth about religion, and his deeper mind responded. Though he was in prison at the time and sorely punished, he brought forth the masterpiece, *Pilgrim's Progress*.

The oak sleeps in the acorn. The bird waits in the egg, and God is waiting in you to be expressed and reproduced on the screen of space. Edison was a "tramp" telegraph operator, and though he was deaf and expelled from school, he had an intense desire to light up the world. The Living Intelligence within him responded to his faith and belief.

Dress up your desire, exalt it in your own mind, beautify it, magnify it, let it captivate you so much that you yearn for it. Fall in love with your desire. The mental picture you have in your mind backed up by faith will be manifested by the sub-conscious mind.

A woman in our audience had tried unsuccessfully to sell a home in another state for over three years. One Sunday morning in this service she got into a drowsy, sleepy state, a state akin to sleep. In this relaxed, quiet, peaceful state of mind, she focused all her attention on the sale of the home. She was in a state of physical immobility which increased the power of concentration. In this state she imagined she had the check for the full price in her hand, she gave thanks for the check, and rejoiced in its possession. She was looking backward at the goal, at the fulfilled desire. She rejoiced, gave thanks, and was filled with the feeling, "It is done!" In this mental attitude all effort was reduced to a minimum. That same day in Ohio the broker sold her home. It was about the same time as she was giving thanks for the sale. She said to me, "I knew I let it go this morning because I had a great sense of relief."

There is an old saying in the Tarot Teaching which says, "Man is what he imagines himself to be." Your idea is an image which comes forth spontaneously from your subliminal depths or from the world without. Your faculty of imagination clothes all ideas and projects them on the screen of space. This is why thoughts are things. One is the inside and the other is the outside of the same reality. Quimby said, "Man moves as he is moved upon. Man acts as he is acted upon."

Your ideas govern you and master you. Your idea this morning is tending to execute itself. The primal faculty of man is his imagination. Use it wisely, judiciously, and constructively. Imagine what is lovely and of good report. *Let us make man in our image.* GENESIS 1:26. God imagines Himself to be the sun, moon, stars, world, and man. He then feels Himself to be what He imagined Himself to be. The idea and the feeling unite (male and female), and the cosmos comes forth. God imagined Himself to be man. Then through feeling He became what He imagined Himself to be.

Give life and confidence to your image, and it will become alive in your experience. This is how you become what you want to become. Troward said, "Whatever you affix to I AM you become." I AM is the Name of God which means pure Being, Awareness, or Life. If you say, "I am sick," you will become sick. If you say, "I am poor," you will become poor. Why unite yourself with the feeling of poverty? Begin to affirm, "I am strong, whole, perfect, powerful, radiant, illumined, and inspired." Feel the truth of what you affirm, and wonders will happen in your life. Do not permit your feeling to unite with an image of limitation as you will generate the consequences of your unholy alliance.

Let us restate some of the salient points of these important truths. You do not put vitality into the seed, but you must deposit it in the soil. You water the seed regularly, thereby accelerating its growth. Let us look at our mind. The seed is your desire to be, to do, or to have. You must deposit it in the receptive soil of your mind, use no force nor mental coercion, and cease trying to make it come to pass. Your job is to keep out the negative thoughts of doubt and fear which tend to neutralize your affirmative prayer. Enter into the feeling of pleasure and satisfaction in imagining the fulfillment of your desire.

Your desire or idea is the substance of things hoped for, and the evidence of things not seen. Your desire is as real as your hand or heart, and has its own form, shape, and substance in another dimension of mind. "Believe that ye have it now, and ye shall receive it." Regard your mental creation or idea as a spiritual reality. Then implicitly trust the Law of growth to bring it to pass and walk in the Light that it is so, until the day breaks and the shadows flee away.

6

THE MYSTERIES AND
WONDERS OF SLEEP

For God speaketh once, yea twice, yet man perceiveth it not. In a
dream, in a vision of the night, when deep sleep falleth upon men, in
slumberings upon the bed; Then he openeth the ears of men, and sealeth
their instruction, That he may withdraw man from his purpose, and
hide pride from man. He keepeth back his soul from the pit, and his life
from perishing by the sword.

—JOB 33:14–18

You spend approximately one third of your life asleep. This is an inexorable law of life. This also applies to the animal and vegetable kingdoms. Sleep is a Divine ordinance, and many answers to our problems come to us when we are sound asleep upon the bed.

Many people have advocated the theory that we get tired during the day and that we go to sleep to rest the body, and that a reparative process takes place while asleep. Nothing rests in sleep. Our hearts, lungs, and all the vital organs function. Our nails and our hair grow while asleep. If you eat prior to sleep, the food is digested and assimilated; also the skin secretes perspiration.

Dr. Bigelow, in his research work on sleep, demonstrated that in our dreams we receive impressions showing that the optic, olfactory, and gustatory nerves are active during sleep, and also the cerebral nerve centers are active. We must remember that there are qualities within us which never grow old, decay, or die. We cannot say that Love, Beauty, Peace, Joy, Patience, Veracity, Justice, Goodwill become fatigued or tired. Our body is composed of a confluence of atoms and molecules which comprise our cells, nerves, tissues, muscles, and bones. What we call matter is Invisible Energy reduced to the point of visibility; matter is characterized by inertia. It moves as it is moved upon. It acts as it is acted upon. The substance of your body is made of the same substance as the planets which have been dancing to the music of the spheres for myriads of years. The planets do not get tired or exhausted as they continue to move along their appointed orbits.

You go to sleep not just to rest your body, but to receive and participate in the Wisdom of God. Your conscious mind, busy in the workaday world, gets involved with the vexations, strife, and contentions of the day, and it is very necessary to withdraw periodically from sense evidence and the objective world and commune with the Indwelling God, thereby being replenished spiritually with wisdom, strength, and guidance enabling you to overcome all difficulties and solve your daily problems. Job reminds you that you may get answers to your problems in a dream and in a vision of the night.

Every night when you go to sleep you take your last waking concept with you into the deep where it is etched on the subconscious mind. In other words, the mood in which you go to sleep determines the experiences you shall have tomorrow, the next day, and the next, except you change your consciousness through prayer and meditation. Whatever you impress on your subconscious mind will be expressed as experience and events. Go to sleep every night feeling that your prayer is answered. Sleep brings counsel.

Dr. John Bigelow of England says, "No part of man's life deserves to be considered more indispensable to its symmetrical and perfect spiritual development than the whiles he is separated from the phenomenal world in sleep."

All of us know that in the sleep process our conscious mind is suspended temporarily, and we are sheltered from the distractions and fascinations of the phenomenal world, without which spiritual growth and development would be impossible.

The late Professor Agassiz, in one of his scientific works, relates a dream which solved his problem. He had been two weeks striving to decipher the somewhat obscure impression of a fossil fish on the stone slab in which it was preserved. Weary and perplexed, he puts his work aside at last, and tried to dismiss it from his mind. Shortly after, he awakened one night persuaded that while asleep he had seen his fish with all the missing features perfectly restored. But when he tried to hold and make fast the image it escaped him. Nevertheless, he went early to the Jardin des Plantes, thinking that on looking anew at the impression he should see something which would put him back on the track of his vision. In vain—the blurred record was as blank as ever. The next night he saw the fish again, but with no more satisfactory result. When he awoke, it disappeared from his memory as before. Hoping that the same experience might be repeated, on the third night he placed a pencil and paper beside his bed before going to sleep.

Accordingly, toward morning the fish reappeared in his dream, confusedly at first, but at last with such distinctness that he had no longer any doubt as to its zoological characteristics. Still half dreaming, and in perfect darkness, he traced these impressions on the sheet of paper at the bedside. In the morning he was surprised to see in his nocturnal sketch features which he thought it impossible for the fossil itself to reveal. He hastened to the Jardin des Plantes, and with his drawing as a guide, succeeded in chiseling away the surface of the stone under which portions of the fish proved to be hidden. When wholly exposed it corresponded with his dream and his drawing, and he succeeded in classifying it with ease.

If you are seeking an answer to a perplexing problem, cease maundering and asseverate quietly and firmly prior to sleep: "God knows the answer; I accept the answer now and give thanks."

You will recognize the answer by the inner silent knowing of your soul, by an inward sense of touch, or a spontaneous idea which may well up from your subliminal depths like toast pops up out of a toaster. When you talk to God, you expect an answer and you listen quietly, lovingly, and knowingly for Him. How can you hear if you refuse to listen? This is well expressed in Alfred Tennyson's "The Higher Pantheism."

Speak to Him thou for He hears,
And Spirit with Spirit can meet—
Closer is He than breathing, and
Nearer than hands and feet.

The nature of Infinite Intelligence is responsiveness. It responds to you when you call upon It. Let me illustrate how the sub-conscious answers you. A young lady who comes to our Sunday morning lectures told me that she had been offered, a few months ago, a lucrative position in New York City at twice her present salary. She was wondering whether to accept or not and prayed as follows prior to sleep: "Father, thou knowest all things, reveal to me the right decision. Thank you for Thy guidance."

She repeated this simple prayer over and over again as a lullaby prior to sleep, and in the morning she had a persistent feeling that she should not accept the offer. She rejected the offer and subsequent events verified her inward sense of knowing, because the company went bankrupt in a few months following their offer of employment to her.

The conscious mind may be correct on the facts objectively known, but the intuitive faculty of the subconscious mind saw the failure of the concern in question and prompted her accordingly. We read in Acts 16:9 of instructions given to Paul when he was asleep. *And a vision appeared to Paul in the night; There stood a man of Macedonia and prayed him, saying, Come over into Macedonia and help us.* This changed the whole course of Paul's life.

During the month of May I gave a series of lectures in Town Hall, New York, under the aegis of the Church of Religious Science, New York. One night I had a dream in which a man said, "Get up and write this down, you are seeing my daughter Anna tomorrow." I awoke and went to the desk in the Algonquin Hotel and rustled through the drawer for a sheet of hotel stationery. He dictated to me as I wrote. I am sure that these instructions were not written by Joseph Murphy even half asleep, even by my subconscious in a half-dream world in which I was.

I believe that it was the father of the girl whom I was to see the following day.

I definitely feel that it was the personality of her father, surviving so-called death, that gave me the instructions which explained in detail where a certain large sum of money was hidden, and also of holdings in the Bahamas with explicit instructions to his daughter whom to contact, etc., all of which was subsequently verified.

The following day Anna visited me at the Church of Religious Science Headquarters. I knew her because I had seen her in my dream the night previously. She knew me, and everything in the office was familiar to her. I believe that our dreams explain a great many of the statements and experiences of people who say, "I've been here before." "I've seen him before." "I've heard that voice." "I have walked this path." There are times when a shining facet of our mind reflects the memories of things unseen objectively but seen subjectively, that which was not consciously known, but was subconsciously perceived and known. All of us dream, but we may not remember our dreams.

All prayer is a form of sleep whereby we become asleep to the world and its appearances and alive to the Presence and Power of God. Prayer means to withdraw and abstract your attention from the problem, difficulty, and evidence of senses, and focus your faith and confidence in God to guide, heal, and reveal the answer. In the prayer process you definitely reject the power of external conditions, and you affirm the supremacy and sovereignty of the Spirit within.

A young man had difficulty locating his father's will, and at night prior to sleep he prayed as follows: "Infinite Intelligence knows where the will is, and it is revealed to me now." He had a dream in which the location of the will was revealed to him.

In sleep there is a complete dissociation from the world in which we live, and our conscious attention to matters which engross our relations during the day are severed. Sleep is the inexorable master and is no respecter of persons. "The morning hour," says a German proverb, "has gold in its mouth."

If you have been upset, harassed, and worried during the day, and at night perhaps you read a psalm praying for peace, entering into the feeling of good will and the spirit of forgiveness to all, notice how you awake refreshed, with strength renewed, your mind serene and clear, your passions calmed, your animosities soothed, and kindlier feeling toward all.

The Bible says: *Remember the Sabbath day, to keep it holy.* EXO-DUS 20:8. The Sabbath means rest in God, a stillness born of the conviction of the ever availability of the God-Presence at all times everywhere. We are in the Sabbath when we have complete trust and faith in God, knowing it is impossible for our prayer to fail. It is a feeling of inner certitude which follows true prayer.

Every night when you go to sleep feeling the joy of the answered prayer, you are in the Sabbath which means you have turned over your request to the Deeper Mind which is full of wisdom and intelligence. It knows the answer and will bring it to pass. There is always an interval of time between the impregnation of the subconscious and the external manifestation, and that is also called the Sabbath, or period of mental pregnancy.

When we are asleep the spiritual side of our life is in the ascendant. We are free from the world's hold upon our thoughts and feelings, and we are actually one with the Universal Life of God, and the Healing Currents of Eternity flow through our whole being while we are asleep.

The Mosaic Law set apart one day in seven for our spiritual reflection, and enjoined upon us to do no manner of work. It is for the same reason we are directed, when we pray, to enter into the inner chamber and shut the door, that we be not distracted by externals while we commune with our Father within. In sleep we are united by abstraction to our Higher Self, and we participate in His Healing Presence.

Yet the Lord will command his lovingkindness in the daytime, and in the night his song shall be with me . . . PSALMS 42:8.

The processes of spiritual growth and development are more than ordinarily active during sleep. Job says that, while sleeping, God openeth the ears of men and sealeth their instruction. We are divinely instructed while asleep; moreover, whatever we take into the Deep as we go to sleep is etched in the subconscious mind which determines how it is to be expressed or made manifest. The many visions, prophetic dreams mentioned in the Bible were apparently given to the illumined men as they slept; perhaps because a Divine Truth was more sure of receiving attention and was less liable to encounter worldly obstruction and distractions during the sleeping than during the waking hours.

Sleep withdraws you from your purpose and hides pride from you, by showing you that while asleep, the whole world continues to function perfectly and that God is running the show.

He keepeth back his soul from the pit, and his life from perishing by the sword. JOB 33:18.

You can always avoid the pit of sorrow, grief, despondency, and the piercing sword of jealousy and anger by surrendering to God prior to sleep. Forgive everyone by pouring out God's love, peace, and joy upon them until there is no sting in your mind. Then talk to God, your Counselor and Guide, and affirm lovingly as you go off to the deep of sleep: "Father, thou knowest all things. Reveal to me the answer, heal me, guide me, comfort me, and let your river of peace flood my mind and heart."

Do this humbly and reverently every night, and you will never sit on a psychiatrist's couch, neither will you ever become neurotic, frustrated, or mentally deranged.

Lack of sleep can cause you to be irritable, moody, and depressed. Dr. George Stevenson of the National Association for Mental Health says, "I believe it can safely be said that all human beings need a minimum of six hours sleep to be healthy. Most people need more. Those who think they can get along on less are fooling themselves."

Medical research scholars investigating sleep processes and deprivation of sleep point out that severe insomnia has preceded psychotic breakdown in some instances. Remember, you are spiritually recharged during sleep, and adequate sleep is essential to producing joy and vitality in life.

Robert O'Brien, in an article, "Maybe You Need More Sleep" in an issue of "Reader's Digest" reports the following experiment on sleep:

"For the last three years experiments have been in progress at Walter Reed Army Institute of Research in Washington, D.C. Subjects—more than 100 military and civilian volunteers—have been kept awake for as long as four days. Thousands of tests have measured the effects on their behavior and personality. Results of these tests have given scientists astonishingly new insights into the mysteries of sleep.

"They now know that the tired brain apparently craves sleep so hungrily that it will sacrifice anything to get it. After only a few hours of sleep loss, fleeting stolen naps called 'lapses,' or micro-sleeps, occurred at the rate of three or four an hour. As in real sleep, eyelids drooped, heartbeat slowed. Each lapse lasted just a fraction of a second. Sometimes the lapses were periods of blankness; sometimes they were filled with images, wisps of dreams. As hours of sleep loss mounted, the lapses took place more often and lasted longer, perhaps two or three seconds. Even if the subjects had been piloting an airliner in a thunderstorm, they still couldn't have resisted micro-sleeps for those few priceless seconds. And it can happen to you, as many who have fallen asleep at the wheel of a car can testify.

"Another startling effect of sleep deprivation was its attack on human memory and perception. Many sleep-deprived subjects were unable to retain information long enough to relate it to the task they were supposed to perform. They were totally befuddled in situations requiring them to hold several factors in mind and act on them, as a pilot must when he skillfully integrates wind direction, air speed, altitude and glide path to make a safe landing."

Every night of your life, as you go to sleep, you are going before the King of Kings and the Lord of Lords, the Living Spirit Almighty. Be dressed for God mentally and emotionally. Go to sleep with the song of God in your heart, with love and good will for every living being in the world. Go into His presence clothed in the robes of love, peace, praise, and thanksgiving. You must be without spot or blemish when you visit God who is Absolute Love—the Immaculate Unblemished Presence. You must be all fair and no spot on thee. Wrap yourself in the mantle of Love, and go off to sleep with the praise of God forever on your lips.

You must remember there are many degrees of sleep, and every time you pray you are actually asleep to the world and alive to God. When you abstract your five senses from your problem or difficulty and focus all your attention on the solution or answer, knowing that the subjective wisdom of God is bringing about a solution in ways you know not of, you are practicing the art of sleep as mentioned in the Bible. You are asleep to the falsehood and hypnotic influence of the world when you accept as true what your reason and senses deny. When you hear of a person getting a nervous breakdown, you are reading of one who wandered away from God, and has cohabited mentally and emotionally with the false gods of fear, worry, ill will, resentment, remorse, and confusion.

Trustful relaxation is the remedy for insomnia. When you retire at night, let go of every worrisome and anxious thought. Cast out all burdens from the mind. Know that God is with you and that He has the answer. Abandon yourself to the thought that "underneath are the everlasting arms." Say over and over in quiet confidence: "I now relax and rest in God. I yield myself to God's river of peace. His peace and love pervade my whole being, and I sleep in peace. God giveth His beloved in sleep."

7

NOT RESIGNED, BUT RECONCILED

Troward says, "There are two ends to a stick." Emerson says, "We meet polarity or action and reaction in every part of nature." All of us know that our thoughts come in pairs. When you think of wealth, the thought of poverty comes into your mind also, and when you think of health, the thought of the opposite rears its head. Let us enumerate some of these opposites such as matter and spirit, negative and positive, darkness and light, evil and good, disease and health, pain and pleasure, misery and happiness, ebb and flow, male and female, in and out, subjective and objective, fear and love, heat and cold, rest and motion, yes and no.

The opposites are the expressions of the cosmos. They are dual expressions of the same principle. We are here to reconcile the opposites and bring harmony, health, and peace into our world. When it is cold you build a fire, when hungry you seek food, if sick you align yourself with the Healing Presence and establish wholeness and perfect health again. When fear strikes you, the thing to do is to mentally unite with the Source—God which is Love. You could read the 27th Psalm slowly, quietly, and lovingly, and as you do you are moving mentally to the opposite which is faith in God. Fear is a denial of the power of God and the goodness of God. Fear is faith upside down. Fear is a shadow in the mind, and there is no power in a shadow. "Perfect love casteth out fear." Fall in love with the good, become emotionally attached to the great Truths of God, and all fear will go away.

If you are fearful, you can rest assured there is a desire within you for that which is opposite to the thing feared. Place your attention on the thing desired, and you will begin to reconcile the opposites. Desire is the angel of God, the messenger of the Divine saying to each one of us, "Come on up higher." Desire is behind all progress. Let your desire captivate and hold your attention. You move in the direction of the idea which dominates your mind. The greater the expected benefit from the desire, the stronger our desire.

I should like to tell you of a singer who failed to get a contract because his voice cracked on three occasions during an audition. Fear was his enemy, and he discovered he could move to the opposite which was faith and confidence through prayer. He stilled the wheels of his mind two or three times a day. He imagined he was singing before a microphone. He saw the imaginary audience. "Act as though I am, and I will be." He began to feel the joy of it all and the thrill of accomplishment. He continued to do this at regular intervals until he got the reaction which satisfied. He succeeded in planting his desire in his subconscious mind, and he felt a great sense of peace and satisfaction. He loved his desire to the point of acceptance and proved to himself that "perfect love casteth out fear."

Love is an emotional attachment, being loyal and devoted mentally to your ideal. As you do this the fear or the negative thought dies, and the ideal becomes real. This man is successful today because he learned how to reconcile the opposites in his life and bring peace where discord was. Give yourself wholeheartedly to your ideal, be loyal to it by mentally and emotionally uniting with it, you are loving it.

A soldier told me that he was cut off from his battalion in the last war and was in the midst of a hail of bullets. His knees were shaking with fear. He repeated the 23rd Psalm and a wave of peace came over him, and he found his way to safety. This soldier realized that if he remained at the extreme of fear he would be frozen to the spot, and the result would have been death and destruction. He let the pendulum of his mind swing to the opposite pole which was faith in God as his shepherd and protector from all harm.

The Bible says, *Ask, and it shall be given you; seek, and ye shall find; knock, and it shall be opened unto you; For every one that asketh receiveth; and he that seeketh findeth; and to him that knocketh it shall be opened. Or what man is there of you, whom if his son ask bread, will he give him a stone? Or if he ask a fish, will he give him a serpent? If ye then, being evil, know how to give good gifts unto your children, how much more shall your Father which is in heaven give good things to them that ask him?* MATTHEW 7:7–11.

These verses from the book of Matthew represent some of the greatest truths of the Bible, and set forth a wonderful formula for prayer. You are clearly told to ask, and you shall receive. To ask in Bible language is to claim your good, and then the Spirit within will honor and validate your claim. In these passages you are told God is your Heavenly Father, and you are to expect from Him all the blessings of Heaven. Look upon God as a loving father, a kindly father who watches over you, cares for you, guides and directs you, and provides for your welfare. As you make a habit of this you will discover that you will always be prospered, guided, and you will find yourself in your true place doing what you love to do, divinely happy, and divinely blessed in countless ways. God is to you what you conceive Him to be.

As long as man thinks that God is punishing him, testing him, or ruling over him with a rod of iron, a sort of jealous, cruel, or capricious tyrant, he will be confused, muddled, perplexed, and in mental conflict. Such thoughts being chaotic, the result is chaos and misery in his life. Man is what he thinks all day long.

Jesus states categorically, definitely, and unequivocally that God is our Father, and that we are His children. Your relationship with God should therefore be on the most friendly and loving terms, that of father and son. Never again during the whole course of your life look upon God as a God of wrath, indiscriminate in his vengeance. Such a concept held in the mind brings untold misery and suffering to the individual who entertains such a belief. Our beliefs are our masters, and all beliefs tend to manifest themselves in our lives.

Believe only that which is true of God; accept that which is lovely and of good report. Believe in the goodness of God, in the love of God, in the guidance of God, in the harmony of God, in the wisdom of the Almighty. Believe in the joy of God, and His abundance. Believe and expect all the blessings of Heaven here and now. *According to your belief is it done unto you.* Recognize the Fatherhood of God—God is your Loving Father; He loves you, and He cares for you. God wants you to be happy, joyous, and free. You are here to express the joy of living and to reproduce all the qualities, attributes, aspects and potencies of God.

I have said ye are gods, and all of you are sons of the Most High. It is fundamental and foundational to say that the offspring must be of the same nature and species of the parent. *I and my Father are one.* This means you and God are one mentally, spiritually, and physically. Infinity is within you, and therefore there is no end to the glory which is man. The journey is ever onward, upward, and Godward. You are capable of infinite growth and spiritual development.

Your greatest prayer is to still the wheels of your mind every morning, and for five or ten minutes feel that you are a channel through which God flows through you as harmony, health, peace, joy, wholeness, beauty, love, companionship, security, true place, and expression. Praying humbly and reverently in this manner you will expand in spiritual awareness until you have transcended even your fondest dreams.

Your glorious destiny is to be united with God and experience the glory which was yours before the world was. Cease being a serf, a slave, a doormat. Never say, "I have to resign myself to my fate." "I must put up with this." "This is God's will and I must put up with my illness." "I'm incurable." "It's hopeless." "Etc." If you make such statements or have the mental attitude that you are here to suffer and that God is punishing you for your sins, you are placing yourself in thralldom, bondage, and degrading your Divine destiny as a son of the Living God here on earth to enjoy the inheritance of your Father.

Ask and ye shall receive is your passport and enfranchisement to freedom, health, supply, beauty, joy, and life more abundant. It could not be stated more emphatically or compellingly. It is absolutely wrong for you from every standpoint to remain in any kind of bondage whether physical, mental, or material. There is absolutely no virtue whatever in resignation or being satisfied with your lot. To resign yourself to sickness or poverty is to sin or miss the mark of perfect health and abundance. Resignation is a mixture of ignorance, fear, superstition, and indolence. Refuse to accept ill health, discord, poverty, loneliness, or unhappiness.

God's beloved intention for you is the life more abundant, happiness, and peace of mind. You are here to let the Light of God shine in your mind, body, and environment. This is the only way you glorify God here and now. God is always successful in all His undertakings. What is true of God is true of you because you are His son and heir to all His riches. It is your sacred task out of love for God to positively and definitely refuse to accept anything less than peace of mind, true place, abundance, and security. Keep on asking and knocking until the day breaks and the shadows flee away. *Knock and it shall be opened unto you.* This means that when you have a definite desire or idea in your conscious mind and have come to a clear-cut and definite decision in your conscious mind, you will then gain a response from your deeper mind which is full of wisdom and power. You refuse to take "no" for an answer because you believe implicitly in the promises of God: *Ask, and ye shall receive.* Keep on claiming your good continuously and untiringly until your prayer is answered.

A tragic and egregious blunder made by orthodox religious people is to think that the will of God for them is bound to be something tragic or evil or downright unpleasant. If the will of God for you were sickness, then all the doctors, psychologists, and nurses in the world would be working contrary to the will of God—this, of course, is the quintessence of absurdity. It is very unfortunate that millions of people look upon God as a hard, cruel, despotic taskmaster. Others believe in a devil that is tempting them. This belief in two powers results in endless confusion and a mental conflict accompanied by all kinds of strange fears and fixations.

Hear, O Israel, the Lord thy God is one Lord. There is only one Power which moves as a unity—this is a mathematical and spiritual necessity. Infinity cannot be divided or multiplied; there cannot be two powers, as one would cancel out the other, and there would be nothing but discord and chaos everywhere. Good and evil are the movements of our own mind relative to the One Being forever Holy, Pure, and Immaculate in Himself.

"I sent my soul into the Invisible, some letter of the afterlife to spell. And bye and bye my soul returned to me, saying I myself am Heaven and Hell." The will of God is the nature of God. God is Life, and Life cannot wish death. God is Peace, and Peace cannot wish pain. God is Love, and Love cannot hate and build a fire where man burns for eternity.

There are many things God cannot do. He cannot violate His own Nature. Life cannot wish death, sickness, misfortune, or accident. We bring these things on ourselves by our own wrong thinking. Your heart would have to be full of hatred if you longed to see others suffer in a fire forever because they didn't belong to your creed or church, or because they erred and made serious mistakes. God is Love, and God is Absolute Harmony, and Harmony cannot wish discord. It is a fact that you can hate, but God is Love—that is the Truth which changes not, the same yesterday, today, and forever. It is a fact that you can create discord by misusing and misdirecting your subconscious mind, but the changeless Truth is that God is Absolute

Harmony. It is a fact that you can lie, cheat, and defraud, but God is Absolute Truth, and the Universe is scrupulously honest, and God is Absolute Justice. There is a great difference between a fact and the Truth. The word fact comes from the Latin *factum*, your ability to create, manufacture in the factory of your mind.

You can use your mind two ways. Learn to use it the right way, and tune in on the Infinite Ocean of God's Love, Peace, Beauty, and Joy, and let these qualities flow through you. You do not create Harmony, Peace, Beauty, Joy, Love, or Health—you align yourself with these qualities of God by mentally tuning in with the Infinite, and letting His Splendor flow through you, in you, and all around you. The Will of God for you is greater freedom, greater self-expression, true place, perfect health, abundance, and blessings transcending your fondest hopes.

If you are a square peg in a round hole, and unhappy, you are not expressing the will of God. Inharmony and confusion will be the result. Resolve to express more and more of God's Love, and you will go from glory to glory. You and your desire are present now—these are the eternal two mentioned in the Bible. Your desire is whispering within you, and fear and doubt arise also. You must determine to resolve the quarrel in your mind so that peace is restored. Our early conditioning, fixed beliefs, and religious training impede and thwart our faith in God and all things good, and we find our mind is a battleground.

Your desire, as we said earlier, is of God and has its own mathematics and mechanics with it. Conditions, circumstances, and environment are not causative—these are effects and are subject to change. The fear thought that challenges your desire must die, and your desire must live. Take your attention completely away from the thought of opposition. This will starve it to death, and mentally and emotionally feast on your ideals. The latter is good, constructive, and wholesome, and will bless you. Your loyalty, devotion, and attention must be given to your goal, ideal, desire. Your thought-image is the first cause relative to the thing you are praying for, and is real on its own plane of reference.

Lift your mind and heart up beyond the problem or difficulty, and picture the fulfillment of your desire, the happy ending irrespective of opposition. Fear and false beliefs must die. Starve them to death by refusing them attention; give confidence and life to your ideal. This is the way of reconciling the opposites.

A famous space scientist, Dr. Von Blenk-Schmidt, who is doing research work on space travel, told me he is always running up against the devil, which simply means resistance, difficulties, and problems. Sometimes fear of failure enters in. He resolves these problems by prayer. He gets still and quiet and asks for the answer, and the creative ideas necessary for the solution come to him sometimes spontaneously out of the blue (the subconscious mind). Engineers, chemists, physicists working with him are trying to overcome atmospheric friction and resistance with various alloys of metals and new designs. There is always a way out, a solution, a happy ending. It is through difficulties and problems that we discover our Divinity. The joy is in the overcoming. If the crossword puzzle were all made out for you, life would be insipid, dull, and uninteresting.

You are here to discover your God-Self. If all your faculties functioned automatically, you could not discover your God-given powers and attributes. You can use your powers two ways, enabling you to deduce a law of life. Man is under the thralldom and bondage of the five senses until he awakens to the Creative Power of God. Realize your thoughts come in pairs.

The fear thought is not real, it denies that which is actual. Be a spiritual paratrooper. Fly over the obstacle with the wings of faith and imagination, and feel, rejoice, and give thanks for the joy of the answered prayer.

Love is the fulfilling of the Law of Health, Happiness, Abundance, and Security. Wish for everyone what you wish for yourself, and fall in love with your ideal. Be faithful and loyal to your ideal, and it shall come to pass, and the Light of God will shine upon you.

8

THE MASTER SECRET
OF THE AGES

And the angel of the Lord appeared unto him in a flame of fire out of the midst of a bush: and he looked, and, behold, the bush burned with fire, and the bush was not consumed.

And Moses said, I will now turn aside, and see this great sight, why the bush is not burnt.

And when the Lord saw that he turned aside to see, God called unto him out of the midst of the bush and said, Moses, Moses. And he said, Here am I.

And he said, Draw not nigh hither: put off thy shoes from off thy feet, for the place whereon thou standest is holy ground.

—Exodus—Chap. 3 Verses 2–3–4–5

And Moses said unto God, Behold, when I come unto the children of Israel, and shall say unto them, The God of your fathers hath sent me unto you; and they shall say to me, What is his name? what shall I say unto them?

And God said unto Moses, I AM THAT I AM: and he said Thus shalt thou say unto the children of Israel, I AM hath sent me.

—Exodus—Chap. 3 Verses 13–14

Man is looking everywhere for God, not knowing that when he says "I Am" he is announcing the presence of the Living God within himself. This is called the master secret of the ages, sometimes referred to as the lost word. "I Am" means Being, Life, Awareness, The Presence of God in man. It is the nameless one.

In ancient times, the secret was given only to the initiated, never to the profane, because the ancient seers said with this knowledge, or awareness, a man can rise to the heights of spiritual illumination or he can sink to the depths of degradation. Hence, it was given only to those who were spiritually awakened and stood the tests that were given them.

This is how a woman applied the master secret in her own life. She attends my lectures at the Wilshire Ebell Theatre on Sunday and wrote as follows: "I am sixty-five years old, a widow with a grown family. I am living alone and am on a pension. I heard you say one Sunday that whatever you attach to I Am, you become and if a woman is lonesome and wishes companionship that she should affirm with feeling 'I am wanted, I am happily married to a wonderful man, and I am secure.' I began to affirm slowly, quietly, and lovingly, 'I am wanted, I am loved, I am happily married to a loving, kind, and spiritual minded man. I am secure.' I kept on doing this every night and morning for about three weeks. A few days ago I went to the corner drug store. The druggist introduced me to a man who was a retired pharmacist. After a few days acquaintanceship he proposed to me and next month we are going on our honeymoon to Japan. He gave me a wedding present of $15,000."

Her prayer was felt as true in her heart and her affirmation sank down by osmosis into the subconscious mind, which is the creative medium. The moment she succeeded in bringing about a subjective embodiment, the subconscious brought about the answer through the law of attraction. The deeper mind full of wisdom and intelligence brought both of them together in Divine order.

Many are sound asleep because they do not know about this gold mine of Infinite Intelligence and Boundless Love within themselves. Whatever you want you can draw forth. A magnetized piece of steel will lift ten times its own weight. Demagnetize this piece of steel, and it will not even lift a feather. There are two types of men. There is the magnetized man who is full of confidence and faith in an Almighty Power to lead and guide him; he knows that he is born to win and to succeed. Therefore his deeper mind responds to Him. There is the other man who is demagnetized; he is full of fears and doubts. Opportunities come, and he says, "I might fail. I might lose all my money. People will laugh at me." This type of man will not get very far in life, because if he is afraid to go forward, he will simply stay where he is.

The magnetized man says, "I am going to succeed. The Power will back me up. I will prosper. There is nothing to stop me." The God Power moves through that man at his focal point of attention. Cease being demagnetized by doubts, fears, anxieties, and demoting yourself by saying, "I don't know the right people. I am too old. I haven't got the right politician," and so forth and so on.

The electrons, the atoms, and the molecules are all the same in the magnetized and the demagnetized steel, but in the magnetized steel all the atoms and molecules are marshalled. They are focused in a certain direction. That is why it is a magnet. In the demagnetized steel, molecules move about at random and are not focused.

The ancients discovered that there was a Power with man, and that when man had confidence and faith in this Power, Lady Luck seemed to bless him in all his undertakings. When he was full of fear (of sickness for example that some germ would attack him), and he lived in that fear, he would create the disease. They realized that there was nothing external that could affect man except it affected him inside in his own mind. Nothing can touch you from the outside without your mental consent.

If you believe Lady Luck is with you, good fortune will smile on you. If you believe a jinx is following you, all kinds of trouble will come upon you. You begin to become suspicious of people and everything goes wrong and awry in your life because of your belief. Man's inner belief creates his personal good and evil. Man is belief expressed. The law of life is the law of belief. The Spirit within man is God. Spirit has no form, shape, or substance. Spirit is timeless and ageless.

This unconditioned Being called God, becomes conditioned by conceiving Itself to be something. The whole world is simply this Being conceiving Itself to be all these things.

The whole world is a dramatization of God's ideas whether they are trees, suns, moons, stars, or continents. They are all God's ideas. God dramatizes Himself by conceiving and feeling Himself to be all these things. Everything in this world is alive, and the world that we see is not really solid at all. This is a world of intensities, frequencies, and densities, and the only difference between one substance and another is the number and rate of motion of the electrons revolving around a nucleus. The whole world is a world of vibrations.

The electron we speak of cannot be seen. The whole world is simply Spirit in differentiation. Matter is energy reduced to the point of visibility. Your thought is energy and it takes form. This is why thoughts are things. You are what you think all day long.

A little boy, fourteen years old, listens to my lectures on Sunday mornings. His father died some years ago and his mother couldn't afford a home. The little boy got a hammer, nails and some wood and built a miniature home. He put this small model on the mantlepiece of their home. The mother said, "What is that?" He said, "Mom, we want a home. If we look at this home, the picture of a new home will go into our subconscious." A man, for whom the boy works occasionally, donated him a home, so that he and his mother could live comfortably. This is the way the Law of Mind worked for this boy.

One day during the course of conversation, the man said, "Why don't you buy a home?" The boy said, "My mother hasn't the money." The man said, "I am going East to live with my son. I am not coming back to California any more. I have all the money I need. I have never done anything for anyone, but you are a nice boy and you deserve a break. You take this deed and give it to your mother." That is the way they got the home. The man never had seen the mother. He liked the boy and he gave them the home.

Strange? There is nothing strange about it. There are people in this country who give millions away.

He saith unto them, But whom say ye that I am? Who do you say this I AM within you is? What is your concept of God? What is your real belief? I am not talking about your intellectual assent. I am talking about your real belief, your deep functioning, abiding faith about this God Power. Your concept, your blueprint, and estimate of God is your whole concept of yourself, and your concept of yourself determines your entire future.

The answer you give to the question, *But who say ye that I Am?* determines your health, environment, social life, financial life, and all phases of your life, because your belief about God determines your whole life.

"I Am the Way." Yes, I Am is the Power that resurrects and makes alive the things that you are seeking, that which you want to be. This is the only Power and Presence, the only cause, the only Intelligence, the only Wisdom, the only Substance.

When you say, "I am poor," and so forth, you are making a poor mental arrangement in your own mind. Chant the beauty of the good and claim, "I am wealthy. I am happy. I am prosperous. I am healthy. I am secure. I am loved, I am illumined, and I am inspired." Watch the wonders in your life as you pray in this affirmative manner.

We have a new body every eleven months. Your thoughts are things and, as you fill your mind with the Truths of God, the electrons and the molecules of your body will undergo a transformation. There will be a dispersal of the old molecules, and the old electrons, which were diseased. "In my flesh shall I see God." You change your whole body through your thought and your feeling, and through your constant identification with the eternal verities.

There is no law compelling you to be depressed, dejected, vindictive, or to have destructive thoughts of poverty, lack, and limitation.

You can be engulfed in the sea of despair, lack, ill will, and gloom, because you have no inner bulwarks to man the ramparts. Learn where the God Presence is. Then you can say, "I am whole. I am watched over by the Love of God. I am surrounded by the whole armor of God and where I Am, God is." This attitude will render all your fears and doubts null and void. The waves of despair and despondency will go back to the seas, and you will walk over to dry land.

Your faith and confidence in God will lift you up and set you on the highroad to freedom, happiness, and peace of mind.

"I AM hath sent me unto you." Wouldn't it be wonderful if you went back to business tomorrow, to your factory, or to your conference and said, "God sent me here to solve all problems, to disperse anxiety, to bring peace where discord is, love where hatred is, joy where sadness is, and to bring forth new ideas." Go forth with that attitude, and you can't fail. All the power and wisdom of God will flow through your focused point of attention—and this is called touching the hem of His garment.

The best way to realize your desire is to claim, feel, and know that, "God gave me this ideal, this goal, this objective, and I am giving my attention and devotion to it now. I picture the end. I feel it and know that all the power of the Godhead is flowing through my mental image, and I am at peace."

There is an acid test for Truth. The fruits of Truth are joy, happiness, peace, love, goodwill, patience, and perfect health. This is the "Melody of God" which man plays. What good is any teaching, any religion? What good is man himself except he becomes an instrument through which these Eternal Melodies are played.

The burning bush is within you, and you can lead your children (ideals, dreams, and aspirations) out of Egypt, out of the darkness, and into the Light of the Promised Land which means the realization of your desires. You are Moses, because you have the capacity to draw out the Wisdom and the Power that is within you.

Ye are the light of the world. This light is the Infinite Intelligence of God, that will illumine your pathway and will reveal to you everything you need to know. "A city that is set on a hill cannot be hid." You are the city of God, and all the thoughts and ideas in your mind are the people who live in this city.

If you are full of faith and confidence in God's Wisdom and believe with conviction that God will guide you, then that Light in you cannot be hid. Everyone will see it, because you are announcing the Presence and Power of God within yourself. You are announcing the presence of peace, of joy, of happiness.

The healing Rays of God flow through your eyes, your ears, and all your organs. You are suffused and submerged in the Holy Omnipresence and feel that God is vitalizing every cell and nerve of your body, so that your whole body dances to the rhythm of the Eternal God.

Feel a transfusion of God's grace flowing through you. Feel and know that this Holy Spirit which created you is now taking over all the processes and functions of your body.

"I Am the Way," "I Am the Truth," and "I Am the Life." "I Am the Door." Your own consciousness is the door to all expression, because what you claim and feel as true within yourself, the Spirit in you will honor, validate, execute, and bring to pass. This is the way all things are made, and there is nothing made that is not made that way.

A wonderful sense of peace fills your soul. Let this Light of God be a torch to you. Lift up your eyes and behold that Light. Affirm, "God shows me the way. He is a lamp unto my feet; He is a light on my pathway." And that is exactly what God will be to you, because that which you believe God to be, He will be that to you. You live in the joyous expectancy of the best. His candle shines upon your head, and by His Light, you walk through darkness.

When the whole world says it can't be done, you will go inside, into the silence of your soul, and say, "It is done." You create the way God creates, by self-contemplation of the Spirit, and what you conceive as true, you can give it conception.

I Am the way. Your own *I Amness* is the power that resurrects, that guides, that heals, makes alive whatever you feel to be true in your heart.

Your body is acted upon by the Creative Intelligence. You are Divine, you are Spiritual. You are joyous. You are surrounded by the Peace of God. The Spirit of God pervades every atom of your being, your children, your home, your business. There is Divine Right action in your life. You are instantaneously healed by the Presence and Power of the Almighty.

There is Divine equilibrium in your body, which you sense and feel, and you rejoice that there is but One Presence and One Power and It is moving as a unity and as a harmony through you. You live, move, act, and have your being in God. You feel that it is impossible for your prayer to fail. The answer comes to pass in due season, in God's own way, and in God's own time, for God is bringing it to pass now in His own way.

When fear or worry comes into your mind, you do not entertain these thoughts. You chant the Beauty of the Good, and affirm, "God is guiding me now. God is taking care of me, and all is well. The Creative Intelligence of God, which is regnant and supreme, brings all my requests to pass in Divine Order. According to my faith is it done unto me. It is wonderful!"

9

YOU ARE WHAT YOU EAT

These are the beasts which ye shall eat; the ox, the sheep, and the goat.

The hart, and the roebuck, and the fallow deer, and the wild goat, and the pygarg, and the wild ox, and the chamois.

And every beast that parteth the hoof, and cleaveth the cleft into two claws, and cheweth the cud among the beasts, that ye shall eat.

Nevertheless these ye shall not eat of them that chew the cud, or of them that divide the cloven hoof; as the camel, and the hare, and the coney: for they chew the cud, but divide not the hoof; therefore they are unclean unto you.

And the swine, because it divideth the hoof, yet cheweth not the cud, it is unclean unto you: ye shall not eat of their flesh, nor touch their carcase.

These ye shall eat of all that are in the waters; all that have fins and scales shall ye eat:

And whatsoever hath not fins and scales ye may not eat; it is unclean unto you.

Of all clean birds ye shall eat.

But these are they of which ye shall not eat: the eagle, and the os-sifrage, and the ospray.

And the glede, and the kite, and the vulture after his kind,

And every raven after his kind,

And the owl, and the night hawk, and the cuckow, and the hawk after his kind,

And the little owl, and the great owl, and the swan,

And the pelican, and the gier eagle, and the cormorant,

And the stork, and the heron after her kind, and the lapwing, and the bat.

And every creeping thing that flieth is unclean unto you: they shall not be eaten.

But of all the clean fowls ye may eat.

Ye shall not eat of any thing that dieth of itself: thou shalt give it unto the stranger that is in thy gates, that he may eat it; or thou mayest sell it unto an alien: for thou art an holy people unto the Lord thy God. Thou shalt not seethe a kid in his mother's milk.

—DEUTERONOMY—CHAP. 14:4–21

All of us have heard the expression, "You are what you eat." If a thing is true, there is a way in which it is true. There is a way in which the verses in the fourteenth chapter of Deuteronomy are true. They are true psychologically and spiritually and represent many of the most profound truths in the entire Bible.

The Bible is a textbook on psychology and the science of living and it cannot be taken literally. The spiritual key to the Bible does away with all superstitions, literalisms, and rescues us from all the seeming contradictions, inconsistencies, and historical dilemmas. Except we have the inner meaning of the Bible, we really do not have any Bible.

I have known people who have had the choicest food and a perfectly balanced diet, according to the laws of nutrition, and yet they developed ulcers, cancer, and other destructive and degenerative diseases. The food we eat is transmuted by the Creative Intelligence within us into tissue, muscle, bone, blood, hair, etc.

If we are hateful, envious, jealous, and full of hostility, the food we eat may well be transformed into various diseases of a psychomatic nature. Our moods and attitudes of mind determine whether our food will build health or disease. If we are full of goodwill and eat our food with joy and thanksgiving, it will be transmuted into beauty, vitality, wholeness, and strength. The bread or meat which you eat, after a few hours, becomes your flesh and blood. This is essentially the doctrine of transubstantiation, when shorn of its superficial wrappings and trappings.

Food for the body is very important. Today some of our foremost research physicians are pointing out the dangers of excessive fat which interferes with the mechanical efficiency of all our vital organs, such as the heart, lungs, liver, and kidneys. We know that many physical and mental diseases can result from lack of certain vitamins and chemicals. Beriberi, a disease characterized by multiple inflammatory changes in the nerves, producing great muscular debility, is brought about by insufficiency of vitamin B. Research experiments on animals depriving them of manganese and other elements bring on mental and physical deterioration and degeneration. We are all familiar with the necessity of sufficient calcium for the pregnant mother. Deficiency of vitamin A has deleterious effects on the eyes and a sufficient amount of protein is essential for our well being. All this is most important, but our own mental and spiritual diet is of the greatest importance.

The Bible says, *Thou shalt not eat any abominable thing,* which means that you should not entertain or enthrone in your mind negative thoughts such as resentment, ill will, cynicism, hate, or anger. Animals in the Bible represent animated states of consciousness. Emotions follow your thoughts. If you think hateful thoughts, you will generate a destructive emotion, which is one of the animals you should not eat of. Emerson said, "You are what you think all day long." The Bible says: *As a man thinketh in his heart so is he.* Distinguished research physicians and other scientists point out that we have a new body every eleven months. You are creating new cells all the time, and if you fill your mind with the eternal verities and spiritual values of life, your brain will send these spiritual vibrations through the medium of your nervous system all over your body, and all the new cells will take on the vibration of these spiritual overtones, so that, like Job, you will be able to say: *Yet in my flesh shall I see God.*

You are eating of the Truths of God when you mentally and emotionally dwell on whatsoever things are just, honest, lovely, and of good report.

Eating in Biblical language refers to our mental and spiritual diet. We are fed daily through the five senses by an avalanche of sights, sounds, sundry concepts—good and bad, but most of this food is highly unsavory. We must learn to turn inward to God and be replenished from the standpoint of Truth. For example, affirm frequently—with feeling, "God is guiding me now, God's Love fills my soul, God inspires me, God's river of peace floods my mind and heart. I hear the Truth, I love the Truth and I radiate love and goodwill to all." This prayer is wonderful spiritual food for your mind. You will find yourself guided in all your ways and that will also refer to the food you select because the Nature of Infinite Intelligence is responsiveness and It responds to the nature of your thought.

You are told you may eat the beasts that parteth the hoof and cleaveth the cleft into two claws, and cheweth the cud such as the cow, the sheep, the goat, etc.

The hoof is a wonderful symbol which means understanding, our capacity to choose, divide, and select. The Bible says, *Choose ye this day whom ye shall serve.* Choose the concepts and ideas which are true. Use your reasoning faculty to discern and discriminate between what is true and false. When you learn to choose correctly, you will no longer choose sickness, accident, poverty, pain, misery, or lack. You may eat of the choicest food and be hungry in your heart for peace, joy, love, happiness, and inspiration. Every day of your life, mentally eat of God's ideas of wisdom, truth, and beauty. You choose the bread of Heaven whenever you turn away from the world and sense evidence, and mentally feast on the Truth that there is only One Power operating through the thoughts, feelings, and imagery of your mind.

When you read the newspapers, listen to the radio and press reports, you read of suffering, war, injustice, crime, poverty, and lack of all kinds. Shakespeare said, "Man's inhumanity to man makes countless thousands mourn." You may feel the strains and stresses of your business or profession. Perhaps the vexations, arguments, and difficulties of the day have unduly upset you. If so, divide the hoof and chew the cud. You must choose the Truth and chew on it in the sense that you appropriate it by meditating on it and absorbing it until the true ideas become a part of you in the same way that a glass of milk becomes your bloodstream. You must meditate on the Truths of God until you feel radiant, happy, and free, then you are one with God and you feel His Presence in your whole being. To divide the hoof is to arrive at the Truth in your mind, and see the spiritual values which never change and are the same yesterday, today, and forever. However, this is not enough, you must now chew the cud like a cow. The cow has several stomachs. She feeds on the grass, passes it from one stomach to another and when she feels contented, she lies down on the field and chews the cud. This is a process whereby she brings the food previously absorbed into her mouth as a sort of bolus, and begins to masticate it all over again until the food is thoroughly digested and appropriated completely by the whole system. You chew the cud by mentally dwelling on God's Wholeness, Perfection, Power, and Wisdom until your mind is lifted up and exalted. As you do this, your mind will be fascinated, engrossed, and absorbed in the great Truths you are feasting on. You will hunger no more, nor thirst any more, for God in His Wisdom becomes a lamp unto your feet and a light on your path.

The swine divideth the hoof, yet cheweth not the cud and is called unclean. The reason for this is obvious to you by now. Many people have a wonderful intellectual grasp of the Truth. They accept the Truth readily with the conscious mind only. Intellectual assent to the Truth is not enough. There are people who agree that honesty is the best policy, but they don't always practice it. Millions perhaps give lip service to the Ten Commandments, but these are constantly broken. When these Truths are accepted by the subconscious mind, and thus assimilated into the whole mentality, a tremendous difference takes place in one's character or life. You can taste clover in the milk of the cow after she has chewed the cud, the reason being, she has appropriated, assimilated, and digested the clover so thoroughly that she exudes the aroma in the milk, which is a part of her. Likewise, when you appropriate, meditate, and feast on the qualities, attributes, and potencies of God you will be under a Divine compulsion to express these qualities as they become a part of your nature. The swine divides the hoof and chews not the cud; it is therefore unclean. There are people who write and talk glibly on how to use the Healing Power of God, yet many live in an unhealthy way, notwithstanding. Many philosophers who write on the wisdom of the ages, and give intellectual assent to the same are extremely unhappy, frustrated, and neurotic. I knew a man who wrote a wonderful book on nutrition; it was quite scientific and very sound. He had acute ulcers and was most unhappy. He had *head* knowledge and failed to let it become heart knowledge. He failed to meditate, reflect, and mentally digest what he wrote so that it would be incorporated into his subconscious. He would then have followed his own physical diet as well as the mental and spiritual vitamins which he also recommended. The Truths of God must be appropriated and impressed into the subconscious, before a real change takes place.

You should not eat of the camel, and the hare, and the coney because they chew the cud and divide not the hoof. There are people who dream about a state and never appropriate it. I have talked to people in England and Ireland and other countries, who suffered from various ailments, such as rheumatism, sciatica, asthma, hay fever, etc. I talked to them about the Healing Presence and the scientific work being done in the psychosomatic field of medicine which listed the mental and emotional factors behind their ailments. They agreed with me and said it was interesting and undoubtedly true, but they did nothing about it. They refused to divide the hoof, and come to a clear-cut decision, that they could be healed and according to their decision would it be done unto them. The moment you come to a clear-cut, definite decision in your conscious mind, that you can be healed, your Deeper Mind which is full of Wisdom and Intelligence will respond accordingly. They refused to change their consciousness and consequently remained as they were. There is the man who is always *talking* about the book he is going to write, the new business he is going to open up. He never does anything—it's all talk. He lacks decision, judgment, and discrimination.

There are a great number of people who chew the cud in this way. They study the various religions of the world, they read a vast number of inspirational books, they study numerology, astrology, various philosophies and become charter members of every new and strange cult. They become muddled, perplexed, and so confused that many of them become mentally and emotionally disoriented and unbalanced. You must divide the hoof by deciding once and for all what the Truth is and build your whole life on that impregnable rock which never changes.

You divide the hoof by selecting what is eternally true, and all your reading, thought, instruction, and decisions must meet and conform to the following standard: *Whatsoever things are just, whatsoever things are pure, whatsoever things are lovely, whatsoever things are of good report; if there be any virtue, and if there be any praise, think on these things.* PHILIPPIANS 4–8.

This is the master spiritual standard which enables you to choose what is noble and God-like for the sanctuary of your own mind. Anything and everything that does not conform to this spiritual standard must positively and definitely be rejected as unfit for the house of God, which is your mind.

All fish that have fins and scales, ye can eat, the meaning of which is quite apparent. Scales represent the armor of God which Paul speaks of. *And the Lord, He it is that doth go before thee.* Your conviction of God's Presence is a mighty armor of protection, which goes before you, making straight, beautiful, joyous, and happy your way. All the highways and byways of your world are controlled by God, making the skies above and the earth beneath a highway for your God. The fish with fins have the power of propulsion and they steer themselves. All of us know the story of the salmon. Driven by inner wisdom he makes his way back across the ocean, overcoming all hurdles and obstacles to the place of his birth, where he dies, bequeathing his life forces to other forms of himself.

Man has fins and scales when he knows that he can choose, direct, and control his own destiny. His thought and feeling control his destiny. Man who does not choose his own thought and fails to meditate on the eternal verities becomes a victim of the race mind and moves along with the flotsam and jetsam of life, becoming subject to all the trials and tribulations of the race mind. If man does not do his own thinking, the race mind, the newspaper, the columnists and the newscasters and his relatives will do his thinking for him. Fish without fins and scales are at the mercy of the tides and are cast upon the beach to die. Cease drifting, steer your ship. Let God lead and guide you. Choose health, choose prosperity. Choose success. Let God lead and be your Silent partner in all your undertakings.

You are a conqueror. The world is not your master. Conditions and circumstances are effects, not causes. Your mind and Spirit are cause. You can change conditions. You are not subject to the political tide, the financial tide, or the tide of national events. Identify with your goal, image it, feel it, and know the Almighty Power of God is moving on your behalf. As you continue to nourish your ideal with faith and confidence, you will experience the joy of the answered prayer. There is nothing to oppose Infinite Intelligence. It is All Powerful, The Ever-Living One, the All-Knowing One, and the All Powerful One.

You shall not eat the vulture, the raven, or the hawk for the simple reason that they are birds of prey. You must not take advantage of others by preying on their weaknesses, lack of understanding, and ignorance. Some men pray together on Sunday and prey on each other on Monday. The vulture hovers overhead to eat the dead carcass. Like many other birds it is a scavenger. Men are scavengers when they feed on grudges, peeves, ill-will, hatred, and resentment. Love, peace, joy, beauty, happiness, vitality, and strength die in us when we eat mentally of these destructive states.

We must not eat the cuckow, because this bird is noted for the habit of laying its eggs in the nests of other birds for them to hatch, instead of building a nest of its own.

Do not have the characteristics or habits of the cuckow. Learn to lean on God, not on others. Stand on your own feet, don't expect others to do all the work for you. You are here to put your shoulders to the wheel, also. You have responsibilities, you have oars in the way of two hands, and a brain also, and you must pull your share. You are a Son of God on a voyage of self-discovery, and you must learn to build your own nest and draw forth the gifts and powers of God within you. You are prohibited from eating the raven, because it is omnivorous and predaceous. If you rob, cheat, or defraud others, this will react on yourself, resulting in loss of health, wealth, and peace of mind. To hurt another is to hurt yourself. Birds have two wings; likewise we have two wings, namely, thought and feeling. If you think evil of another and your mind being creative, will create what you think, thereby polluting your own soul.

Every creeping thing that flieth is unclean. This means that man must cease thinking of himself as a worm of the dust, apologizing for being alive and judging everything according to appearances. We can fly in our imagination to any heights or depths. Imagination is the workshop of God, but many misuse, distort, and diabolically pervert this God-given faculty. Imagination enables us to soar aloft above the storms and stresses of life and see and feel the happy ending, the Divine solution, the answered prayer.

I shall illustrate this by telling you about a man who crawled along the ground in the mud and mire of fear, hatred, and ill will. His wings were clipped, and he ceased to move onward, upward, and Godward. He had been smarting from a letter received from his general manager. His attitude was, "This is the last straw—this I can't take." He was boiling and seething with resentment, saying to himself, "This I can't forgive after all my years of faithful service, etc."

He was crawling in the mire of resentment and revenge. At my suggestion, he used his wings and imagination the right way. Every night before he went to sleep, he sat humbly down imagining the general manager had written him a letter which praised him and his work, and which satisfied him in every way according to the Golden Rule, the Law of Love and Goodwill. He saw the words in the imaginary letter. He rejoiced in reading them. He said to me, "I kept it up every night. I would read that letter over and over again and look at the general manager's signature." All hatred left him as he continued to do this. To quote him again, "The queerest thing in all the world happened!" The general manager wrote him a letter praising and promoting him. The letter was the essence of what he had been imagining and feeling for several days.

Every creeping thing that flieth is unclean—the man no longer used his imagination from a creeping, crawling, muddy standpoint, but with the wings of faith and imagination, he pictured conditions as they ought to be. He substituted the mood of love and goodwill for the feeling of ill will and hostility. Orage, a student of Ouspensky, used to give a wonderful technique for solving personal problems as follows: "Compose a letter, written as from your friend to yourself, which would completely satisfy you if you received it. Put into it such words as you would like your friend to do or write to you." The above mentioned young man rejoiced in reading the contents of the imaginary letter, and the All-Wise Deeper Self cast the spell of God around the general manager, causing him to respond in kind. Give love and you will receive love.

Ye shall not eat of anything that dieth of its self.
Thou shalt not seethe a kid in its mother's milk.

We should always eat of the nourishing Truths of God which live forever and never die. Fear, hate, jealousy, condemnation, revenge, ill will, etc., should die in us. We should take our attention away from all negative states and feast on goodness, truth, and beauty all the days of our lives. Opinions, theories, creed, dogmas, philosophies, conditions, circumstances pass away—they die of themselves. Do not eat of these things which undergo change and decay but meditate on God's eternal Love, Light, Truth, and Beauty, which are the same yesterday, today and forever. "Change and decay, all around I see, O Thou who changeth not abide with me!" All things in this world pass away. Dwell on the great truths of life which never pass away and you will become what you contemplate.

You shall not seethe a kid in his mother's milk. Many people will not drink milk with meat, as they take the Bible literally. A kid is a symbol of sacrifice. Milk is a universal food, a symbol of nourishment. Do not nourish a grudge or dwell on resentment. If you do, you are giving attention to the kid and you will become the goat. Whatever you give your attention to magnifies and grows in your experience. You should sacrifice the kid (grudge, hate, etc.), by consuming it in the fire of Divine Love, for your God is a consuming fire. Radiate love, peace, joy, and goodwill to the other until all the roots of ill-will are burned up. If you nurse the grudge and emotionalize it (mother's milk), you may develop tumors, growths, and other discordant bodily states, causing you to become the *goat*. (You don't really want to ride the goat).

Watch your mental and emotional diet. Divide the hoof by choosing what is true, noble, and God-like. Choose your thoughts from the standpoint of God and hang the walls of your mind with pictures of whatsoever things are lovely, and of good report. Choose the mood of faith, expecting the best, and fill your mind with God's Love. Chew the cud morning, noon, and night by lighting the fire of Divine Love in your heart, which will keep you warm and cheerful at all times. Absorb the truths of Life, let them saturate and gestate in your soul and you will become like a tree planted by the rivers of water, and whatever you do will prosper.

Go thy way and eat thy food with joy and let the joy of the Lord be your strength now and forevermore.

10

THE MAGIC QUALITY
OF SELF-CONFIDENCE

Now faith is the substance of things hoped for, the evidence of things not seen. For by it the elders obtained a good report. Through faith we understand that the worlds were framed by the word of God, so that things which are seen were not made of things which do appear. But without faith it is impossible to please him: for he that cometh to God must believe that he is, and that he is a rewarder of them that diligently seek him.

—HEBREWS 11:1, 2, 3, 6

The eleventh chapter of Hebrews is the greatest chapter in the Bible on building self-confidence. Confidence means *with faith*. Faith is an awareness of the presence and power of God within you.

Man may have confidence in stocks, bonds, real estate, in his ancestors, academic distinction, and perhaps in his qualifications, etc., all of which is good in its own way, but all these things pass away and are not stable. Man must have confidence in the Principle of Life which responds to his thought and never fails him.

Many people have faith in a system of theology, in certain ecclesiastical dogmas, but they have no working faith at all, and their lives are chaotic. Others who have a system of theology have a workable faith. They express it in their business, in their talents, in their homes, and in their relationship with people.

Confidence gives you a light in your eye, a new stance, and a fresh grip on life. You wear a smile. You are filled with vitality and energy. A person reflects his confidence in himself by his posture, manners, gestures, speech, and by the look in his eyes. Every part of him reveals his estimate or blueprint of himself. In that way many people can read character by watching a person walk. Others can read character by listening to a man talk. This is why psychologists and psychiatrists listen to their clients, who reveal themselves in their speech and in the timbre and tone of their voice.

Approve of yourself and have a high estimate of yourself because you are an individualized expression of God. You are a son or expression of the Living God. Adopt this attitude of mind, and you will lose the sense of inferiority. I know people whose faith seems to be in the money they can make in the stock market; but the stock market rises and falls. Your faith must be in that which never changes, namely the spiritual values of life, the laws of your mind, and the Principle of Life which remains the same yesterday, today, and forever. Theologies, philosophies, governmental operations, fiscal values, etc., wax and wane, come and go. Governments topple, wars and strife cause money to lose its value. Sometimes floods, hurricanes, and other cataclysms of nature sweep cities, towns, and homes away.

Everything in this world passes away and is subject to change. *Change and decay all around I see. Oh, Thou who changeth not abide with me.*

To really acquire self-confidence, you must have faith in the Eternal Principle of Life within you which created you and also the world. You must by study and application develop confidence in the two phases or functions of your mind, namely the conscious and subconscious. The subconscious mind responds to your habitual thinking. You can choose your thoughts, imagery, reactions, and response to life. You can channel your emotions constructively. You can develop confidence in the subconscious mind in the same way you would have confidence in chemistry, physics, mathematics, or electronics in building a radio or television set. A doctor has confidence when he begins to operate, because he knows surgery, anatomy, physiology, and other basic sciences dealing with the human body.

Many people say, "I am shy; I am timid; I am no good; I am abashed; I was born on the wrong side of the tracks; I did not have a good education; I did not go to college." All these negative thoughts pass through the minds of people then comes self-protection. Some retreat into themselves saying, "I want to be alone." They shun company and become self-centered, and their mentalities become warped. They are afraid of getting hurt, so they will not go to other people's homes or to a local party, lest their psychic boil get hurt.

This attitude of mind is due to a sense of rejection, which is primarily due to the fact they have no confidence in the God-Self within. Furthermore, many of these psychic traumas go back to childhood, when the parents may have said, "You are no good, you will never amount to anything. You will be a drunkard like your father, etc." The way to overcome all sense of inferiority and rejection is to realize that you can change your concept of yourself, and that conditions, circumstances, and events are not causative, these are effects. The basic cause of all fear is to believe that externals are causative. The cause of all is your own mind and spirit.

The Bible says, *If God be for me, who can be against me?* Take this statement of Truth and feel that the God-Presence is flowing through you as strength, beauty, love, peace, security, and true place. Realize that you are one with God, and that as you think of harmony, health, peace, joy, power, and happiness, the God-Presence responds, bringing all these qualities to pass in your life. As the God-Presence flows through these patterns of thought, you become creative, and you become what you want to be, to do, and to have, irrespective of what other people say, do, or think.

You can banish all sense of inferiority by affirming, feeling, and knowing the truths in the following prayer: "I am a channel for God's Life, Love, Truth, and Beauty. I am an expression of God. God is my Father. God loves me and cares for me. I am a unique expression of God, and there is no one in all the world like me. God seeks to express Himself in a unique and extraordinary way through me. I am a pipeline for His power and strength, and every day of my life I am expressing more and more of my hidden power. I radiate love and good will to all, and I wish for everyone what I wish for myself. I am one with my Father, and my Father is God."

Dwell on the above truths several times a day and particularly prior to sleep at night, and you will find all sense of inferiority and rejection disappear. Remember that when you give life-giving thoughts and new mental patterns to your subconscious mind, the latter accepts the new imagery, and the past is obliterated and expunged from the subconscious mind. Prayer changes the subconscious mind by eliminating all the subjective patterns which were causing all the trouble. Prayer is filling your mind with the Truths of God, thereby crowding out of the mind everything unlike God, or the Truth.

The late Henry Hamblin, editor of the Science of Thought Review, London, England, told me that one Sunday morning he received a call from the local Congregational minister. This was when he first started to write along spiritual lines. The minister wanted him to deputize for him that morning. He had never conducted a Congregational service, and did not know the routine or procedure. He said that he was panic stricken, filled with consternation, foreboding, and cold shivers ran down his spine. He began to ask himself, "Where is my confidence? Where is my faith in the things that are right?" There was no time to open the Bible or to prepare a sermon. He walked onto the podium, and the people began to sing their hymns, and entered into their thanksgiving prayer.

He began to say to himself, "God guides and reveals to me what to say." Suddenly, the quotation, *Turn your eyes unto the hills from whence cometh your help,* came to him, and he mentally surrendered affirming, "I surrender, God takes over and speaks through me." Instantaneously the burden of fear was dissipated. He was lifted up by the Spirit so that he saw intuitively into the hearts of all the people present. He saw them struggling, striving, scrambling, squabbling for the baubles of life. They did not seem to know where they were going. He said that he apparently saw into the hearts of all humanity.

This was a cosmic vision given to him by the Spirit. He saw people's hopes, fears, their loves and hates, their joy, frailties, their shortcomings, and their derelictions—all simultaneously.

A divine compassion for them seized him. Just as suddenly as it came, the vision vanished, and he began to talk, and the entire congregation was held spell-bound. They were seized and imbued by the Holy Spirit. It was his recognition of the Spirit within which gave him the confidence he needed. All members of the audience felt the intangible, invisible spiritual overtones which permeated them subjectively. He discovered the Power that moves the world and which answers when called upon. This is the way to build up self-confidence.

But without faith it is impossible to please Him: for he that cometh to God must first believe that He is, and that he is a rewarder of them that diligently seek Him.

When you turn to God, God turns to you. His nature is responsiveness, and you are rewarded according to the nature of your thought and the measure of your acceptance. A young man, who listens to the writer on the radio in the mornings, wrote me saying that he was too shy and timid to propose to his girl, and that every time he tried, he became tongue-tied and panic stricken. Fear held him in bondage.

In talking to him I suggested that every night prior to sleep he imagine he is acting the way he desires to act when in the presence of the girl. He pictured himself as the ardent lover and said, "This is the way I am proposing to her now." He would dramatize the imaginary act over and over again every night. He made this mental movie as vivid as possible. He emphasized that he would actually behave that way and that he was completely calm and poised. On the twentieth evening he went to her home and with faith, fervor, and confidence proposed and was accepted.

Too many people have a churlish timidity toward life. Put on the whole armor of God by knowing that God thinks, speaks, and acts through you. If you feel inferior in the face of a dilemma, some perplexing situation, or certain assignment, begin to think of all the reasons why you can overcome, achieve, and arrive at a happy solution. Say to yourself, "I shall conquer through the Power of the Almighty." All of us know that Abraham Lincoln felt inferior to the task assigned to him of making a speech commemorating the battle of Gettysburg. He prayed for guidance, studied parts of the Bible, and asked God to give him counsel and strength. He approached the subject with humility, simplicity, and with a deep reverence for things Divine. *He that cometh to God must believe that He is, and that he is a rewarder* . . . Lincoln believed that God always answered prayer. His simplicity, devotion to Truth, and humility before God caused him to produce the greatest address in history.

When you face a difficult problem, become aware of the Divinity within and say to yourself, "This problem is divinely outmatched because I see God, and whatever is necessary for me to know and to do, God reveals it to me." Go ahead and tackle the situation doing the best you can, and you will find Infinite Spirit will aid and assist you. The dawn will appear, and all the shadows will flee away.

Do not waste your energy. Watch the expenditure of your thought by saying to it that all your thoughts are invested wisely. Remember that the law of parsimony must prevail in your mind, and you must economize in your mental assumptions. You must assume that God is and that He answers you. *Faith is the substance of things hoped for* . . . Faith is to perceive the reality of the idea, thought, or image in your mind. You have faith when you know that the idea of a book, play, composition, or invention in your mind is as real as your hand or heart. This is the substance of things hoped; this is the evidence of things not seen. I do not see the new invention in your mind, but as you accept it and give it attention, the law of growth will take place. Like the seed in the ground, you will attract everything necessary for its unfoldment. What you give attention to you will experience.

It is very strange how people expect to get ahead in life, be happy and healthy without organizing their mental faculties, or even knowing anything about them. You would not operate an automobile if you had no experience, neither would you operate a chemical laboratory if you knew nothing about chemistry. Thinking is a process as real and as definite as the making of sodium hydroxide or bicarbonate of soda. You think with your own mind, and you can make wonderful mental combinations which will transform your life. Thoughts are things, and *as a man thinketh in his heart, so is he.*

To worry is to deflect your attention deliberately away from the good and to mentally focus on the negative aspects of life. Your thoughts go round and round as you dizzily seek a way out of the dilemma. Come back from the periphery to the center, where God abides, and find the answer within.

When we attempt mental imagery we must feel the picture. There must be an emotional tone to vitalize it. The pictured scene is a dramatization, a series of mental patterns, which you feel as true. The majority of people go to business and other activities with the wrong mental imagery, bringing about all kinds of trouble in their lives. Their minds are naked. Your mind must be clothed with faith in God and all things good. You must believe in the goodness of God and in the guidance of God, and in His Overshadowing Presence at all times. When your mind is thus clothed, you are wearing the garments of God. You would not go in sport clothes to a presidential banquet, nor would you wear evening clothes in the swimming pool. Are you dressed mentally for God, or is your mind full of rags, and of torn and tattered garments? You must wear psychic clothing for all occasions. When going on a journey know that, "Divine Love goes before me, making straight, beautiful, and joyous my way."

The Bible states clearly that if you wear the mental garment of faith that you will be *like the men who through faith subdued kingdoms, wrought righteousness, obtained promises, stopped the mouth of lions, quenched the violence of fire, escaped the edge of the sword, out of weakness were made strong, waxed valiant in fight, turned to flight the armies of aliens.* HEBREWS 11:33–34.

These are the wonderful things, which confidence in God accomplishes. You actually find that, as you build up your awareness of the Power of God in your mind, all the so-called insuperable obstacles are overcome by you. There are people who have escaped fires, floods, hurricanes, disasters at sea, subdued lions, and the ravages of war. Nothing touched them; they seemed to lead charmed lives. The spell of God was around them. They were God intoxicated, having acknowledged and received the Divine Antibody, the Presence of God in the midst of them, mighty to heal, save, and protect.

William James said, "Believe in the good life, and believe that Life is worth living, and your belief will cause this to become a fact."

Cease identifying with failure, lack, and limitation. Unite with your goals and aspirations. Timidity is a state of mind. The timid are usually consummate egotists who try to hide their blatancy in mental retreat. The timid must do the things that they fear to do, and the death of fear is certain. We have to win with pleasure in the game of life and lose with a smile.

Demosthenes stuttered badly. He decided to become a great orator, and he persevered until he won the battle. Victory was assured because of his confidence in the Almighty to which all things are possible to him that believeth.

All of us remember the great soul stirring classic sermons of Henry Ward Beecher. You will recall that as a boy he was full of fear, and was bashful, shy, and retiring. His speech was very defective because of an enlarged and abnormal palate. He was given to constant prattle which was a subconscious compensation for his handicap. He believed that he would become a great preacher. He became what he believed he would be—the famous preacher of Plymouth Church. Discouragement seldom depresses the man whose focus is on the unfoldment of an ultimate desire. He who finds God within himself loses his misery and suffering.

The Greeks said that laughter is for the gods. Laughter is a medicine for many troubles. Man is the only being in the world who can laugh. Animals can't laugh. Laughter restores your perspective, takes your attention from yourself, and lets you think clearly and decisively. Make it a special point to laugh at your fears. Be sure to laugh when people irritate you, and by all means laugh at all the foolish, silly mistakes you made during the day. Laugh at yourself for being so stuffy and so serious. The greater the problem, the more humor you need. There is no self-pity nor self-condemnation where the laughter of God in the soul of man takes over.

I heard a boy the other day saying to his mother, "I laughed because I did not want to cry." The boy let the eggs and the milk fall on the street and instead of crying, he laughed. There is no use in crying over spilled milk.

Come back to the center within yourself where God abides.

Here all is peace, bliss, harmony, and joy. Here you live beyond time and space. You are alone with God. You are in the sacred center of God's Eternal Love. On this rock you stand. You are impervious and invulnerable, and all the negation of the world cannot touch you. God by his very nature is for you, so who can be against you? There is no power in all the world to withhold from you success, achievement, and the realization of your heart's desire because *one with God is a majority.*

11

THE MASTER KEY TO HARMONIOUS HUMAN RELATIONS

Judge not, that ye be not judged. For with what judgment ye judge, ye shall be judged: and with what measure ye mete, it shall be measured to you again. And why beholdest thou the mote that is in thy brother's eye, but considerest not the beam that is in thine own eye? Or how wilt thou say to thy brother, Let me pull out the mote out of thine eye; and, behold, a beam is in thine own eye? Thou hypocrite, first cast out the beam out of thine own eye; and then shalt thou see clearly to cast out the mote out of thy brother's eye.

—MATTHEW 7:1–5

The master key to happy relationship with people is the application of the Golden Rule and in discovering that there is no one to change but yourself. As you would that men should think about you, think you about them in like manner. As you would that men should feel about you, feel you also about them in like manner. As you would want men to act toward you, act you toward them in like manner.

A study of the above mentioned verses and the application of the inner truths therein contained would transform our entire life. These verses teach the emancipation of man and reveal to him the solution to his individual as well as world problems.

We are told to *judge not that ye be not judged.* To judge is to think, to arrive at a mental verdict or conclusion in your mind. For example, I had a conversation with a man about fifty years old who had lost his position, and his financial situation had gone from bad to worse. He was extremely critical of the management in his former place of employment; he had a deep grudge against them. I explained to him that his negative, resentful attitude was highly destructive to him, that his hatred, resentment, and hostility were mental poisons which were robbing him of vitality, enthusiasm, strength, guidance, and peace of mind.

He began to see that the suggestion we give to another we give to ourselves because our mind is the creative medium. Therefore we actually create what we think and feel about the other. This is why the Bible says, *For with what judgment ye judge, ye shall be judged.* He ceased thinking negatively of his employers and sincerely wished for them health, happiness, and peace. He began to claim as follows: "God opens up a new door of expression for me. I am divinely guided every step of the way, and I follow the lead which comes to me. I sincerely wish for every man what I wish for myself." He found a new position, and is now on the way to the fulfillment of his dreams.

The good we do for others comes back to us in like measure; and the evil we do returns to us by the law of our own mind. If a man cheats and deceives another, he is actually cheating and deceiving himself. His sense of guilt and mood of loss will return to him some way, some time. His subconscious mind is a recording machine that faithfully reproduces what is impressed upon it. We cannot escape the law of our mind. Reward and retribution are reactions of our own mind based upon the way we directed our meditation. Our subconscious mind is impersonal and unchanging, neither considering persons nor respecting religious affiliations or institutions of any kind. It is neither compassionate nor vindictive. The way we think, feel, and act toward others returns at last upon ourselves.

Ask yourself now, "How am I behaving internally toward this other fellow?" This interior attitude is what counts. A woman wrote me about her husband, saying that he goes into a rage when he reads what certain newspaper columnists write in the newspaper. He came to see me, and I expatiated on the way our mind works and how emotionally immature it was to get angry because others write things with which we disapprove or disagree. My explanation to him was more or less along the following lines:

"Begin now to observe yourself; observe your reactions to people, conditions, and circumstances. How do you respond to the events and news of the day? It makes no difference if all the other people were wrong and you alone were right. If the news disturbs you, it is your evil, because your bad mood affected and robbed you of peace and harmony. You do not have to react negatively to the news or the comments of the broadcaster. You can remain unmoved, undisturbed, and poised, realizing he has a right to his expression and beliefs. It is never what a person says or does that affects us; it is our reaction to what is said or done that matters."

This explanation was the cure for this man, and he realized that with a little practice he could master his morning tantrums. His wife told me subsequently that he laughed at himself and also at what the columnists say. They no longer have power to disturb, annoy, and irritate him. He knew that he had been irritating himself in the past and blaming others for his discomfiture.

If all the people in the office or factory annoy you, isn't it a possibility that the vibration, annoyance, and turmoil may be due to some subconscious pattern or mental projection from you? We know that a dog will react ferociously if you hate or fear dogs. Animals pick up our subconscious vibrations and react accordingly. Many undisciplined human beings are just as sensitive as dogs, cats, and other animals.

A private secretary was very bitter toward some of the girls in her office because they were gossiping about her, and as she said, spreading vicious lies about her. She admitted that she did not like women. She said, "I hate women, but I like men." I discovered also that she spoke to the girls who were under her in the office in a very haughty, imperious, irritable tone. She pointed out that they took a delight in making things difficult for her. There was a certain pomposity in her way of speaking, and I could see where her tone of voice would affect some people unpleasantly.

I suggested a process of prayer, explaining to her that when she began to identify herself with spiritual values and commenced to affirm the Truths of life, her voice, mannerisms, and hatred of women would completely disappear. She was surprised to know that the emotion of hatred shows up in speech, actions, in our writings, and in all phases of our life. She ceased reacting in the typical, resentful, and angry way. She established a pattern of prayer which she practiced regularly, systematically, and conscientiously in the office.

The prayer was as follows: "The Infinite One thinks, speaks, and acts through me now; this is my real self. I now radiate love, peace, tolerance, and kindliness to all the girls who criticized and gossiped about me. I salute the Divinity in them. God speaks through me as peace, harmony, and love. Whenever I discover that I am about to react negatively, I say firmly, 'This is not the Infinite One speaking or acting.' Divine Love, Light, and Truth flow through me now."

The practice of this prayer transformed her life, and she found that all criticism and annoyance ceased. The girls became coworkers and friends along life's journey. She discovered that *there is no one to change but myself*.

Do you observe your inner speech? For example, you may be polite and courteous to the boss in the office, but when his back is turned, you are very critical and resentful toward him in your mind.

One day a salesman came to see me and described his difficulties in working with the sales manager of his organization. He had been with the company ten years and had received no promotion or recognition of any kind. He showed me his sales figures which were greater proportionately than the other men in the territory. He said that the sales manager did not like him, that he was unjustly treated, and that at conferences the manager was rude to him and at times ridiculed his suggestions.

I explained that undoubtedly the cause was to a great degree within himself, and that his concept and belief about his superior bore witness to the reaction of this man—*the measure we mete, shall be measured to us again*. His measure or concept of the manager was that he was mean, cantankerous, and he was filled with bitterness and hostility toward him. On his way to work he conducted a vigorous conversation with himself, filled with criticism, mental arguments, recriminations, and denunciations of his sales managers.

Whatever we give out mentally, we are inevitably bound to get back. This man realized that his inner speech was highly destructive, because the intensity and force of his silent thoughts and emotions and personally conducted mental condemnation and vilification of the sales manager entered into his own subconscious mind, bringing about the negative response from his boss, as well as creating many other physical and emotional disorders.

He began to pray as follows: "I am the only thinker in my universe. I refuse to give power to any person, place, or thing to annoy me or disturb me. I am responsible for the way I think about my boss. I know that God indwells him. I salute the Divinity in him. He is a spiritual being, living in God's universe, and he is governed over by God. I see him as God sees him. He is full of God's love, light, and truth. Whenever I think of him I say to myself, 'What is true of God is true of you.'"

He repeated this prayer out loud slowly, quietly, and feelingly, knowing that his mind is the garden of God, and whatever he plants in the garden will come forth like seeds after their kind. He practiced mental imagery every night prior to sleep this way: He imagined that his sales manager was congratulating him on his fine work, on his zeal and enthusiasm, and wonderful response from customers. He felt the reality of all this, felt his handshake, heard the tone of his voice, saw him smile. He made a real mental movie, dramatizing it in his own way, according to the Golden Rule and the Law of Love. Night after night he conducted this mental movie, knowing that the subconscious mind was the receptive plate on which his conscious imagery would be impressed. Gradually by a process of what may be termed mental and spiritual osmosis, the impression was made on the subconscious, and the expression automatically came forth. The sales manager called him up to San Francisco, congratulated him, and gave him a new assignment as Division Sales Manager over one hundred men with a big increase in salary. He changed his concept and estimate of his boss, and the latter responded accordingly.

Like attracts like; birds of a feather flock together. Is it not possible that your associate's crotchety, petulant, critical attitude is a reflection of your own inner frustrations and suppressed rage? What this person says or does cannot really hurt you, except you permit him to disturb you. The only way he can annoy you is through your own thought. For example, if you get angry, you have to go through four stages in your mind: You begin to think about what he said. You decide to get angry and generate a mood of rage. Then you decide to act; perhaps you talk back and react in kind. You see that the thought, emotion, reaction, and action all take place in your mind. When you become spiritually mature, you do not respond negatively to the criticisms and resentment of others. To do so would mean that you had descended to that low mental vibration and become one with the negative atmosphere of the other. Identify yourself with your aim in life and do not permit any person, place, or thing to deflect you from your sense of oneness with the Infinite One who thinks, speaks, and acts through you.

You have the faculty to enter into the Secret Place of the Most High and commune with God. Here you live beyond time and space. In this spiritual union with the Divine you have a sense of inner peace. You are one with God. You refuse to descend from this high level of awareness. Your inner peace and sense of oneness with the Infinite One is your impregnable fortress. You never surrender your inner poise and sense of inner peace. "One with God is a majority." "If God be for you, who can be against you?"

Freud said, "Unless the personality has love, it sickens and dies." Love is understanding, good will, and it is respecting the God in the other person. The more love and good will you radiate, the more comes back to you. If you puncture the other fellow's ego and wound his estimate of himself, you cannot gain his good will. Recognize that every man is an incarnation of the Almighty, and that he wants to be loved, appreciated, and important to the world. Recognize that the other is conscious of his true worth and that he feels the dignity of being a son of the Living God. As you do this consciously and knowingly, you build the other person up, and he returns your love and good will.

Begin to see sermons in stones, tongues in trees, songs in running brooks, and God in everything. Begin to see God in everybody, and you will find that God begins to shine through that other in all His pristine glory. You owe every man respect and love. You must respect the God in him and identify yourself with the Creative Love in him.

During a lecture series in Town Hall early this year for Dr. Raymond Barker, Minister of Religious Science, an actor told me that the audience booed and hissed him on his first appearance on the stage. He said the play was a bad one and that undoubtedly he did not play a good role. He pointed out that for months afterward he hated audiences. He called them dopes, dummies, stupid, gullible, etc. He quit the stage in disgust and went to work in a drug store for a year. One day he entered Town Hall and heard Dr. Barker speak on "How to Get Along With Ourselves." That lecture changed his life. He went back to the stage and began to pray for the audience and for himself. He poured out love and good will, and every night he claimed that God's peace filled their souls, and that they were lifted up and inspired. For ten nights or more he claimed that God's peace filled his mind and that he was expressing himself at his highest level through the wisdom and intelligence of the Almighty. All during the performance he sent out love vibrations of God's grace to the audience. Today he is a great actor, and he loves and respects people. Your good will and esteem will be transmitted to others and be felt by them.

Information or news is constantly brought to your attention all day long through the medium of your five senses. You are the one who determines what your mental responses are going to be to the news conveyed. You can remain poised, serene, and calm, or you can fly into a rage, and as a result get an attack of migraine or experience some other form of pain.

The reason two men react differently to the same situation is based on the nature of their respective subconscious conditioning. Your personality is based on the sum total of all your opinions, beliefs, education, and early religious indoctrination. This inner attitude of mind conditions your response. One man will get angry when he hears a certain religious program, but his brother may enjoy it because one is prejudiced, and the other is not. Our subconscious convictions and assumptions dictate and control our conscious actions.

You can recondition your mind by identifying with the eternal verities. Begin now by filling your mind with concepts of peace, joy, love, good humor, happiness, and good will. Busy your mind with these ideas. As you do, they will sink into the subconscious level and become orchids in the garden of God.

There are difficult people in the world who are twisted and distorted mentally. They are mal-conditioned. Many are mental delinquents, argumentative, uncooperative, cantankerous, cynical, and sour on life. They are sick psychologically. You would not condemn a person who had tuberculosis. Many people have deformed and distorted minds, probably warped during childhood. Many have congenital deformities. No one, for example, hates a hunchback; there are many mental hunchbacks. You have compassion and understanding. To understand all is to forgive all.

The hateful, frustrated, distorted, and twisted personality is out of tune with the Infinite. He resents those who are peaceful, happy, and joyous. Usually he criticizes, condemns, and vilifies those who have been very good and kind to him. His attitude is this: "Why should they be so happy when I am so miserable?" He wants to drag them down to his own level. Misery loves company.

A girl told me that she hated another girl in her office, the reason being that she was prettier, happier, had wealth, and was engaged to the boss of the company where they worked. After the marriage had taken place, one day the crippled daughter (by a former marriage) of the woman whom she hated came into the office. The child put her arms around her mother and said, "Mommy, mommy, I love my new daddy! Look what he gave me!" She showed her mother a wonderful new toy.

She said to me, "My heart went out to that little girl, and I knew how happy she must feel, and I got a vision of how happy this woman was. All of a sudden I felt love for that woman, and

I went into the office and wished her all the happiness in the world, and I meant it."

In psychological circles today, this is called empathy, which simply means the imaginative projection of your consciousness into that of another. She projected her mentality into that of the other woman and began to think from her brain. She was thinking and feeling as the other woman, and also as the child, because she likewise had projected herself into the mind of the child. She was looking out from that vantage point on the child's mother.

If tempted to injure or think ill of another, project yourself into the mind of Moses and think from the standpoint of The Ten Commandments. If prone to be envious, jealous, or angry, project yourself into the mind of Jesus and think from that standpoint. The words will come like a melody of God, *Love ye one another.*

No matter what the problem is, or how acute it may be, or how difficult the person, there is in the final analysis no one to change but yourself! When you change yourself, your world and environment will change. Begin with number one—yourself!

Don't permit people to take advantage of you and gain their point by temper tantrums, crying jags, or so-called heart attacks. These people are dictators who try to enslave you and make you do their bidding. Be firm but kind, and refuse to yield. Appeasement never wins. Refuse to contribute to their delinquencies, selfishness, and possessiveness. Remember, do that which is right. You are here to fulfill your ideal and remain true to the eternal verities and spiritual values of life which are eternal.

Give no one in all the world the power to deflect you from your goal, your aim in life, which is to bring more and more of

God's wisdom, truth, and beauty into this world. Remain true to your ideal. Know that God guides you and that right action is yours, and whatever contributes to your peace, happiness, and fulfillment must of necessity bless all men who walk this earth. The harmony of the part is the harmony of the whole, for the whole is in the part, and the part is in the whole. The other fellow is an incarnation of God. All that you owe him is Love, and Love is the fulfilling of the Law.